PORTRAIT OF PEMBROKESHIRE

Portrait of PEMBROKESHIRE

by

Dillwyn Miles

GWASG DINEFWR PRESS
2003

Copyright © Dillwyn Miles 1984
First published in Great Britain 1984

Re-published 2003

All rights reserved. No part of this publication may
be reproduced, stored in a retrieval system,
or transmitted, in any form or by any means,
electronic, mechanical, photocopying, recording
or otherwise, without the prior permission
of the publisher.

ISBN 1-904323-03-0

For Marilyn

Printed, published and bound in Wales by
Gwasg Dinefwr Press Ltd.,
4 Rawlings Road, Llandybie
Carmarthenshire, SA18 3YD

Contents

	List of Illustrations	7
	Preface	9
1	The Face of Pembrokeshire	11
2	A Historic Legacy	16
3	Along the Teifi	26
4	South of Presely	36
5	The Barony of Cemais	47
6	The Last Invasion	64
7	Around Treffgarne	81
8	Dewsland	92
9	Town and County of Haverfordwest	108
10	The Rout of Colby Moor	121
11	Milford Haven	132
12	Dale and the Isles	148
13	Canaston to Carew	163
14	Pembroke	174
15	The Manor and Island of Pŷr	192
16	Tenby	201
17	The National Park	212
	Welsh Place-names	217
	Index	219

Illustrations

Between pages 48 and 49

Carn Briw, Bronze Age cairn
The Presely Hills
Carreg Goetan cromlech, Newport
Pilgrims' Cross at Nevern
Vitalianus Stone, Nevern churchyard
Foel Drygarn
Castell Mawr fort
Cilgerran Castle
Rosebush slate quarry
Pentre Ifan cromlech
High Cross at Nevern
Mounting-block at Nevern
Cwmyreglwys Church
Bedd Morris, Bronze Age standing stone
Dinas Island
Mathry

Between pages 96 and 97

Poll Carn rhyolite outcrop
Whitesand Bay
The Howards of Rudbaxton
Seasick voyager, misericord at St David's Cathedral
Bishop's Palace, St David's
St David's Cathedral
Trefrân colliery stack
Haverfordwest Castle
Old warehouses, Haverfordwest
Bethesda Chapel, Haverfordwest
Wiston, shell keep
Llawhaden, bishop's castle
Stack Rock Fort

Friends' Meeting House, Milford
Oil tankers in Milford Haven
Milford Docks

Between pages 160 and 161
View from look-out at Abereiddi
Nab Head, mesolithic site
Carew Castle
St Govan's chapel
Pembroke Castle, Great Keep
Tudor Merchant's House, Tenby
Tenby harbour and castle
Five Arches, Tenby
St Mary's Church, Tenby
Tomb of Margaret ap Rhys of Scotsborough
Thomas White and son John, St Mary's, Tenby
Begelly Church watch-tower
How many miles ...?

All photographs taken by Roger Worsley

Map   *page* 12-13

Preface

Sea-girt on three sides and fringed on the fourth by mist-laden moorland, Pembrokeshire was set apart as *Gwlad hud a lledrith*, the land of magic and mystery, for magic there was, and spells cast, and bewitchery was not unknown. It lay beyond *llengel*, the concealing veil, and it was close to *Annwn*, the other-world, where the shades merged with Elysian meadows, and off its coast lay the green isles of enchantment for all with second-sight to see.

Such was the Pembrokeshire into which I was born, and in my childhood nurtured on legends of bravura, the riveting escape stories of fishermen and poachers, and the tales of *The Mabinogion* that seemed no less old than those of the Book of Genesis. With a few interruptions, I have lived in Pembrokeshire all my life: I am a Pembrokeshire man. I have seen the change that has come over it, and I wish I could say that it was for the better.

I have attempted to present a portrait of Pembrokeshire as I see it. I have written of its past, for no one can get to know Pembrokeshire without being aware of its uncommonly rich heritage. I have deliberately not dwelt on descriptions of the scene: with so much beauty, repetition would become tedious, and the language exhausted of its superlatives. Yet I plead to the prejudice of an earlier writer, Giraldus Cambrensis, who claimed, eight hundred years ago, that his native Pembrokeshire was the most delectable corner of Wales.

The substance of this book has been gathered over many years, and I have endeavoured to pass on those things which are of interest to me and which others, I trust, will find equally interesting. Roch Castle is a castle is a castle, but it also has a bodeful ophidian legend attached to it; it was held by ancestors of a king's mistress and of the Princess of Wales, and it stands on a plug of rock which is as old as any there is, and which gave it, and its builders who are still known in Ireland, their name.

Pembrokeshire has been fortunate in its chroniclers. Giraldus Cambrensis accompanied the Archbishop of Canterbury, preaching the Third Crusade in 1188, and did 'not pass over in silence the circumstance that occurred' or fail to record a tale that he heard on his travels. George Owen of Henllys, lord of Cemais, admirably portrayed Pembrokeshire in the sixteenth century, and marvelled at its 'divers wonders'. Richard Fenton could leave no stone unturned, and recorded his excavations and his observations in his *Historical Tour through Pembrokeshire* published in 1811. They lifted the veil on life in their time, at intervals in the long history of the shire, and their example has been followed by others nearer our time.

Pembrokeshire was Pembrokeshire for $8\frac{1}{2}$ centuries, for twice as long as other counties in the Principality, and was therefore known as 'the premier county of Wales'. With the reorganization of local government in 1974, however, it was bundled with the neighbouring counties of Cardigan and Carmarthen to create the new county of Dyfed. It was divided into two districts: Preseli, a misspelt misnomer, and South Pembrokeshire, and the former county is referred to by the bureaucrats as Preseli/South Pembrokeshire. But its name survives, and will survive, in its institutions: the Pembrokeshire Health Authority, the Pembrokeshire Agricultural Society, the Pembrokeshire Cricket Club, and Her Majesty the Queen, we hope, will be allowed to continue to have her favourite Pembrokeshire corgis around her.

I wish to acknowledge my debt to my friend Wynford Vaughan-Thomas, at whose suggestion this book was written, and to express my gratitude to Major Francis Jones, Herald of Arms Extraordinary, and Judith Graham-Jones for their encouragement. I wish to thank Antony Wood for his guidance and help, and Eileen Goodall for her care in typing the manuscript.

Dillwyn Miles

1
The Face of Pembrokeshire

The outstanding natural beauty of Pembrokeshire is born of the variety of its scenery: smooth green hills, moorland royally mantled in purple and gold, deep wooded valleys and wide estuaries, tall cliffs and long stretches of sand.

In the beginning, it was a land of explosive volcanoes and flowing molten magma that cooled into rock, a thousand million years and more ago. Outcrops of these, the most ancient of rocks, the Pre-Cambrian, still stand on St David's peninsula, at Roch and Treffgarne, at Benton, Johnston and Talbenny. The Cambrian sediments, laid down when Pembrokeshire was deep under the sea, are displayed in the cliffs at Whitesand Bay and on Ramsey, at Caerfai and Caerbwdy, at Porth-y-rhaw and at Solva, and disclose the first sign of life in their fossils: water fleas, brachiopods and foot-long trilobites.

The northern part of Pembrokeshire is covered by Ordovician sandstone, grit and shale laid down in the same sea at a time of further volcanic activity. The resistant igneous rocks form the headlands of Penclegyr and Penmaendewi and remain in the monadnocks of Carn Llidi and Penbiri and stretch the length of the Presely Hills.

The Silurian rocks are exposed in isolated strata: from St Dogmael's to Newport Sands, from Narberth to Haverfordwest, from Freshwater East to Freshwater West, and from St Ishmael's to Skomer and beyond to the Smalls. Towards the end of this period, about 400 million years ago, the Caledonian orogeny rumpled the sediments into folds, so evident in cliff faces at Pen-yr-afr and Ceibwr, and radically transformed the geography of north Pembrokeshire by imposing upon it an east-north-east to west-south-west trend.

Old Red Sandstone and Carboniferous rocks underlie south

PORTRAIT OF PEMBROKESHIRE

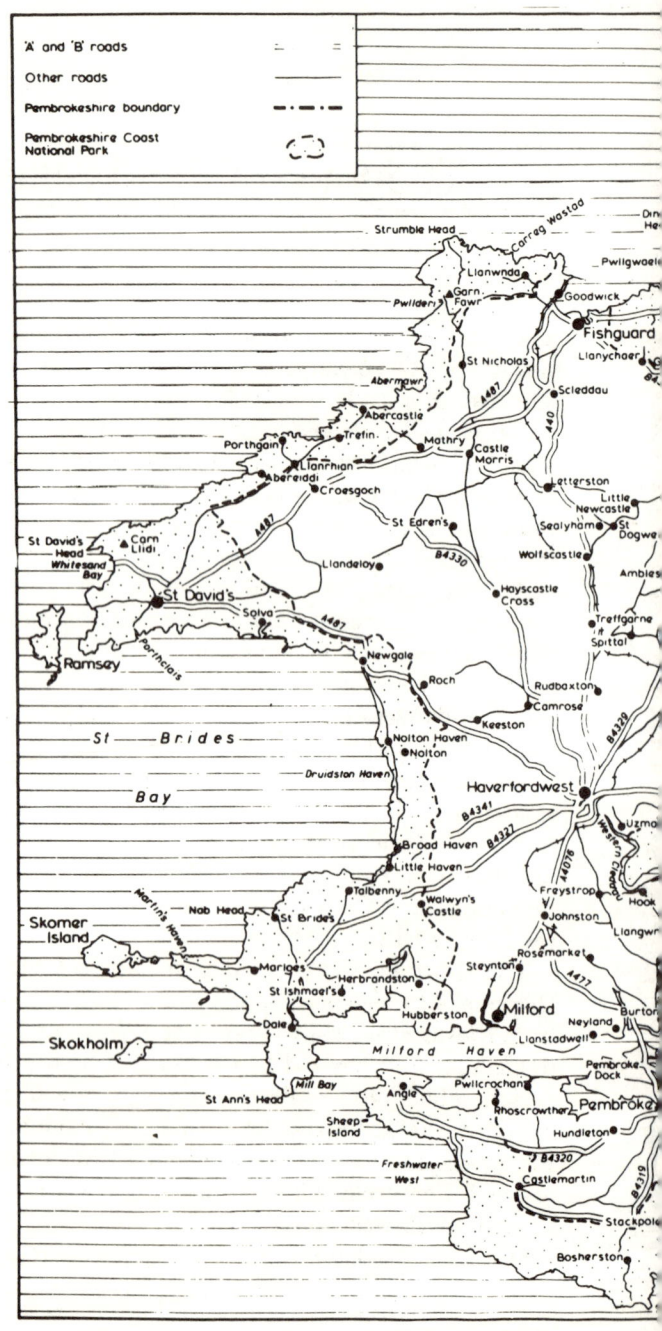

Pembrokeshire

THE FACE OF PEMBROKESHIRE

(Based upon the Ordnance Survey map with permission of the controller of Her Majesty's Stationery Office. Crown Copyright Reserved.)

Pembrokeshire, where the limestone cliffs provide some of the most spectacular scenery. Coal measures are exposed along the coast from Monkstone Point to Amroth and from Talbenny to Newgale.

At the end of the Carboniferous period, another earth movement known as the Armorican orogeny, as it was centred on Armorica, now Brittany, pressed south Pembrokeshire up against the north and produced a trend lying east-south-east to west-north-west. The Three Chimneys stand on end at Marloes Sands in consequence.

The sea has covered the land on more than one occasion. Two million years ago, it was six hundred feet above the present and reached the base of the Presely Hills, leaving a plateau that survives to the north-east of Newport and around Maenclochog. At a later date, the sea level fell to four hundred feet, forming a level surface that is traceable between Dinas and Fishguard, at Hayscastle Cross and around Mathry and Croesgoch. Later still, it was two hundred feet above its level today, when it planed a platform that covers south Pembrokeshire and much of the coastland.

The presence of ice-scratched rock surface on Carn Llidi and the widespread occurrence of boulder clay and fluvio-glacial gravel indicate that Pembrokeshire was completely submerged beneath glacier ice about a hundred thousand years ago. Erratic boulders and pebbles brought from Scotland, Cumbria and the Isle of Man are scattered over south Pembrokeshire: some have been used as tombstones in a churchyard.

In north Pembrokeshire, sub-glacial meltwater channels, under a waning ice cover, cut into the upland, isolating Carn Ingli from the Presely Hills, to form the the Gwaun Valley, and created a complex of channels south of Fishguard before escaping southward through the deep cleft of the Treffgarne gorge. The erosive action of meltwater also separated Dinas Island from the mainland and cut a channel from Porthgain to Abereiddi to isolate Barry Island.

When the ice finally melted, the sea rose again to its present level and drowned the valleys of the Nevern, the Solfach and the Ritec: the pre-glacial course of the Daugleddau is now the deep-water channel of Milford Haven. Ancient forests were submerged and sometimes lie exposed at low tides at Newport,

Abermawr, Whitesand Bay, Newgale, Freshwater West, Freshwater East, Manorbier, Lydstep, Saundersfoot and Amroth.

Some time, before these land surfaces were submerged, man appeared on the scene.

2
A Historic legacy

It was cold winter all the year long when man first came to this westernmost peninsula of Wales and sought shelter in the limestone caves on Caldey, around Tenby, and at Catshole Quarry on the Pembroke river, the most westerly site of occupation by palaeolithic man. A fire kindled at the cave entrance kept him and his family warm and protected them against the wild beasts that roamed through forests and over moors that are now the bed of the sea. They left the bones of the animals they hunted for food on the cave floors, and their weapons and implements, made of flints found on the local beaches, were such as to identify them with the culture of people who lived in caves at Cresswell Crags in Derbyshire.

As the ice retreated northward and the weather improved, people were not so confined to caves. Some built themselves flimsy dwellings on coastal sites and estuaries as at Nab Head on St Bride's Bay, Small Ord Point on Caldey, Swanlake at Manorbier, and the banks of the Nevern at Newport, the only known site in north Pembrokeshire. Here they sat and fashioned flints into microlithic artefacts which they mounted on bone shafts to make arrows and harpoons, and left the flakes and the chips on their chipping-floors as evidence of their occupation of the coastal lands, some ten thousand years ago. Low-lying lands became swamped as the sea level rose with the melting of the glaciers, and now and again, at low tide, the sunken forests appear as ebonized stumps of trees, at Newgale, Newport, Freshwater West and Amroth. Flint arrowheads found among the ribs of a wild pig on the submerged land surface at Lydstep provided evidence of a quarry that a mesolithic hunter had failed to retrieve.

The memory of sunken lands remains in the legend of Cantre'r Gwaelod, the Lowland Hundred. The kingdom of Gwyddno

Garanhir lay between the north Pembrokeshire coast and the Lleyn peninsula and was protected from the encroaching sea by a dyke in which there were floodgates. Gwyddno had placed responsibility for the floodgates in the hands of Prince Seithenyn, but one night he got drunk at a feast and forgot his duty. The sea came in and drowned Cantre'r Gwaelod's sixteen noble cities and their 'marble wharves and churches whose towers resounded with beautiful peals and chimes of bells'.

The neolithic people are remembered by their chambered tombs, for their dwellings were perishable except where stone was more readily available. The only evidence of their habitation here is at Clegyr Boia, an igneous monadnock to the west of St David's, where Audrey Williams, excavating the site in 1943, was able to trace the foundations of a rectangular house and an oval building, the roof of each having been supported by timber posts set in sockets in the rock. The round-bottomed bowls used by the inhabitants were similar to those found in burial chambers, both here and in Ireland. Their axes were made of local stone, possibly at axe-factories on the Presely Hills, and they brought with them the arts of agriculture which had originated in the Middle East.

The cromlech, or chambered tomb, comprised a large capstone resting on stone pillars covered by a mound of earth or stones. It was intended for collective burial over a period of time, and there are some indications of funerary ceremonial. The elements and the hand of man have denuded the mounds, and in some cases the tombs themselves have been vandalized, but there remain over thirty chambers, most of them in north Pembrokeshire, to testify to the importance these people attached to the burial of the dead. Outstanding among them is Pentre Ifan cromlech, with its symbolic portal and crescentic façade. Its relationship to the Irish court-cairns indicates that its builders came originally from Ireland. Other tombs have a polygonal chamber set in a round mound with access provided by a passage-way, an example of which is the Longhouse cromlech, near Mathry. Burial chambers on St David's Head and Pencaer have capstones supported on low uprights or even on natural ledges of rock, which also happens in the case of the King's Quoit chamber at Manorbier.

The tombs have been the objects of man's conjectures and beliefs for many years. They have been regarded as the altars of druids, the graves of giants, blacksmiths' anvils and the 'quoits' of kings, of the devil, of Arthur and of Samson. The capstone of Llechydrybedd, 'the stone on the trivet', was hurled from the summit of Carn Ingli by Samson, as effortlessly as he had carried away the gates of Gaza. Every girl knew that, if she crawled round a cromlech at full moon, she would see her lover standing in the moonlight, but if a man fell asleep under its capstone, he would either die or go raving mad or become a poet.

The Presely Hills have long been known as a source of stone implements, and evidence goes to show that there were two centres of axe production. One used the spotted dolerite found in the 'bluestone' area of Carn Menyn and surrounding outcrops as its raw material, and the other, somewhere at the eastern end of the range, manufactured axes of rhyolite tuff. The products of these factories have been found as far afield as Carclinty Bog in County Antrim and, in some abundance, in Wessex where the trade in these implements undoubtedly related to the transport of the bluestones to Stonehenge.

'Stonehenge stands as lonely in history as it does on the great plain,' wrote Henry James of this most remarkable of prehistoric monuments in Britain. The Welsh poet Aneirin pronounced it, in the seventh century, to be the work of giants, and John Aubrey, its first investigator, misled generations by advocating that it was the Temple of the Druids; one historian averred that it had been erected by Appalachian Indians, while Dr Hastings Banda wished he could take it to Nyasaland to show his people that Britain once had a savage culture. Geoffrey of Monmouth's statement that it had been brought by Merlin from Ireland may have been based on a belief in a western origin.

While carrying out a survey of south Pembrokeshire in 1922, Dr H.H. Thomas of the Geological Survey found some boulders of spotted dolerite and traced their origin to outcrops at Carn Menyn and the surrounding area. Here also were found the rhyolite and volcanic ash pillars that, with the spotted dolerite, constitute all the foreign stones found at Stonehenge, with two exceptions.

Some time during the third millennium BC, more than eighty stones, weighing over 250 tons in all, were transported from the Presely Hills to Salisbury Plain. Professor R.J.C. Atkinson has carried out experiments to prove that they could have been hauled over land by sledge and rollers, probably to Canaston

Bridge, the tidal limit of the Eastern Cleddau, and thence taken by water to Milford Haven, along the coasts of the Bristol Channel, up the Bristol Avon and the Frome, then over land to Warminster, down the River Wylye and on to their final destination. That the stones were shipped out of Milford Haven is proven by the fact that the two pillars that do not come from Presely have been identified with the micaceous sandstone found near Llangwm and at Mill Bay, near Cosheston. A bluestone found in a long barrow at Heytesbury suggests that the stones may have been used on a site other than Stonehenge in the first instance. The recent theory that the stones were carried by glacier ice from Presely and Milford Haven and deposited conveniently on Salisbury Plain is one that most people find difficult to accept.

The motives that prompted the effort to transport the foreign stones over such a distance may be found in the veneration in which the Presely Hills were held by neolithic people. Professor Atkinson has expressed the view that the cloud-capped summit of Presely Top must have seemed to them 'no less the home of gods than did Mount Ida to a voyager in the Cretan plain'.

Although early maps showed the Presely Hills dotted with stone circles, there is, in fact, only one, at Gors Fawr, near Mynachlogddu, and its stones are low, none exceeding three feet in height.

The most common prehistoric stone monument in Pembrokeshire is the *maenhir*, or standing stone, and, at the same time, the most puzzling. Giraldus Cambrensis was of the opinion that they marked the victories of King Harold over the Welsh in 1063 and states that they were called Harold Stones on that account, but there is no evidence that the last of the Saxon kings visited the area, and certainly not Skomer Island, which has a Harold Stone. Some are the last surviving uprights of burial chambers, and others are associated with Bronze Age barrows: some may have been waymarks, or monuments, or cult objects with a phallic connotation. Excavation at the Rhos y Clegyrn stone, near St Nicholas, produced evidence of elaborate ritual practices. They sometimes appear in pairs, one taller and more tapering than the other, 'male' and 'female' like the stones at Avebury. An alignment of eight stones at Parc-y-meirw, near Llanychaer, is one of only eight in Wales.

A people with a different tradition from the neolithic tomb-builders arrived around 1800 BC and brought with them weapons of bronze and bell-shaped beakers, and they buried their dead in single graves under round barrows. The barrows are usually on high ground and often along the ancient trackways. The most outstanding are the three cairns which give its name to Foel Drygarn, and a group of six barrows occupies a prominent site at Crugiau Cemais, while there are other concentrations at Ridgeway, Dry Burrows and Wallaston in the south. The trackways were followed by Bronze Age prospectors travelling between Wessex and Ireland where a flourishing metal industry had developed.

The early Bronze Age people buried their dead usually in a crouched position, and placed pots, or beakers, containing food with the body. From about 1500 BC cremation took the place of inhumation, and the burnt remains were placed in an enlarged urn, which was sometimes accompanied by a small decorated 'pygmy cup'.

Those who came during the Early Iron Age, from about 500 BC, are known from their settlements, which were built with defence in mind. Their hill forts crown the summits of Carn Ingli, Garnfawr and Moel Drygarn and other eminences, some with a single rampart, and others multivallate for greater protection against slings and arrows. The coast was girt with promontory forts protected by banks and ditches, and jutting scarps in inland valleys were similarly defended; occasionally hill slopes have earthwork defences, some with concentric rings of bank and ditch resembling the camps found in south-west England and in northern Spain. Apart from the fortified sites there are groups of hut dwellings on the slopes of Presely, and field systems on Skomer Island and St David's Head.

These were the early Celts who brought with them a proto-Celtic language that became divided into the Brythonic – Welsh, Cornish and Breton – and the Goidelic – Irish, Gaelic and Manx – languages, identifed as P and Q groups, as the Brythonic Celts used a *p* sound for the Goidelic *q* or *c*. The Welsh *pen*, 'head', is *ceann* in Irish, 'five' is *pump* in Welsh and *cuinc* in Irish.

From early times, Pembrokeshire has lain at the crossroads of the western seaways: the northward Atlantic sea-route from the coasts of France and Spain, and the east-west passage between the Continent and southern Ireland. Professor V.G. Childe saw 'the grey waters of the Irish Sea bright with neolithic argonauts', and Bronze Age traders were no less busy, lured by the copper and gold in the Wicklow Hills; the sea was no barrier, any more than language, to the early Celts.

In the late fourth century, or early fifth, AD, an Irish tribe, the Deisi, came from Deece in County Meath, under their leader, Eochaid Allmuir, to colonize Pembrokeshire and to establish a dynasty that was to rule it for several centuries. They are remembered in place-names and in the ogham writing on inscribed stones. Apart from providing the earliest written evidence, these stones bear witness to the introduction of Christianity before it had reached other parts of Britain. They were erected in memory of personages of some account during the fifth, sixth and seventh centuries, and the inscription is frequently in Goidelic ogham and in Latin. The ogham alphabet was invented in southern Ireland and consisted of up to five lines, indicating a manual basis, and the characters were notched on the arris, or edge, of a stone. Stones bearing incised crosses belong to a later period, culminating in the decorated high crosses at Nevern, Carew and Penally, which are of the eleventh century.

The early Church was organized on a monastic level, with a *clas*, or religious community, that concerned itself with missionary work. The Celtic missionaries, or 'saints', travelled freely between Ireland and the Continent, using the transpeninsular routes across Pembrokeshire and Cornwall, and established cells that later became churches dedicated to them.

The inhabitants of Pembrokeshire at the beginning of the Christian era were referred to by the geographer Ptolemy as the Demetae, and their land was known as Demetia, the Latin form of the modern Welsh name Dyfed. Whether the Demetae were too much of a handful for the Romans to tackle or, perhaps more likely, came to terms with them, may never be known, but the fact is that the quadrilateral Roman occupation of Wales did not extend into this western peninsula. There are traces of buildings, however, that had Roman characteristics, at Ford, Castle Flemish and Trelissey, which appear to have been fortified farmsteads occupied by natives between the first and third centuries AD. The recent discovery that slate ballast taken from the Presely Hills was used to metal the third-century wharves at Caerleon, and to repair the south coastal highway, indicates a legionary communication by sea, and it is thought that Roman ships patrolled the Pembrokeshire coast against Irish sea-raiders and may even have sought shelter in Milford Haven.

The fury of the Norsemen visited St Dogmael's and St David's, but there is no memory of them save in the place-names of coastal settlements, features and islands. The only material evidence of their visitations is a leaden tablet found on the shore at Freshwater West.

The Dark Ages were no less dark in Pembrokeshire than in the rest of Europe. While the known story is one of fratricidal strife among the Welsh princes, there are thin shafts of light to show that native culture was far from dead. A poem written in praise of the hospitable lord of Tenby, Bleiddudd ab Erbin, survives from the ninth century, and Asser, a boy from Pencaer, was sufficiently outstanding to become the trusted adviser to King Alfred, while the tales of *The Mabinogion* which have their setting in pre-Norman Pembrokeshire portray a way of life that was both civilized and colourful.

The Norman Roger de Montgomery struck across Wales, made for the richer pastures of south Pembrokeshire and created a linguistic divide that exists to this day. In the north, Robert FitzMartin sailed over from Devon and conquered the cantref of Cemais, but there the Normans intermingled with the native populace and the Welsh language survives. The rest of Pembrokeshire became feudal lordships based largely on the old Welsh hundreds, except for Dewsland that was never conquered, but its bishops, nevertheless, were henceforth Anglo-Norman with military tenants occupying episcopal fiefs.

Before they could complete their occupation of Pembrokeshire, the Normans built over fifty castles, most of them never more than earthworks, but some were built of stone, usually near water so as to maintain the marine communication that was necessary to bring supplies and reinforcement. Around the castles there grew towns, in a land where there were only villages, and the towns were granted charters that gave them fairs and markets and mayors. The Normans endowed monasteries and built churches with tall towers that are landmarks still. Despite the linguistic 'landsker', the racial division was not so sharp, and there was much intermarriage. Welsh families in the north bear Norman surnames, and Welsh place-names survive in the south, though many have been corrupted beyond recognition.

The Normans encouraged the English to settle in south Pembrokeshire, and in 1108 some Flemish immigrants were introduced by Henry I who, 'being very liberal of that which was not his own', gave them land in Rhos and Daugleddau in mid-Pembrokeshire. Giraldus Cambrensis states that they had been brought as a defence against 'the unquiet Welshmen', whom they grew to hate, and he describes them as 'well-versed in commerce and woollen manufactories ... a hardy race, equally fitted to the plough and the sword'.

The Tudor period began as Henry Tudor, born at Pembroke Castle, returned to his native county and set foot ashore at Mill Bay, near Dale, at sunset on a Sunday evening in August 1485 and unfurled his banner bearing the red dragon of Cadwaladr. At dawn, next day, he set off with his motley army of two thousand French, Breton, English and Welsh soldiers, on the long march to Bosworth Field.

Pembrokeshire had its own great Elizabethans: George Owen of Henllys, the historian; George Owen Harry and George William Griffith, genealogists; Robert Holland, translator of the *Basilikon Doron*, and Thomas Phaer who translated Virgil's *Aeneid* into English; Robert Recorde, the mathematician, and Sir John Perrot, Lord Deputy in Ireland.

The Civil War found Welsh Pembrokeshire staunchly Royalist, while the anglicized south was for Parliament, but there were many changes of allegiance on both sides. General Rowland Laugharne, commander of the Roundheads, later garrisoned Pembroke Castle against Cromwell. Cromwell's orders to destroy castles were carried out half-heartedly, and more damage was done by pillagers.

William Walter went to London to claim compensation for the damage done to his castle at Roch and took his daughter, Lucy, with him. She became acquainted with the Prince of Wales, later King Charles II, and in consequence the mother of the Duke of Monmouth.

The latter half of the seventeenth century was notable for the rise of religious dissent. Early Quakers were persecuted and prosecuted, and some sought freedom to worship in Pennsylvania, where they settled and gave their townships the names of Haverford and Narberth. The Methodist revivalists came and preached to the multitudes in fields as there were no edifices large enough. John Wesley visited the county on fourteen occasions and was entertained by the leading families. The Moravians built their only church in Wales at Haverfordwest.

Pembrokeshire had a reputation for piracy and for harbouring pirates during the eighteenth century. Bartholomew Roberts from Little Newcastle, who drank nothing stronger than tea, was probably the most successful pirate of all time. Sir John Wogan of Boulston, Vice-Admiral for South Wales, was prosecuted for piracy, and Sir John Perrot had to account to the Privy Council for the presence of the notorious John Callice at Haverfordwest. But Admiral Thomas Tucker of Sealyham is credited with the dispatch of the infamous Bluebeard, and the county also produced Admiral Sir Thomas Foley, who fought with Nelson, Admiral Sir Erasmus Gower and Admiral William Vaughan of Trecwn. Its most famous military figure, General Sir Thomas Picton, distinguished himself in the Pensinsular War and later, though badly wounded at Quatre Bras, led his men the next day, against desperate odds, at Waterloo.

The great excitement of the century occurred at its close, with the French landing near Fishguard, a short-lived fiasco that led to widespread alarm and suspicions but served to expedite measures for the defence of Milford Haven.

The sharp rise in population during the first half of the nineteenth century caused sufferings and disquiet that found expression in the tearing down of toll gates by farmers and farm workers who disguised themselves, as their counterparts had done in England a century earlier, in women's clothes. The 'daughters of Rebecca' assembled at Efailwen on 13 May 1839 and destroyed the gate and burned down the toll house; from there the riots spread, until toll gates were removed and the roads improved. Soon after, the railroad came and reached Haverfordwest and Neyland, Milford, Pembroke and Fishguard, places that had hitherto prospered as ports and harbours.

The prosperity of Milford as a new town, harbour and fishing port did not last long, but the demand for deep-water facilities for tankers, carrying a quarter of a million tons, led to its development as the leading oil port in Britain, with four giant refineries and an oil terminal.

Agriculture, the main industry for centuries, has acquired a new significance with modern farming methods. Pembrokeshire early potatoes are exported in lorry-loads by the score to Lincolnshire and Lancashire, Yorkshire and the Midlands, while Pembrokeshire turkeys are a byword in households throughout the country.

The designation of the Pembrokeshire National Park in 1952 brought into conflict the need to conserve those things that should be kept unspoilt for future generations and the provision of opportunities for their enjoyment by the public. The National Park has proved an attraction not only for holiday-makers but also for those who seek beauty unspoiled and a measure of wilderness.

3

Along the Teifi

St Dogmael's meanders at the behest of the Teifi, a river that rises beyond Strata Florida and, having held Ceredigion in its lap, empties itself into the sea at Poppit Sands. The Welsh name for the village, Llandudoch, derives from an unknown saint to whom an early church may have been dedicated, and there was, by all accounts, another dedication to St Dogfael, commemorated in the English name. The parish church of St Thomas the Martyr is styled *'Ecclesia Sancti Thome apostoli de Sancto Dogmaele'* in the *Valor Ecclesiasticus* of 1291, while the abbey is dedicated to St Mary the Virgin.

The Normans regarded it as an act of piety, once their conquest was complete, to establish and endow a place of worship, and so it was that Robert FitzMartin, having possessed himself of the old Welsh cantref, or hundred, of Cemais, founded a monastery at St Dogmael's and brought thither a prior and twelve monks from the abbey of Tiron, in the diocese of Chartres, in 1115. Tiron had been established by St Bernard of Abbeville for his followers, who wished to observe a more strict interpretation of the rule of St Benedict and a greater devotion to manual labour. In 1120 the consent of the abbot of Tiron was obtained to raise St Dogmael's to the status of an abbey, and its first abbot, Fulchard, was enthroned by Bishop Bernard of St David's in that year.

The presence of a number of inscribed stones suggests the existence of an earlier Christian settlement on or near this site, and an early Welsh poem speaks of 'a disturbed house on the banks of the Teifi' and warns that the marauding Norse from the Isle of Man will 'break the bell of the monks of Llandudoch' and reduce their house so that it will be no more than a resort of wild pigs – *'namyn gwarwyfa gwyddfoch'*. This 'prophecy' was probably written after the sacking of St Dogmael's by the Norse in the year 987.

Robert FitzMartin endowed the abbey with lands in Pembrokeshire, Devon and County Wexford, and his mother, Geva, made a gift of Caldey with its Celtic monastery which became a subordinate priory to St Dogmael's.

The abbey was suppressed in 1536 and purchased by John Bradshaw of Presteign, in Radnorshire, and formerly of Lancashire, who converted the abbot's dwelling into a residence.

The cruciform abbey church and the cloisters, the abbot's lodging, the presbytery and the infirmary were built during the twelfth century and the first half of the thirteenth. Early in the fourteenth century the church and cloister ranges were rebuilt following a disaster, and the chapter house and guest house were added. The north transept was reconstructed and covered with an elaborate vaulted roof in the sixteenth century.

Among the several inscribed stones found within the precincts of the abbey was the Sagranus stone, dating from the early sixth century and now resting in the nave of the parish church but once used as a gatepost. On one face of the stone is the Latin inscription SAGRANI FILI CVNOTAMI while on the angle, or arris, is inscribed in ogham writing SAGRANI MAQI CUNATAMI, indicating, both in Latin and in Gaelic, that the stone was intended to commemorate a local chieftain, probably of Irish ancestry, by the name of Sagranus, the son of Cunotamus.

Archbishop Baldwin of Canterbury and Giraldus Cambrensis slept the night at the abbey while preaching the Third Crusade in 1188, and were 'handsomely entertained', both there and at Cardigan Castle, by Prince Rhys ap Gruffydd, the Lord Rhys.

St Dogmael's, now a holiday resort, was one of the boroughs of the lordship of Cemais, with a portreeve elected annually by the burgesses at the Court Leet. Its menfolk have long connections with the sea, as mariners or fishermen. The fishermen divide into crews, each with its captain, and draw lots to drag recognized beats of the Teifi, or a half-moon in the bay, with long seine-nets. At the start of the season, the nets are blessed at a ceremony held on the river bank.

Higher up the Teifi, Cilgerran was a borough, until the Municipal Corporations Act of 1883 abolished small boroughs, where newly sworn burgesses were toasted by the portreeve in a horn of ale at the Court Leet, and where St Lawrence Fair was held each year on 10 August, the feast day of that saint who was martyred on a gridiron.

Cilgerran Castle is spectacularly sited, high above a gorge of the Teifi. It inspired artists, like Peter de Wint, Richard Wilson and J.M.W. Turner: the Wilson hangs in the National Museum of Wales, and the Turner at the Tate. And it provided the setting for Joseph Warton's *King Arthur's Grave*, from the erroneous belief that Cilgerran derives from 'the cell of Geraint', one of the Knights of the Round Table.

The original castle may have been built by Roger de Montgomery during his advance to Pembroke in 1093: it was certainly in the hands of Gerald de Windsor, constable of Pembroke, ten years later. It was captured, in 1164, by the Lord Rhys, whose sons held it until 1204, when it was retaken by William Marshal, Earl of Pembroke. Llywelyn the Great took it in 1215, but it was recaptured in 1224 by William Marshal the Younger, who began to rebuild the castle in local slate. It was held by five of his sons in quick succession and then, in 1245, by his daughter, who had married William de Braose, lord of Abergavenny, from which time it came under that lordship and remained so until it reverted to Lawrence Hastings, Earl of Pembroke, in 1339. The castle had been neglected meanwhile and was in ruins by 1326. When it was feared that the French would invade South Wales, following the defeat of the English fleet at La Rochelle in 1372 under John Hastings, Earl of Pembroke, Edward III ordered the repair of Cilgerran, but it was slighted again in 1405 during the rising of Owain Glyn Dŵr. When the last of the Hastings died in 1389, Cilgerran passed to the Crown, and Henry VII granted its custody to William Vaughan of Merioneth. It later passed to the Pryses of Gogerddan and remained in that family until 1938 when it was purchased by Mrs Colby of Ffynnone nearby and presented to the National Trust. It is now under the guardianship of the Department of the Environment which has undertaken extensive restoration of the remains.

Recent excavation has revealed traces of the original motte-and-bailey that stood on this commanding site. The inner ward occupies the place of the motte and is separated from the outer ward, which covers the extent of the bailey, by a rock-cut ditch. The two circular towers and the gatehouse, with its double portcullis, were built by William Marshal the Younger to protect the inner ward. The rectangular tower in the north-west corner of the inner ward dates from the following century, and there are traces of other buildings that include a kitchen and a medieval limekiln. Between the limekiln and the gatehouse, and outside the curtain wall, are remains of walls that probably belong to the twelfth century.

The church of St Llawddog has memorials to the Gower family which included Admiral Sir Erasmus Gower, born at Glandovan in 1742, who served with Rodney and Cornwallis and was Commander-in-chief and Governor of Newfoundland from 1804 to 1807. An alms dish, among the unusually rich church plate, is the only eucharistic vessel in Pembrokeshire that bears a Welsh inscription. In the churchyard, among the tombstones, is a stone, inscribed in Latin and in ogham, commemorating Trenegussus, son of Macutrenus, who lived in the sixth century.

A Norwich man who had married the daughter of William Vaughan of Forest, Cilgerran, came to settle there in 1543 upon his appointment as solicitor to the Council of the Marches. His name was Thomas Phaer and, apart from being the author of legal works, he wrote several medical treatises and a translation, through the French, of *Regimen Sanitatis Salerni*, which first made medical science intelligible in English. In addition, he published a number of literary works, including a long poem entitled *Howe Owen Glendower being reduced by false prophecies who upon him to be Prince of Wales*. He is best known in English literature for his translation of Virgil's *Aeneid*, the first seven books of which were published in 1558 and dedicated to Queen Mary, and he had completed two more books and was working on the tenth when he died at Forest in 1560.

John Roland Phillips, born at Cilgerran in 1844, became the first stipendiary magistrate for West Ham. An essay, for which he won the prize at an eisteddfod at Cardigan in 1866, was later published as the *History of Cilgerran*, and among his other works were *Memoirs of the Ancient Family of Owen of Orielton*, *A List of the Sheriffs of Cardiganshire* and *Memoirs of the Civil War in Wales and the Marches*.

Giraldus Cambrensis states, in 1188, that here were found the last beavers in Wales, or even in England, and tells how they elude the stratagems of the well-armed hunter, who is watching them from the opposite banks of the river. When the beaver finds he cannot save himself from the pursuit of dogs who follow him, that he may ransom himself his body by the sacrifice of a part, he throws away that which by natural instinct he knows to be the object sought for, and in the sight of the hunter castrates himself, from which circumstance he has gained the name of Castor; and if by chance the dogs should chase an animal which had been previously castrated, he has the sagacity to run to an elevated spot, and there lifting up his leg, shows the hunter that the object of his pursuit is gone.

'The chiefest weir of all Wales' lay below Cilgerran Castle, according to George Owen, made of strong timber frames in which as many as twelve dozen salmon had been captured in one day. The weir was levelled in the thirteenth century because it interfered with the passage of boats carrying stone and timber to Cardigan Castle, but in 1314 it was reinstated, allowing room for vessels to pass. It was said that the people who lived at Coedmor, the house above the gorge, used to hang a net across the river, and from it a string was connected to a bell in the house, that rang whenever there was a catch of salmon.

The reaches of the Teifi between Cilgerran and Llechryd have always yielded the greatest abundance of salmon, and at one time there was hardly a cottage in the neighbourhood without its coracle hanging by the door.

The coracle was originally covered with the skin of a beast, but nowadays unbleached calico, waterproofed with a mixture of pitch and linseed oil, is stretched over a framework of split willow rods secured at the ends with hazel twigs to form a plaited gunwale. A twisted oak sapling, pushed through holes in the wooden seat, is used for carrying the coracle upstream, and men doing so look like so many giant beetles. The paddle, made of ash, is sculled in front of the craft, with one hand. Coracles drift down river in pairs, with a seine-net between them, held by guidelines of horsehair and rings of polished cowhorn. The netted salmon is dispatched with a truncheon cut from an apple tree and known as 'the priest'. An Act of Parliament of 1935 prohibited the issue of fishing licences to coracle men on the Teifi above Llechryd Bridge, where the river now ceases to be tidal.

Llechryd Bridge has the date 1638 on its Pembrokeshire side. Below its four arches are the remains of *Y Gored*, a fish trap that yielded £900 worth of fish annually until it was destroyed by the Rebecca Rioters in 1843. Freshwater mussels were plentiful until the river was polluted, and many a 'swan pearl' was found by the mussel-fishers. A Llechryd angler, it is claimed, was the inventor of the *coch-a-bonddu* fly.

Pig iron and limestone were hauled in horse-drawn barges from the port of Cardigan to feed the Coedmor forge established nearby in the seventeenth century. Fifteen years after it ceased to function, in 1765, the Penygored tinworks was opened on the opposite bank of the river, near Castle Maelgwyn, and provided employment for up to three hundred men producing twelve thousand boxes a year for the next forty years.

At the battle of Llechryd Bridge in 1087, Rhys ap Tewdwr, Prince of South Wales, supported by Irish and Norse mercenaries he had brought from Ireland, beat his adversaries, the sons of Bleddyn ap Cynfyn, Prince of Gwynedd, and is said to have handed over a great number of captives to the Irish.

James ap Gruffydd of Castle Maelgwyn was arrested and lodged in the Tower of London for his alleged complicity in the treason for which his cousin, Sir Rhys ap Gruffydd, was executed in 1531, but he was pardoned and left for Scotland where he joined the Scottish King, until Queen Mary came to the throne and he was able to return to Castle Maelgwyn. The present house, now a country hotel, was built at the end of the eighteenth century by John Hammett, who was responsible for the Penygored tinworks.

Two of the box pews at Manordeifi church have fireplaces, in front of which the gentry would stretch their legs and smoke their pipes during sermons. A coracle had to be kept in the church porch to rescue the prayer books during times of flooding. The church is now ruinous but a service is held in the churchyard each summer, when the strains of thanksgiving hymns floating down the valley provide an experience that stays long in the memory. A tablet in the church commemorates the Welsh poet Alun, the Reverend John Blackwell, who was appointed vicar in 1833; another remembers a soldier mauled to death by a tiger in Rawalpindi. A church built on higher ground in 1899 has a pulpit and a font, of marble and mosaics, that were removed from the private chapel of Pentre, a nearby country house.

Thomas Rocyn Jones (1822-77) learnt how to cure cattle on his father's farm at Manordeifi and applied the skills thus acquired to the treatment of human injuries. His inventiveness in devising splints and wedges established him as an eminent bone-setter half a century ahead of his time.

On a day in 1763, Howel Davies, 'the Apostle of Pembrokeshire', was travelling along the road from Abercuch to Boncath when he suddenly flung his whip into a clump of gorse and proclaimed: 'Here shall we build a new chapel.' And, on land given by Squire Colby of Ffynnone, the chapel was built. The chapel, and after it the village, was called New Chapel to distinguish it from the earlier chapel of Woodstock, on the mountain road from Cardigan to Haverfordwest. The village school was provided by John Colby, ten years later, at a cost of £1,000, and houses were built for those who were employed in the surrounding stately homes.

Ffynnone was originally designed, in 1793, by John Nash, and although the house has been re-modelled, the interior is Nash. Cilwendeg, now a home for the elderly, is a Georgian house built by Morgan Jones from money derived from the Skerries lighthouse, off Anglesey. It has a grotto with shell-lined walls and intricate flooring.

The church at Capel Colman is dedicated to St Colman of Dromore, one of the traditional Twelve Apostles of Ireland, who is also represented at Llangolman. In his *View of the State of Religion in the Diocese of St David's in the beginning of the 18th Century*, Erasmus Saunders complains that some churches were 'totally neglected ... and which if they are not converted into barns and stables, which is the case of many churches in England as well as Wales, do only serve for the solitary habitations of owls and jackdaws, such are ... Capel Colman and others in Pembrokeshire'. A pillar-stone inscribed with crosses on the back and front, which formerly served as a gatepost, is now safe in the church.

Boncath – Welsh for 'buzzard' – grew as a railway village when the Whitland and Taf Vale line was extended to Cardigan in 1885.

Castell Crychydd, 'heron's castle', is a fine motte-and-bailey built by the Normans to consolidate their advance into Pembrokeshire.

In the course of digging a bog near Henfeddau farm, in the

parish of Clydai, in the autumn of 1859, a farmer came across a hoard of bronze implements, mainly swords and spearheads, most of which appeared to have been damaged intentionally, perhaps to prevent their use by an approaching enemy. In 1903 a dugout fashioned from a single baulk of oak was retrieved from a peat bog at Nant Ifan nearby.

Clydai church has inscribed stones commemorating, in Latin, Solinus, son of Vendonius, and bilingually, in Latin and ogham lettering, Etternus, son of Victor, and Dobitucus, son of Evolengus, all dating from the fifth or sixth century.

Pwyll, Prince of Dyfed, 'was minded to go out and hunt and the part of his dominions in which it pleased him to hunt was Glyn Cuch'. As soon as he had loosed his hounds, he heard the cry of other hounds, the like of which he had never seen before, 'for their hair was of a brilliant shining white and their ears were red, and as the whiteness of their bodies shone, so did the redness of their ears glisten.' Even so, Pwyll drove them away and set his own hounds on the stag they were chasing, and in penance he had to change places with the King of Annwn, the Other World of the Celts, whose hounds they were. So begins the first tale of *The Mabinogion*, a collection of stories dating from the Celtic era, committed to writing about the year 1300 and then, and now, regarded as a masterpiece of medieval European literature.

The vale of Cuch is as enticing today as it was for Pwyll.

The village of Abercuch has long been known for its wood-turners who, until recently, employed methods that were used two thousand years ago to produce ware that corresponded closely to that found at lake dwellings in Glastonbury. James Davies's pole lathe consisted of a long ash pole anchored at one end and resting on a forked stick, with a piece of string, passed round the lathe chuck, joining the other end to a foot treadle. I once found him turning a bowl, black and smooth as ebony, from a piece of oak which had lain for centuries beneath the mill wheel beside his workshop. He was making it, he confided in his quiet voice, as 'a present for our new Queen', as Queen Elizabeth the Queen Mother then was.

The Penrhiw Inn, now no more, was the home of John Morgan Gibbon, who became minister of the Congregational chapels at Highgate and at Stamford Hill, while at the 'Nag's Head' was reared Evan Herber Evans, principal of Bala-Bangor College and one of the most appealing preachers of the last century. At Pontsely, the sculptor James Milo Griffith, whose works include 'The Four Evangelists' at Bristol Cathedral and 'The Fine Arts' on Holborn Viaduct, was born in 1843.

The Court Leet and View of Frankpledge of the lordship and manor of Castellan, in 1854, resolved, 'after solemn consideration', that the Elizabethan chalice that belonged to 'the chapelry of Castellan should be deposited in some suitable place for safe custody and preservation' and requested the lord of the manor, William Henry Lewis, to allow it 'to be deposited in some convenient place at his mansion at Clynfiew', near Abercuch. The chalice, which is inscribed *'Poculum capelle de Castellan'*, is probably 1574.

The chapel of Castellan was annexed to the parish of Penrhydd and was granted by William Marshal, Earl of Pembroke, to the Knights Hospitallers at Slebech. It was in ruins by 1684 when the rector reported that the bier had been stolen, 'but by whom we cannot tell'.

I was first taken to Crymych, as a small boy, in a pony and trap, and thought that I had arrived in Abilene. There were horses and horse-drawn carriages along the wide street, and ponies tied to posts outside the shops and the 'saloons' – the Crymych Arms and London House inns. I almost expected Joseph (the real) McCoy and Wild Bill Hickock to swagger by.

Crymych began as a farmhouse, standing on the convergence of six roads, and its growth as a village began with the coming of the Whitland and Taf Vale Railway in 1875. The Congregationalists had already established Antioch Chapel in 1858, and the Baptists built Seion in 1902. There is no church.

According to legend, a leaden chest filled with gold lies buried on the slopes of Freni Fawr, guarded by 'some tremendous phantom with tempest in his train', while *The Dream of Macsen Wledig*, one of the tales of *The Mabinogion*, tells us that Macsen, that is Magnus Maximus, the Roman soldier who proclaimed himself Emperor of the West, went forth to hunt and 'came so far as the top of Freni Fawr, and there the emperor pitched his tent. And that encampment is called Cadair Facsen to this day.'

Moel Drygarn, to the west of Crymych, has a cockscomb of three barrows of the Bronze Age, which give it its name, and its summit is girt by the defences of an Iron Age hill fort.

In the burial ground of the chapel at Hermon is the tomb of Nathaniel Williams, 'Minister of the Gospel to Jeneral Baptists', hymnologist, theological controversialist and amateur doctor whose works included *Pharmacopoeia, or Medical Admonitions in English and Welsh* and whose hymns were of such excellence as to be mistakenly attributed to the great Ann Griffiths.

The slate quarry at Glogue was worked by the Owen family of Glogue Farm from about 1685, and until the arrival of the railway in 1873, slates were dispatched by sea from Cardigan and Newport. By 1885 the output of the quarry was close on two thousand tons a year.

Llanfyrnach takes its name from St Brynach, to whom no fewer than nine churches in north Pembrokeshire are dedicated. The church was appropriated to the Knights of the Commandery at Slebech, together with a hundred acres of land, some time before 1165. A silver lead mine at Llanfyrnach produced a thousand tons of ore per annum before it was closed in 1888, when a ton fetched £13.

In the graveyard of the chapel at Glandwr stands a pillar bearing the name, in ogham writing, of Efassangus Asegnus, who appears to have been a man of consequence in this area some fifteen hundred years ago. Inside the chapel is a memorial to Lazarus Howel 'who entered his disembodied state Jan. 15th. 1776'. Thomas Phillips of Waunbwll buried his lame mother beside the churchyard gate, so that she would not have far to travel on Judgement Day. Twm Waunbwll, as he was known, was a celebrated local character, of whom many a tale is told. On one occasion, two surveyors came to survey Twm's land with a view to placing a railway line across it, but they were refused access. When they produced a 'blue paper' of authority, Twm consented, and then turned a bull into the field they were surveying. As the bull was chasing the men round the field, Twm sat on the five-barred gate and shouted: 'Show *him* the blue paper!'

4
South of Presely

In the graveyard of Bethel chapel at Mynachlogddu lies Thomas Rees of Carnabwth, pugilist and riot leader. On the night of 19 July 1839 a large crowd of people assembled at the tollgate at Efailwen, on the road from Crymych to Narberth, having disguised themselves by blackening their faces and by wearing women's clothes. Thomas Rees was alleged to have been the leader on that occasion, and it is said that there had been some difficulty in obtaining female garments to fit him until he succeeded in borrowing those of Big Becca, a large lady who lived in the adjoining parish of Llangolman. In consequence, the leader of the mob was addressed as Becca, and the protesters were known henceforth as the Rebecca Rioters. Rees took no further part in the riots, by all accounts. In 1847 he lost an eye in a fight following a drunken argument with a gypsy, but he later became a devout member of Bethel, and his sudden death, at the age of seventy, is the subject of the epitaph on his tombstone:

Nid oes neb ond Duw yn gwybod
Beth all ddigwydd mewn diwarnod,
Wrth gyrchu bresych at fy nghinio
Daeth Angau i fy ngardd i'm taro.

(No one but God knows what can happen in a day. While I was fetching a cabbage for my dinner, Death came into my garden and struck me down.)

The manor of Mynachlogddu was granted to the abbey of St Dogmael's by Robert FitzMartin, lord of Cemais, in the twelfth century, and the inhabitants of Plwyf Bach, in St Dogmael's, had a right of summer pasture there for their cattle.

North of Mynachlogddu bridge is the Gors Fawr stone circle, the only ring of free-standing stones in the Presely Hills and one that is typical of the upland areas of Wales. Sixteen low igneous boulders stand unevenly spaced in a near circle, some seventy feet in diameter, on a level piece of moorland. Towards the north-east are two outlying pillars, each about six feet high, which are probably associated with the circle.

The collapsed megalithic monument at Mountain Farm appears to have been a portal dolmen, and judging from the size of its fallen supporters, it was an impressive tomb standing on the saddle of a pass and on a route that must have been used by prehistoric man. Above it stands Foel Drygarn, with its three Bronze Age burials and Iron Age hill fort, and the outcrops that yielded the Stonehenge bluestones, while the valley below has standing stones and round barrows. On the open mountain nearby, at Croes Mihangel, recent excavation revealed a number of Bronze Age burial urns dating from about 1500 BC; there is a local belief that malefactors were hanged here. Crugiau Dwy has two cairns on its summit, and the tale goes that two females, some say goddesses, who were in love with the same man, or god, retired to the hill top to fight it out with stones, while the loved one acted as umpire: the combatants, sadly, both perished in the fight, and the disconsolate lover gathered the boulders and erected them into cairns on the grave of each.

Carn Menyn was the main source of the spotted dolerites transported to form the bluestone circle at Stonehenge about 1700 BC.

Pembrokeshire slates were renowned for their soft colours and tough quality. They were used to roof the Temple of Peace at Cardiff, Llandaff Cathedral, the Kensington Museum and abroad, as far as South Africa, on the Cape Town town hall. And it may be that not many members of the House of Lords and the House of Commons are aware that the silver-grey slates on the Palace of Westminster were quarried at Llangolman.

St Teilo was buried in three places, it was claimed: at Llandaff, at Llandeilo Fawr, in Carmarthenshire, and at Llandeilo Llwydarth, near Maenclochog. His tomb at Llandaff was desecrated by pirates from Bristol and was restored, in 1480, by Sir David Mathew. For his piety Sir David was given St Teilo's skull, encased in gold, by the Bishop of Llandaff, and it passed, but without its gold, to a branch of the Mathew family at Llandeilo Isaf Farm in the seventeenth century. William

Melchior came over the hills from Newport to marry the heiress of Llandeilo Isaf, and the Melchiors remained custodians of the skull, which they kept in the drawer of a table in the parlour until 1927, when it was returned to Llandaff. Water from St Teilo's Well nearby was reputed to be a cure for tuberculosis, whooping cough and asthma, provided it was drunk out of St Teilo's skull and handed to the sufferer by the head of the custodian family. The skull, on examination, however, was considered to be that of a young woman.

Two inscribed stones found at Llandeilo, and removed to Maenclochog church for safety, may commemorate two brothers who lived here in the sixth century or even earlier. One pillar bears the name, in Latin, of Coimagnus, son of Cavetus, and the other, in Latin and in ogham, that of Andagellus, son of Cavetus. Another stone, inscribed *Curcagni fili Andagelli*, was taken from Maenclochog to Gellidywyll, near Cenarth, in about 1770, and placed by the squire on the grave of his favourite filly!

The Curcagnus stone was found, in 1743, on the roadside by Bwlch-y-clawdd, then the home of William Lewis, an ancestor of the late Lord Butler of Saffron Walden, who told me that he had miniatures of the Misses Lewis of Bwlch-y-clawdd on his mantelshelf at Trinity College, Cambridge, when he was Master. The house was rebuilt as a hunting lodge, reputedly by John Nash, and named Temple Druid after a cromlech, a 'supposed druid altar', that stood nearby. Leo Walmsley wrote *The Happy Ending* here, and a picture of the house appears on the dust jacket.

The village green at Maenclochog is an unusual feature in north Pembrokeshire. It surrounds the church, and on it were held the monthly fairs and September hiring fair. Fenton maintained that Maenclochog had more fairs than anywhere in the country, and in 1843 attempts were made to establish yet another so as to avoid the payment of tolls at Newport's St Curig's Fair.

The church stands on a raised churchyard. It is a simple Victorian building but it has a square font, probably Norman, with a depression on one side pierced by a round hole, and it contains the inscribed stones, to the sons of Cavetus, that were found at Llandeilo Llwydarth.

Water from St Mary's Well was used for baptism at the

church. The well was formerly covered by a huge capstone which, on being struck, sounded like a bell, and this stone, it was said, had given the village its name: even so, it was smashed because it frightened passing horses. The name derives, however, from the Welsh *maen* and the Irish *cloch*, both words meaning a stone or rock.

Craig y Castell, the castle rock, rises sharply near the site of the small castle that was taken by Llywelyn the Great in 1215 and by Llywelyn the Last in 1257. The village's two chapels, both Independent, remind one of the story of the Welsh sailor who had been marooned on a desert island and, when found twenty years later, was asked why he had built, beside a house, two chapels. 'The one on the left,' he answered, 'is the one I don't go to.'

The pale green velvet slopes of the Presely Hills, now heavily clad with dark conifers, bear the scar of a disused slate quarry at Rosebush. The quarry was acquired by Edward Cropper, Member of Parliament for Penshurst in Kent (who bore cropper pigeons on his canting arms). Cropper had married, for his second wife, Margaret, sister of Thomas Babington, Lord Macaulay, and for his third, Margaret, the widow of Macaulay's brother, Henry William. On Cropper's death in 1877, his property passed to his children but the management of the Rosebush enterprise was entrusted to his stepson, John Babington Macaulay, and he was supported in its development by Colonel John Owen, second son of Sir John Owen of Orielton, who had married Cropper's widow.

The quarry flourished and the four hovels that had been Rosebush were replaced by twenty-six quarrymen's cottages, still known as 'The Street', with water from a pool in the quarry piped to them, and the population quickly grew to 179 souls. Extensions to the quarry were undertaken at a cost of £30,000, and a windmill was constructed to provide power, but it got out of control in a high wind and damaged the working machinery.

To carry the slates away, Cropper signed an agreement with the Great Western Railway in 1871 to build a railway from Clunderwen, a distance of eight miles, but climbing eight hundred feet, with stations at Llanycefn and Maenclochog. The line was opened on 19 September 1876, and on that day free rides were provided along the flag-bedecked route while the dignitaries were entertained to a grand luncheon in a marquee erected at

Maenclochog, at which the Narberth Town Band and the band of the Haverfordwest Volunteers provided music between the lengthy speeches. A regular passenger service was provided at a return fare of one shilling, and in 1877 nearly 24,000 passengers were conveyed, providing an income of £515, while the carriage of 8,628 tons of freight brought in £782.

The Rosebush and Fishguard Railway Act of 1879 authorized an extension of the line through Puncheston and Letterston to Fishguard, but the track was not completed until 1899. After the closure of the quarries in 1906, the railway survived for the conveyance of a dwindling passenger traffic and a daily tonnage of dead rabbits until the Great War, when the lines were lifted and shipped to France to make guns, but the ship conveying them sank and the rails ended up at the bottom of the sea. The line was relaid after the war, and efforts were made to encourage tourists to use it, but without success. The last passenger train ran in 1937, and although the line was used for trials of a new type of armour-piercing shell during the last war, the North Pembrokeshire railway line was finally closed on 16 May 1949 when the last freight train laden with children and their elders journeyed past villages and farms hooting its farewell, while the bereft parishioners waved flags and sang hymns and fired guns to mark its passing.

Colonel John Owen of Rosebush was educated at Rugby, where he was 'fag' to Thomas Hughes, the author of *Tom Brown's Schooldays*. Hughes was a keen boxer, and Owen had to follow him into the square ring and became so adept in the noble art as to be known as 'Owen Square'; under that pseudonym he wrote his *Memories of Above Half a Century* in 1889 in which he gives a contemporary account of the activities at his 'Arcadia' in Rosebush.

The bracing air of Rosebush and its accessibility by rail had made it appear to Owen and Macaulay the ideal place for development as a mountain holiday resort. For the accommodation of the tourists a hotel was built, albeit of corrugated zinc, and gardens were laid out and planted with trees and shrubs among aritificial lakes, stocked with trout and tench, goldfish and gudgeon, and embellished with grottoes and fountains. A poster featuring the facilities and extolling the virtues of 'the resort of those who seek scenery and repose' was widely displayed.

Rosebush failed to prosper as a spa, but the hotel flourishes and remnants of rhododendrons emerge from long grass.

As a young gentleman of fortune, Owen undertook the Grand Tour not only of Europe but also to visit the family estates in the Antipodes. On a shooting expedition in Tasmania, with the Governor and the Lord Chief Justice, he took them to lunch at Orielton, a porticoed house with a stone staircase set in spacious parkland, named and partially designed after the ancestral home near Pembroke. While they were sitting at lunch, Owen wondered what his fellow-guests would say if they knew that their host had been born in a lowly cottage, named Temperness, near Rosebush, and had been transported for stealing a sheep.

The summit of Foel Cwm Cerwyn at 1,760 feet is the highest point of the Prescly Hills. In the autumn of 1806 Richard Fenton excavated 'the most conspicuous barrow in the county' here, one of four Bronze Age burials, in the presence of 'a party made of all the beauty and fashion of the country ... a cavalcade of ladies and gentlemen in carriages and on horseback, with their attendants, followed by the sumpter cart', but the weather changed and clouds gathered so that the cart and the company had to repair to the inn at Maenclochog where they partook of a 'plentiful collation'. Among Fenton's finds was an encrusted urn which contained 'a large quantity of charcoal ashes, and small pieces of bone, not perfectly calcined'.

When King Arthur and his knights gave chase to the Twrch Trwyth, the legendary wild boar, after it had landed from Ireland at Porth Clais, they came to Cwm Cerwyn where the boar stood at bay and slew four of Arthur's champions; after it slew another four, it was wounded, but on the morrow, it slew four more and many a man of the country, before going east towards the Severn and into Cornwall and into the sea.

Mute and mysterious references to Arthur litter the hills: Carn Arthur, Bedd Arthur, Cerrig Meibion Arthur and Cerrig Marchogion – his cairn, his grave, the cairns of his sons and of his knights, and many a cromlech bears the name Coetan Arthur with the claim that he had hurled the capstone, quoit fashion, from a distant place.

From Foel Eryr, on a clear day, Bardsey may be seen and Snowdonia and the hills of Wales, Dunkery Beacon and the Wicklow Mountains.

Morvil is remote, its stillness only broken by the language of sheep and the curlew's call, yet it bears a name known in Normandy, given to it by a follower of Robert FitzMartin who is said to have fought a skirmish here during his invasion of Cemais. There is no trace of that past save the little church, rapidly becoming ruinous. In the churchyard stands a stone pillar inscribed with a ring-cross over a thousand years ago, and the tombstone of Andrew Thomas and his sister, Eliza, who sang near-forgotten folk songs by their culm fire in the ingle-nook of their cottage, Pencnwc, until we had them recorded and preserved for posterity. Their neighbour, John James of Penterfyn, went into service and became first footman to the Marquis of Lansdowne and, later, house steward to Queen Victoria's fourth daughter, the Princess Louise, and her husband, the Duke of Argyll. His book, *The Memoirs of a House Steward*, tells of his rise from a moorland croft to Kensington Palace and provides an amusing insight into private lives in a vanished age.

A bridge over a narrow lane that hangs with blackberries in autumn carries the North Pembrokeshire Railway that ran through the fields and over the moors from Rosebush to Fishguard Harbour.

The Norman knight who settled at Puncheston undoubtedly hailed from Pontchardon in Normandy, for that is how the name of the village first appears in its recorded history. The castle he built above the steep valley of the River Anghof was one of a line of small earthworks along the southern slopes of the Presely Hills which mark the limit of Anglo-Norman penetration from south Pembrokeshire, and it may have been sited on the stronghold of a Welsh leader Mael from whom the village takes its Welsh name, Casmael. The Drovers' Arms was for the convenience of those who travelled the drovers' road that followed the prehistoric ridgeway to Crymych and on to the Midlands or to Smithfield.

That 'ancient servant of the Lord' Richard Davies the Quaker had difficulty in finding Puncheston when he came there again in 1668, having lost his way 'among the peat or turf pits and other dangerous places', until he came to the house of Thomas Symmons where he had stayed on his previous visit in 1665. It was late at night and when he knocked at the door, he was refused admittance. Symmons and his wife 'being in bed, answered they thought no good Friend were out that time of night', but when he 'told them in Welsh, Richard Davies was there, Symmons hastily came and opened the door'. Thomas Symmons was one of 'several persons called by the name of Quakers' who had refused 'communion with the Church of England' and had 'suffered meetings at his house', for which crime he had his cattle taken away and also his household goods.

John Gambold was born the son of William Gambold, rector of Puncheston, who compiled a Welsh dictionary but failed to find money to publish it. While studying at Christ Church, John came to know Charles and John Wesley, and under their influence he joined the Oxford Methodists, but he accepted the living of Stanton Harcourt in 1735. Through John Wesley he met the Moravian missionary Peter Boehler and acted as interpreter for him and, later, for Count von Zinzendorf, the founder of *Unitas Fratrum*, the United Brethren, as the Moravians called themselves. He resigned his living in 1742 and kept a school for a while in Market Street, Haverfordwest, but moved to London in 1744, joined the Moravians and was consecrated a *chorepiscopus*, the Moravian equivalent of bishop, in 1753, receiving no income and delighting 'in appearing poor and slovenly'. In 1768 his health broke down and he returned to Pembrokeshire to minister to the Moravian congregation at Haverfordwest where he died in 1771 and was buried in the graveyard of the Moravian chapel that had been established on St Thomas's Green by his brother, George Gambold, and a local 'exhorter', John Sparks.

In a humble cottage called Bwlch Wil, in 1853, was born the poet Evan Rees, better known by his bardic title 'Dyfed'. The family left Puncheston for Aberdare where Evan began to work in the mines at the age of eight; he then became a railway porter and, later, a Methodist minister at Cardiff. He won the chair at the National Eisteddfod on four occasions, and also at the Chicago International Eisteddfod in 1893. In 1906 he was appointed Archdruid and was the last to hold that office for the period of his life, until he died in 1923.

No one has been able to identify Henry who built a motte (not a moat) at Henry's Moat. He may have been Harry to his friends for the name was often written 'Harry's Mote' in medieval times. The knight's fee was held of the lord of Cemais by William

Corbet in 1326. The motte stands by the parish church, which is typically rural and one of the many dedications to St Brynach, who also has a well and a ruined chapel at Ffynnon Brynach, *anglice* Bernard's Well. To the south of the motte is an Iron Age fort sliced at one end to make way for a country road.

The connection between the Tufton Arms and the Earl of Thanet would not be immediately apparent unless one carried a hundred-year-old copy of Burke's *Landed Gentry* under one's arm. There one would find that Joseph Foster-Barham, Member of Parliament for Stockbridge in Yorkshire, was born in 1760, the son of Joseph Foster and his wife, Dorothy, the daughter and heiress of Erasmus Vaughan of Trecwn, near Fishguard. Joseph Foster-Barham married Caroline Tufton, daughter of the eighth Earl of Thanet, and chose to place her family's name on the sign of the limewashed hostelry that stands on the mountain road from Haverfordwest to Cardigan.

Blaenwern Farm, near Tufton, was the birthplace of William Penfro Rowlands, precentor at Tabernacle Chapel, Morriston, and composer of one of the most popular of Welsh hymn tunes, which he named *Blaenwern*.

New Moat was so named to distinguish it from the other motte, at Henry's Moat. The castle mound is grown over with trees, and little is known of its origin. Nearby stood the mansion house of the Scourfield family who claimed that the manor was granted by Edward I to Sir Fulk Scourfield who came from Kendal in Westmorland. The Scourfield escutcheon bears racing greyhounds 'scouring the field' and symbolizing the agreement between two contending heirs that he whose greyhound won a race would inherit the estate. The bones of the fortune-bringing hound are honourably interned among the lead coffins of the Scourfield squires.

William Scourfield, who died in 1622, lies in an altar tomb in the parish church. His son, John, was Sheriff of Pembrokeshire in 1635, at the age of twenty-eight, and in that year, while taking ship money to the Privy Council, he fell into the river at Eynsham and was drowned; the money lost, amounting to £43, had to be made good by his sorrowing father.

Sir John Philipps, who assumed the name of Scourfield on inheriting the estate from a childless uncle, was popular as a satirist and wit whose verses were much in vogue in the Victorian age. *The Wonderful Lamb* lampooned William Lamb, Viscount Melbourne, the Queen's favourite Prime Minister but unloved by the Tories; his contemporary ode *Stultissimi Epistola ad Sapientissimum*, 'The letter of a very big fool to a very wise man', addressed to Archdeacon Williams, Warden of Llandovery College, whose anti-English stance displeased Scourfield, was written in English and in Latin, and he was equally fluent in French, Italian and Greek. He was Member of Parliament for Haverfordwest, and later for Pembrokeshire, and was created a baronet by Disraeli in 1876. His son, Sir Owen, the last of the Scourfields, possessed an encyclopaedic industrial knowledge and a mania for collecting railway engine numbers, to such an extent that he was left behind on the platform at Cardiff station while going on his honeymoon.

Despite its inland situation, Llys-y-frân was famous for its master mariners. One sailed his sailing ship from Bristol to San Francisco in record time, and Captain George emphasized his distant voyaging by naming his daughters Fareast and Farwest.

When Parliament refused to allow a tidal barrage to be constructed across the Daugleddau, in 1958, other means had to be found to provide water for the growing needs of industry in Milford Haven. This was done by building a dam across the valley of the Syfynwy at Llys-y-frân and impounding the water so as to create a reservoir covering 187 acres, with a capacity of 2,000 million gallons and a safe dry-weather yield of 13 million gallons a day. The work, begun in September 1968, was completed in May 1971, and the reservoir was officially opened by Princess Margaret in May 1972. It was stocked with brown trout, and a slipway provides access for rowing and sailing boats; its surrounding area was developed as a country park, with car-parks, viewing points and picnic sites.

The Baptist chapel at Rhydwilym is the mother-church of the denomination in west Wales. It was established by a handful of the faithful in 1668 under the leadership of the Reverend William Jones, the dissenting vicar of Cilymaenllwyd, who got himself baptized by immersion and set out to proselytize his neighbours as Baptists of a new breed. The early Baptists were mainly wealthy, educated urban dwellers in the English towns, but William Jones's recruits were drawn from the rural peasantry, poorly educated but unshakeable in their belief and adherence to the strict communion. By 1689 their numbers had increased to 113 members, and in 1701 the first chapel on the present site was built, at his own expense, by John Evans, who had also given the land. Initiates were immersed in the baptistry beside the river, as they are to this day. A sundial above the vestry door is an unusual feature of a Nonconformist chapel.

A farm servant and a milkmaid were once hired at the Maenclochog hiring fair, the man to groom the horses of Bletherston and the maid to milk the cows at Tref Elen, only to find that they both went to work on the same farm. Bletherston is a hybrid name, meaning the settlement of Bleddri, a Welshman, but its Welsh name is Tref Elen, for its bellcoted church, standing in a small triangular churchyard surrounded by a deep ditch cut in the rock, is dedicated to St Elen, the Welsh wife of the Roman Emperor Magnus Maximus.

5

The Barony of Cemais

The village sign announcing Eglwyswrw is a subject of discussion among passing English visitors, who swear they have never seen such a scramble of ciphers. They are not to know that *w* is a vowel in Welsh, as well as being a consonant, and that *y* has two sounds, *ee* and *uh*. It is simply *Egg-Lewis-oorrooh*: the church of St Wrw, who was buried in the chantry chapel in the churchyard and the parishioners believed that any other corpse interred therein would be cast out the same night. 'They hold opinion,' George Owen tells us, in 1600, 'that their holy saint would not have any bedfellows.'

The medieval Sergeant's Inn has heavy oak beams and a snuggly fireside nook, the traditional but fast-disappearing *simne fawr*, or open chimney. Its black and white exterior featured in a pretty painting by Vernon Ward, which came on a Christmas card when I was in Jerusalem during the war and brought nostalgia to the brim. It has been held that the inn was named after the serjeants-at-law who called there on their way from Haverfordwest to Cardigan, but a more likely origin is a military one, as depicted on an early sign. Across the road, in Elizabethan times, was built an armoury which 'for beauty, strength and good order ... excelled any other in all Wales', and an armourer was appointed at the common charge of the hundreds of Cemais and Cilgerran. The trained bands, after their exercise in a nearby field, were able to store their arms in the armoury and, no doubt, assuage their thirst at the inn.

The motte-and-bailey marked on the Ordnance Map is now known to have been a partial ringwork, and it may have had a tower. The Court was 'a house both of account and strength', moated on three sides, its lawns green with chamomile. In 1296 it was the residence of David Martin, son of Nicholas FitzMartin, lord of Cemais, who was created Bishop of St David's in that year, as the personal nominee of Boniface VIII after he had journeyed to Rome to respond to a claim by a rival, for which he owed the Pope and the cardinals 1,500 gold florins.

Parnassus School was opened at the house of William Edwards, sailmaker, in 1831, 'for teaching penmanship in six easy lessons, stenography in four, and ready reckoning or tradesmen's arithmetic'.

In the adjoining parish of Whitechurch even the meanest ploughman was skilful at chess in medieval times, and used Welsh names for the pieces. The pawns they called *paenod bach*, the bishop *Elphin*, and the rooks, *brain Owen ap Urien*. Owen was the son of Urien, King of Rheged, on the northern shores of Solway Firth, who bore a raven on his banner. In the *Dream of Rhonabwy* Owen played chess with King Arthur, with gold pieces on a board of silver, while Arthur's knights battled with Owen's host of ravens. Within the parish, it was said, there was never an adder seen, which was considered one of the wonders of Pembrokeshire, but the same was said of the parish of Whitchurch, which adjoins St David's and through which St Patrick passed on his way to Ireland.

George Owen Harry, who was instituted into the rectory at Whitechurch in 1584, was one of the 'Three Georges', Elizabethan scholars and antiquaries of considerable note: the other two were George Owen of Henllys who, as lord of Cemais, had presented Harry to the living, and George William Griffith of Penybenglog. George Owen Harry was the author of *The Genealogy of the High and Mighty Monarch, James, by the Grace of God, King of Great Brittayne, &c., with his lineall descent from Noah, by divers direct lynes to Brutus* ..., compiled at the request of Robert Holland, rector of Prendergast, Haverfordwest and published in London in 1604, and of *The Wellspring of True Nobilitie yielding forth an ocean of Heroical descents and Royall genealogies of the renowned Kinges, Princes great states nobilitie and gentry of the famous Ile of Brittaine* ..., of an equally interminable title, which was also meant to be a tribute to King James but appears to have been too substantial a work to find a publisher.

St Meugan in Cemais, near Llanfair Nantgwyn parish church, was a centre of the Roman Catholic religion long after the

Carn Briw, Bronze Age cairn

On the Presely Hills

Carreg Goetan cromlech, Newport

Pilgrims' Cross at Nevern: cross cut in relief on the face of the rock, with kneeling place or recess for offerings

Vitalianus Stone, Nevern churchyard

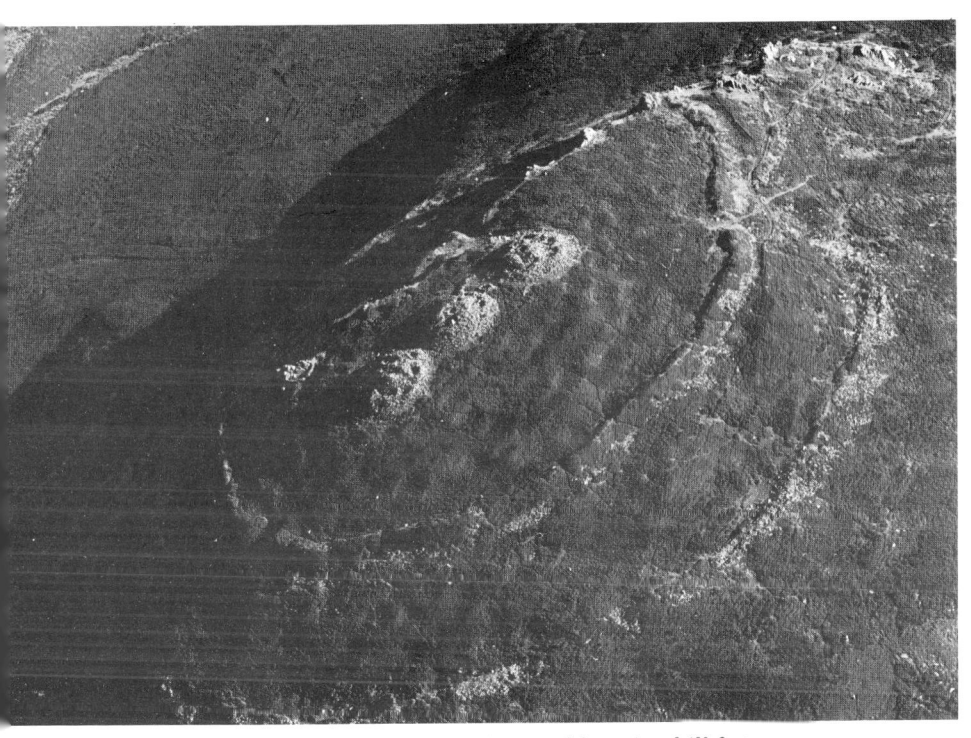

Foel Drygarn – Bronze Age cairns and Iron Age hill fort

Castell Mawr fort above the Nevern Valley

Cilgerran Castle

Rosebush slate quarry

Pentre Ifan cromlech

Eleventh-century High Cross at Nevern

Mounting-block outside church at Nevern

Cwmyreglwys Church

Bedd Morris, Bronze Age standing stone

Dinas Island from above Newport at Carneddfychan

Mathry, a classic medieval village site

Reformation, and certain well-affected gentlemen were required, in 1592, to repair with all convenient speed 'to the place called St Meugan's, where some offerings and superstitious pilgrimages have been used, and there to cause to be pulled down and utterly deface all relics and monuments of that chapel, not leaving one stone thereof upon another'. Pistyll Meugan, a holy well near the chapel, gave forth three streams of water, one of which healed warts, another sore eyes and the other diseases of the heart.

St Meugan's was also the main centre for the unruly game of knappan, which was played at Newport Sands on Shrove Tuesday between the parishes of Newport and Nevern; at Pontgynon on Easter Monday between Meline and Eglwyswrw; at Pwll-du in the parish of Llanfihangel Penbedw on Low Sunday between the men of that parish and those of Penrhydd, and at St Meugan's on Ascension Day and on Corpus Christi when the men of Cemais combined to face the men of Emlyn and of Cardiganshire. These two latter were the major events, with upwards of two thousand men taking part, mounted and on foot, and witnessed by a great multitude of onlookers, towards the regaling of whom there were booths, stalls and standings providing food and drink in plenty.

The men stripped naked, save for a pair of light breeches, and play began with the tossing between the teams of the knappan, a wooden ball of yew, box, crab or holly that had been boiled in oil to make it slippery. The object of the game was to carry the ball to one's own parish, and play would often not cease until nightfall. The mounted participants were armed with cudgels which they were allowed to use on players refusing to yield the ball, and no quarter was given or expected. George Owen of Henllys, who had suffered while playing the game towards the end of the sixteenth century, and carried the scars on his head, hands and other parts of his body, complained that it had become an occasion to pay off private grudges and was, on that account, abandoned.

The story goes that the land to build the little chapel at Brynberian was given to the cause by a local squire whose pastime was cock-fighting, but when the day came to lay the foundation stone, an invited preacher inadvertently chose to denounce the Battle-Royal and the Welsh Main. The infuriated squire withdrew his offer, and the congregation had to move the foundations to the other side of the hedgerow onto common land. Albeit, the chapel became the centre of the Congregational movement in north Pembrokeshire, from the time of its foundation in 1690. Those who ministered there had to travel the twelve miles from Llechryd each Sunday, until 1743 when David Lloyd was inducted minister.

When I was a small boy, Brynberian would become the centre of the universe on Whit Mondays, when the *Pwnc* was held in the chapel. *Pwnc* was a festival invented before people could read. A chapter was selected, usually from the New Testament, to be learnt by heart at Sunday School and rehearsed, for many Sundays in preparation for the festival, in a rhythmic half-musical intonation. The whole gathering would chant the opening verses, then the young girls would stridulate the next few; the growing lads, with voices breaking, would skedaddle discordantly through theirs; then, in turn, the middle-aged, female and male, the croaking old ladies and, finally, the old men, with a thunderous boom, before the mass came in again with the closing verses. Then followed a searching catechetical session. Each of the neighbouring chapels of the denomination would attend the festival, each unadmittingly vying with the others for perfection of cantillation and knowledge of hidden mysteries.

The undulating green outside the chapel was hung with laburnums at that time of the year, like the gardens of Babylon I used to think, and below a furzy bank there was a stream of clear water where trout lazed with gentle motion.

On the open moorland, near Brynberian, among the purple and gold of heather and gorse, lies an oblong mound, some sixty feet in length, that covers a gallery grave. When the site was excavated by Professor W.F. Grimes, he described it as 'an exceptional site in Wales'. The gallery has two parallel rows of around a dozen megaliths, lying a yard apart. Jacquetta Hawkes considered it was 'hardly megalithic' because the stones were so small. It is a type of tomb that is not uncommon in southern Ireland. Its name, *Bedd yr Afanc*, could be translated as the grave of a monster, or of a beaver, but the scholarly Sir John Rhys considered it signified a dwarf's grave.

The hills around are grazed in common and, once a year, tens of thousands of sheep are gathered in a ceremony known as *Y*

Stra, the stray. The sheep are identified by ear-marks, as individual as fingerprints, which are kept in a register by the Presely bailiffs. Any strays, not bearing an ear-mark, are placed in a pound and sold, and the proceeds are divided among the commoners.

The megalithic burial chamber at Pentre Ifan is one of the most impressive in the country. Its high portal and crescentic façade make it look like a petrified elephant, while a bird's-eye view would remind one of a horned beetle. The semi-circular setting of standing stones, which is normally associated with the court cairns of Northern Ireland and which may have been added to an existing tomb, formed a forecourt where any funerary ceremonial would take place. The site was excavated by Professor W.F. Grimes in 1936, but the finds were meagre, consisting of pottery sherds from a shouldered bowl and a triangular flint arrowhead. The cairn contained alignments of small stones and some ritual pits, one of which had contained a fire, and the chamber would originally have been enclosed by upright stones and drystone walling. The monument was probably built by neolithic settlers who migrated across the Irish Sea some time after they had first settled in Ireland, about 3000 BC, and whose origins are traceable to the Atlantic coastline between Brittany and the Iberian Peninsula.

Felindre Farchog takes its name from an old mill that stood opposite the Salutation Inn, and, were it a village in England, it could well be known as Knight's Milton. It lies deep in a tree-clad amphitheatre: just a few houses and a chapel and the inn, and also 'The College', built by George Owen of Henllys to provide education for children and young people who, in his estimation, wasted their youth in shepherding and herding cattle. The inscription on the wall reads '*Llys Dŷ Arglwyddi Cemmes 1559-1620*' – 'the court house of the lords of Cemais'.

George Owen was born at Henllys in 1552. The house stood above Pont Baldwin where, it is claimed, Archbishop Baldwin of Canterbury, in company with Giraldus Cambrensis, preached the Crusade in 1188. The house, in those days, had gardens and ponds and fisheries, and Owen had cockshoots for woodcock, in the nearby forest of Pencelli, where he also kept sparrowhawks. His father, William Owen, had purchased the lordship of Cemais, and George spent much of his life in litigation over manorial rights, yet he found time to compile *The Description of Penbrokshire*, among many other works which portray life in Pembrokeshire during the sixteenth century. Below the house is the splendidly defensive promontory fort of Castell Henllys, now excavated and restored to a resemblance of its state during the Iron Age.

No house in north Pembrokeshire could claim to have provided such patronage for the Welsh bards as Penybenglog. The patron was George William Griffith, descended from Cuhelyn Fardd, fancifully described as one of the peers 'that bore golden swords before King Arthur at his coronation feast at Caerleon' but nevertheless a historical character of the twelfth century, and his wife, Gwrangen Feindroed, 'the little noblewoman of the slender foot'.

Rhys ap Rhydderch ap Howel Gawr of Penybenglog fought at Poitiers with James Audley, lord of Cemais, it is claimed, and for his valour his arms were counter-floried with the arms of France. His grandfather, Howel Gawr, 'the giant', was said to have defeated the French king's champion in his time, for which 'he got for his arms *gules* a lion rampant *or* in a true lover's knot *argent* between four fleurs-de-lys their stalks tending to the centre of the escutcheon, of the second.' The knot, of four bows, is borne by the Bowen family of Llwyngwair in its arms and is known in heraldry as the Bowen knot.

George William Griffith, who married Maud Bowen of Llwyngwair, was at one time seneschal of Cemais. He assisted George Owen of Henllys with historical research and compiled a number of genealogical manuscripts. Penybenglog was plundered by the Royalists during the Civil War on account of Griffith's 'affection to the Parliament'. He died in 1655 and was buried at Meline.

From Penybenglog to the Mansion House in London, and then to die a debtor, such was the career of Watkin Lewes, born the son of the rector of Meline in this ancient house in 1740. He was educated at Shrewsbury and Magdalene College, Cambridge, and was called to the Bar in 1766. His marriage to Rebecca Popkin of Forest, near Swansea, brought him a considerable fortune. He contested Worcester unsuccessfully four times but, meanwhile, became Sheriff of London and Alderman for the Lime Street Ward, and received a knighthood in 1773. He was

Lord Mayor in 1780 and a Member of Parliament for the City of London from 1781 to 1796. He presented the Freedom of the City to William Pitt at Number 10, Downing Street, but a year later he was embarrassed by the publication of 'An authentic narrative of the singular and surprising conduct of Sir Watkin Lewes, knight, respecting his detention and concealment of an old Latin deed delivered to him about ten years ago for the purpose of making out and establishing the title of a poor person in Pembrokeshire to the large estate of Thomas Selby, esquire, late of Wavendon, Bucks'. Even so, his aldermanic brethren made him 'Father of the City of London', but his electioneering expenses and litigation had eaten up his fortune, and he was arrested for debt and ended his days 'at his apartments at the London Coffee-house, Ludgate, within the Rules of the Fleet prison'.

The hamlet of Nevern breathes an air of antiquity, and of sanctity and tranquillity. There is an inn, a few houses and a closed school where Ioan Siencyn, cobbler and schoolmaster, wrote poems praising his patron Thomas Lloyd of Cwmgloyn or seeking favours – a staff to lean on or a cast-off periwig for his bald pate. On the pointed cutwater top of the medieval bridge my grandmother sat and played five-stones when she was a child at school and went home, at times, with a wooden tablet around her neck stamped WN, the Welsh Not, which was passed by one child to another heard speaking Welsh, and the one who carried it the following morning had the stick.

A dark avenue of ancient yews leads to the church door, casting a green light upon grey tombs. One of the yews drips 'blood' from a broken branch – where an innocent was hanged, some say, while others maintain that it bleeds for a broken heart. Beside the church door a stone pillar is inscribed VITALIANO EMERETO in Latin while the ogham fingers on its arris spell VITALIANI, remembering one Vitalianus Emeretus who lived here in the fifth century.

The twelfth-century tower, peeping out of the yew trees, is more solid and less tall than those of the south. It is all that remains of the Norman church built on Brynach's site; the rest is fifteenth-century Perpendicular, much restored in 1864. The north transept has a priest's chamber over, and two pillars, found in a passage leading to it, are now embedded in the window sills. One is decorated with an interlaced cross of the tenth century. The other is inscribed MAGLOCVNI FILI CLVTORI in Latin and MAGLICUNAS MAQI CLUTAR in ogham writing, a monument to Maglocunus, or Maelgwyn, the son of Clutorius, or Clydor, who deserved to be remembered in the late fifth century.

A brass tablet commemorates George Owen of Henllys, lord of Cemais and celebrated historian, who was buried at Nevern in 1613. The tablet bears his coat of arms, a wild boar chained to a holly bush.

The church is dedicated to St Brynach, referred to as Brynach Wyddel, 'the Irishman', who was soul-mate or chaplain to Brychan Brycheiniog, eponymous Irish lord of Brecknock, and is sometimes said to have married his daughter, Cymorth. After a pilgrimage to Rome and a sojourn in Brittany, he landed on the Cleddau where the daughter of a nobleman fell in love with him. He fled from her and came to Pontfaen, where he built a church, and then he was visited by an angel who told him that he should travel until he saw 'a white sow and her piglings and there dwell'. He found them on the banks of the brook Caman, and there he established his religious settlement, where the church now stands.

St David came by one day, the story goes, carrying a thirteen-foot stone cross on his shoulder, which he gave to St Brynach in exchange for some bread. The high cross really dates from the eleventh century and is similar to the one at Carew, a royal memorial erected about 1035. It is heavily decorated with panels and plaits, Stafford knots, frets and diaper key pattern, but the sculptor slipped up on one leg of a swastika on a front panel, below which is an inscription that has defied decipherment. On the opposite side of the pillar are inscribed the letters *dns* which may be an abbreviation of *dominus*. Each year, on 7 April, the feast day of St Brynach, the cuckoo came and sang first on its return to this country upon this stone, according to ancient legend, and the parish priest would not begin Mass until the bird had appeared. One year, the cuckoo was late arriving, and priest and people waited. At last it came and, alighting on the stone, uttered a faint note and fell down dead. This tale, George Owen advises, 'you may eyther beleave or not without perill of damnation.'

In the churchyard, among the tombs of the Bowen family of

Llwyngwair, is an epitaph to the children of David Griffiths, vicar, and his wife, Anne Bowen, which reads:

> They tasted of life's bitter cup,
> Refused to drink the potion up,
> But turned their little heads aside
> Disgusted with the taste, and died.

Nearby is the tomb of the Reverend John Jones, known throughout Wales by his bardic title *Tegid*, taken from Llyn Tegid, or Bala Lake, beside which he was born. After graduating at Jesus College, Oxford, he became chaplain of Christ Church, where he published a new version of the Book of Isaiah, and transcribed *The Red Book of Hergest* for Lady Charlotte Guest to help her with her translation of *The Mabinogion*. In 1842, through the influence of Lady Llanover, he was given the Lord Chancellor's living of Nevern, where he remained until his death ten years later. As he was lying on his death-bed on a Sunday morning, we are told, the voice of a neighbouring clergyman who had come to take the service in his place 'was suddenly drowned by the beautiful song of a thrush that filled the whole church', and it was later 'ascertained that at that very moment the soul of Tegid left his body for the world of spirits'. Lady Llanover presented him with a vine at the Abergavenny Eisteddford of 1848, which he planted by the vicarage door, and when my father visited the vicar of those days, I was allowed, as a small boy, to feast upon the grapes of that vine.

Off a bend on the road leading to Nevern Castle is a wayside cross cut in relief in the face of the rock, with a hollow below it, that is often described as a kneeling place but is really too narrow for that purpose and must have been meant for some other use, perhaps as a recess for offerings.

Nevern Castle stands on the edge of a gorge through which the Caman flows and provides it with a natural defence on its eastern flank. The triangular bailey has a lofty motte and powerful defensive banks, and its eastern corner was later isolated by a deep ditch clean cut in the shaly rock leaving a small platform protected on all sides. The platform was surrounded by a curtain wall and mounted by a square tower, the fragile remains of which are now exposed. The castle was built on the site of the stronghold of a Welsh chieftain by Robert FitzMartin, the Norman conqueror of Cemais. His grandson, William Martin, married Angharad, the natural daughter of Prince Rhys ap Gruffydd, and although Rhys 'had solemnly sworn by the most precious relics' not to disturb his son-in-law, he seized Nevern in 1191 and Martin found a site at Newport and built a castle there. Giraldus Cambrensis regarded it as divine retribution when Rhys was later imprisoned at Nevern, in his own castle by his own sons.

Llwyngwair sits in a sylvan setting on a bank of the Nevern and was 'in former time the original seat of the Cole family', one of whom was 'the first that found out marl in Kemes for mending the land, and he learned the same in France and brought from thence an augur to find it out', according to George Owen, who was a great advocate of employing marl, a limy clay, as manure. It was purchased from the Coles by Sir James Bowen of Pentre Ifan in about 1540 for his son Mathias Bowen, who was the first of the family that was to settle there and to remain there for the next four hundred years. They were patrons of the early Methodists. John Wesley called at Llwyngwair on his travels and found it 'an agreeable place and an agreeable family'. William Williams, Pantycelyn, is said to have been inspired to write 'O'er the gloomy hills of darkness', later translated by his son to become one of the most popular Welsh hymns, when he looked out from Llwyngwair and caught Carn Ingli in one of its glowering moods. The house is now a country hotel.

Moylegrove was the dowry of Matilda, who became the wife of Robert FitzMartin, and was one of the twenty knights' fees of the lordship of Cemais.

Little ships discharged cargoes of coal, culm and limestone at Ceibwr, on the estuary of the Awen, that flows through the village. A local vicar complained of a French invasion of Ceibwr, in 1807, that was more disastrous than the landing at Carreg Wastad thirty years before, and one that kept the people of the surrounding area in subjection. The enemy was not *La Légion Noire* but Cherbourg cognac, a contraband trade in which was carried on at this quiet creek.

Ffynnon Alwm, near Castell Treruffydd, is a chalybeate well 'inferior to none for that property but for the Tunbridge water'. Pwll-y-wrach (the witch's cauldron) is a collapsed blowhole, or gloup, through which water is forced by the rising tide. Along the coast, grey seals bask on the stony beaches and off-shore rocks; fulmars glide and choughs fly on fingered wings by the tall cliffs. In spring and early summer the cliff-tops are matted with vernal squill, thrift, sea campion, red campion, stitchwort, celandine and primrose.

Llechydrybedd cromlech has a massive wedge-shaped capstone which gives it a more impressive appearance than the nearby Trellyffant cromlech, which has a double chamber and a surviving capstone whose upper surface is covered with thirty-five cupmarks.

Giraldus Cambrensis relates how Seisyllt Esgair-hir (Cecil Longshank), who lived at Trellyffant in the twelfth century, was attacked by a host of toads and consumed by them even though his friends had put him in a bag and hauled him up into a high tree: an onomastic tale to justify Trellyffant as 'toad's town'. A black marble toad was formerly set over the mantelpiece in the parlour of the house, sent by Sir Richard Mason, Knight of the Green Cloth to James II, from Italy to his relatives who bore a toad for a crest.

The first people to set foot in north Pembrokeshire did so at Newport. Small flint implements found on the river bank below Newport Bridge were used by mesolithic man who settled there perhaps ten thousand years ago. The estuary was also a convenient landing place for neolithic people who came from Ireland and buried their dead in burial chambers at Carreg Coetan Arthur, Llechydrybedd, Trellyffant and Pentre Ifan. Cerrig y Gof, a unique agglomeration of five rectangular chambers, may have been the megalithic mausoleum of those who made land at Aber Rhigian. The more warlike people of the Early Iron Age sought safety on the summits of Carn Ingli and Carnffoi, and those who followed in more peaceful times appear to have occupied a settlement near the sea, hence Trefdraeth, 'the town on the shore'.

William Martin, driven out of Nevern by his father-in-law, Rhys ap Gruffydd, chose a spur overlooking the estuary upon which to build a castle. The garrison town that sprang up below the castle was incorporated and given the unimaginative name *Novus burgus*, or Newport, meaning 'the new town'. The Martins divided their time between here and their lands in

Somerset and Devon. When a later William Martin was drowned in the moat of Barnstaple Castle while returning from a stag hunt one night in 1326, the drawbridge having been lifted, he died childless and the barony of Cemais passed to his sister who had married Nicholas, Lord Audley of Heleigh in Staffordshire. When James Touchet, Lord Audley and lord of Cemais, was impeached for treason after the battle of Blackheath and beheaded, in 1497, his lands became forfeit to the Crown. In 1543 the castle and the barony were purchased by William Owen of Henllys, who was succeeded by his son, the historian George Owen.

The castle was captured by Llywelyn the Great in 1215 and by Llywelyn the Last in 1257, and suffered under Owain Glyn Dŵr in 1405. By the sixteenth century it was in utter ruin and remained so until 1859, when the gatehouse and one of its flanking towers were converted into a residence by Sir Thomas Davies Lloyd.

Along the curtain wall from the gatehouse, facing the town, is the Hunters' Tower, which has traces of an Early English fireplace and, behind it, the stump of a tower which may have housed the kitchens. At the south-east corner of the ward is a formidable tower jutting out into the moat, and beside it a vaulted chamber is all that remains of the chapel.

The charter granted to Newport by Nicholas Martin around 1240 decreed that 'the burgesses ought to have a reeve', or mayor, appointed 'by consultation with the lord', but this is a confirmation of an earlier charter granted by his father some time before 1215. The mayor is still appointed by the burgesses 'in consultation with the lord', and presides over the Court Leet in the manner of his predecessors in office for close on eight centuries.

St Mary's Church was established by William Martin, possibly on the site of an earlier foundation of St Curig to whom a pilgrimage chapel and a well were also dedicated, and a fair was held on his feast day, the sixteenth day of June. The thirteenth-century tower has stepped buttresses, and the church retains its original cruciform plan. It has a fine cushion-type Norman font, and in the vestry there is a fourteenth-century stone slab bearing a face and a floriated cross and a legend in curtailed Latin stating that a nameless one 'lies here: may God have mercy on his soul'. Above the west door is a pair of escutcheons that seem to bear the arms of the Touchets, lords of Cemais from 1392 to 1497: 'ermine, a chevron gules'. A stone pillar bearing a ring-cross of about the seventh century outside the west door stood head down as a gatepost before it was rescued and brought here.

Sheltered by Dinas Head from the prevailing westerlies, Newport Bay would have made a fine harbour but the dangerous sand bar across the mouth of the river hindered its development. Even so, it was a busy port that rivalled Fishguard in its trade in the sixteenth century. *The Saviour* of Newport took 11,000 slate stones and a pack and fardel of frieze to Bristol in July 1566 and returned with whale oil and alum, pitch and tar, soap and teasels and a bolt of Poldavi. Slates quarried from the cliffs were 'sent by water to Haverford, Pembroke, Tenby and diverse parts of Ireland', and herrings were exported to the Mediterranean. By the end of the eighteenth century Newport had a thriving shipyard. *The Hawk*, launched in 1770, was the subject of a classic poem by Ioan Siencyn, the poet of Nevern, but was sunk by the French. The *Charming Peggy*, a sloop of sixty-three tons built in 1789, was totally lost off Thurso. From 1810 to 1820 Newport built the highest tonnage of any port in Pembrokeshire, but a sharp decline followed.

The brig *Albion*, sailing from Caernarfon in May 1818 with Welsh emigrants to the United States of America, anchored in Newport Bay while the master, Llywelyn Davies, went ashore to bid adieu to his wife and children.

In 1825 a quay was constructed and trade increased with up to a hundred smacks and schooners crossing the bar, in and out of the harbour: *The Lerry*, with coal from Cardiff, the *Kate* from Hook carrying culm, the *Spreadeagle* with salt from Gloucester, the *Heather Bell* with limestone from Caldey, the *Christiana* bringing bricks from Cardigan, the *Emily* with barley and the *Lord Exmouth* with manure. At the sight of the mast tips below Pen Catman, I would rush, as a boy, to the Parrog to see the *Mary Jane Lewis* sail in on the tide; forty years later I saw her skeleton on the beach at Angle. The last of them all was the *Agnes*, which came with its cargo of coal in September 1934.

The slate-stone quay walls still stand, and the last of the five storehouses has been converted into a boat club. The limekilns have been destroyed, save one uniquely double kiln. The four inns on the Parrog – the Queen's, the Parrog Arms, the Sloop and the Mariners – have long since ceased to provide cheer for the jolly sailors.

Two fiery lovers contending for the same heart fought it out on Bedd Morris, they say: the standing stone marks the grave of the one who lost the day. Others say that Morris, a robber who waylaid travellers, was hanged here and buried beneath the pillar. It is a parish boundary stone, and the initials carved upon it are those of Sir Thomas Davies Lloyd, lord of Cemais from 1820 to 1877. Boys are beaten here at a revived beating-the-bounds ceremony so that, when they are old men, they will remember where the boundaries are.

Cnwc-y-grogwydd, 'the gallows tump', was the site of the manorial gibbet.

Dinas Island, now a promontory, was at one time cut off from the mainland by a glacial melt-water channel which formed a narrow strait running from Cwmyreglwys to Pwllgwaelod. Indigenous wild goats used to frequent its grassy slopes until the last war. Foot-like markings on a rock at Dinas Head are none other than those of the Devil himself when he left Ireland in one long leap across the Irish Sea.

Cwmyreglwys was a fishing hamlet of some thirty families in its heyday, and to serve their needs, and those of the crews of the little ships that brought in their cargoes, there were three taverns.

The church, dedicated to St Brynach, was washed away, save for its bellcoted west wall, in the great storm of 1859, when over a hundred vessels were wrecked off the Welsh coast. The sea had already encroached upon the church, for the rector complained in 1827 that 'the north side of the churchyard, with hundreds of dead bodies, and the whole of the chancel, have already been swept away.' The present church, built on surer ground at a cost of £789 on land that had been bought for £3.10.0, was consecrated in 1861.

An earlier establishment appears to have existed at Brynhenllan, 'old church hill', on the site of Tŷ Gwyn, 'the white or blessed house', a term that was used for a stone-built, rather than a timber, church.

Pwllgwaelod was once busy with little ships, as is indicated by the presence of a limekiln and an inn. There was a fairy city under the sea here, they say, and when the sea was calm and the tide low, the golden spires of marble palaces came into view. Once, when a local fisherman cast anchor in the bay, a little man climbed up the rope and complained that it had gone through the roof of his house.

Time stood still in Cwmgwaun, the Gwaun Valley, when its people paid no regard to the change made to the Julian Calendar by Pope Gregory XIII in 1582. In fact, the change was not adopted generally in this country until 1752, when 2 September was followed immediately by the 14th. And although there was an outcry and people demanded: 'Give us back our eleven days', they eventually accepted the new date – but not in the Gwaun Valley. There they still celebrate the New Year on the thirteenth day of January, in the traditional manner and with great neighbourly fellowship in farm and cottage. The children collect *calennig* – New Year gifts of money and apples or oranges – in the morning, before returning home to a feast of goose and plum pudding. In the evening, neighbours gather around selected hearths to tell and re-tell tales and to sing old songs over foaming pots of home-brewed ale.

The small bellcoted churches of Cilgwyn, Pontfaen, Llanychllwydog, Llanychaer and Llanllawer served their own segments of the narrow valley and the surrounding sparsely peopled upland countryside. Each bears evidence of an early association with Christianity by the presence of inscribed stones dating from the seventh century onward. Llanychllwydog has four stumpy cross-incised stones in its churchyard set on each side of the church, which is now a sad ruin in its sylvan setting.

Facing the entrance to Pontfaen church are two slender stone pillars inscribed with Latin crosses, and between them, incongruously, stands a modern tombstone lettered in gold leaf. The church was rescued from the ruin that it was in 1861, with its 'three stone altars still remaining within the abandoned walls and its font open to all the birds of heaven', when it was restored and later embellished by the Arden family of Pontfaen House.

Pontfaen was a house of substance: the Hearth Tax List of 1670 reveals that it had five hearths, and in 1835 it was described as 'a handsome mansion, pleasantly situated and surrounded with thriving plantations'. Its first known occupant, in the fourteenth century, was descended from Gwynfardd, 'regulus' of Dyfed in the eleventh century, and by marriage it passed in 1491 to John Vaughan of Abergavenny, grandson of Sir Roger Vaughan who had been created a knight banneret at Agincourt. In 1625 Lettice Vaughan, the heiress of Pontfaen, married Francis Laugharne of St Bride's, and the estate remained in the family for another two hundred years. In 1863 it was purchased by Richard Edward Arden, a London barrister and a Deputy Lieutenant for the county of Middlesex, who was the benefactor of Pontfaen church and of other churches in the locality. He was appointed High Sheriff of Pembrokeshire in 1872.

The citadel of Nonconformity in the Gwaun Valley is Jabez Baptist Chapel. The chapel hall was the gift of William Evans who left the valley and made his fortune from the invention and door-to-door promotion of Corona mineral water drinks.

Castell Cilciffeth was 'the seat of the monarchs of our mountain squires', according to Fenton, and was the stronghold of Dafydd Ddu who settled there soon after the Normans came. The earthwork has the features of a promontory fort, standing above the Gwaun, and is locally regarded as spooky. In the early seventeenth century Cilciffeth, nearby, was the mansion house of Thomas Lloyd, who was High Sheriff of Pembrokeshire in 1596 and again in 1613, when, to mark his shrievalty, he conveyed lands to establish and endow the Haverfordwest Grammar School for 'the sons of such as should be of the poorer sort of people'. The present farmhouse retains some medieval features, including a low vaulted passage.

On either side of the entrance gate to Llanllawer churchyard are two stone pillars bearing incised crosses of about the eighth century, and outside the churchyard wall is 'a sainted well, abundantly supplied with the purest water, that once had the reputation of most miraculous efficacy in various disorders', for which coins and pins were thrown in. If evil were wished against anyone, a bent pin was used. In the angle of the nave of the church is a weeping stone, which never dries out.

East of the church is the largest of the eight stone alignments in Wales. It has eight stones ranging from five to twelve feet in height: four have fallen and the other four are embedded in a hedgerow, extending over a length of 160 feet but not uniformly spaced. The purpose of an alignment remains a mystery, although it has been suggested that it may have been a lunar observatory of megalithic man. A cromlech nearby was destroyed in 1844, and only the capstone remains: the supports were used to build a house, and the householder later confessed that it 'had not brought him good luck'. The field next to the alignment is known as Parc y Meirw, the field of the dead, and there is a local belief that it was the scene of a bloody battle and that the stones were raised to commemorate the dead. There are also those who believe that a lady in white walks along a trodden way across the field on dark nights, and those who had occasion to walk that way after dark would sooner make a detour of a mile and more. I passed the field early one morning and saw that it was completely covered with gossamer, except for the path.

6
The Last Invasion

The presence of prehistoric sites around Fishguard Bay suggests that voyagers found shelter and safe landing here from early times. The Welsh called the settlement Abergwaun, 'the estuary of the Gwaun', and it is likely that it was the Norse, who visited these shores from their bases in Ireland, who likened it to a 'fish-yard'.

When the Normans came over from Devon to occupy north Pembrokeshire, under Robert FitzMartin, according to one theory they landed at Fishguard where, although the natives rolled boulders down upon their ships, they managed to land and pitch camp at Cronllwyn, on high ground above the Gwaun, before moving on to Morfil, where they met with some opposition, and eventually to Nevern.

The manor of Fishguard was held of the lord of Cemais by Jordan de Cantington and his descendants until it was granted, in 1378, to St Dogmael's Abbey. Following the dissolution of the monasteries, it was leased by the Crown to John Bradshaw as part of the abbey lands, but it reverted to the Crown in the seventeenth century, and in 1810 Richard Fenton states that it still belonged to the Prince of Wales, who appointed a steward, an office then filled by Lord Kensington. Soon afterwards, it was purchased by a Mr Hamlet of Cavendish Square, London, who exceeded his powers as lord of the manor by building cottages on manorial waste land and was taught a lesson by the inhabitants, who tore down the walls.

Fishguard was one of the boroughs of Cemais, with a portreeve, or mayor, appointed under a charter granted during the reign of King John. The charter was lost during the Civil War, and in 1683 it was reported that no mayor had been appointed 'for nine years past'. There was a revival of civic interest in the nineteenth century, however, for a court leet was held in 1822 and a mayor was installed each year until 1855. Since the reorganization of local government in 1974, the Fishguard and Goodwick Town Council is able to appoint a town mayor.

The town itself is divided into an upper part and the much older Lower Town, or Cwm, formerly referred to as the hamlet of Capel Llanfihangel, that was outside the borough. Lower Fishguard was described as 'a good harbour' trading with Ireland, but even in 1567 its people were too impoverished to repair its ruinous quay.

On 15 September 1779 the cutter privateer *Black Prince* appeared off Fishguard and demanded a ransom of £500 for a merchant ship it had seized and which belonged to Samuel Fenton, and a further £500 in ransom for the town. The cutter was commanded by Captain Stephen Manhant, who had a crew of English and Irish smugglers. The Dewsland Volunteers were summoned to no avail, for the cutter, on being refused the ransom money, bombarded the town, hitting some chimneys and the roof of St Mary's Church, and injuring Mary Fenton in the foot. The master of an armed smuggler, that happened to be in port, returned the fire with his cannon and drove the *Black Prince* away empty-handed. As John Paul Jones, the naval adventurer, was known to be active at that time, it was soon rumoured that he was the culprit, but in fact he was in the Firth of Forth on that day, preparing to hold the city of Edinburgh to ransom.

The incident led to the building of a fort, on an inaccessible tongue of land jutting into the harbour. It was equipped with eight nine-pounder guns, manned by three invalid gunners from Woolwich, and would have been of little use in defending either the harbour or the town of Fishguard.

The historian Richard Fenton maintained that his great-grandfather John Lewis of Manorowen had first discovered the advantages of the situation of Fishguard for commerce and had erected several houses in the lower town, beside the estuary, and a large brick building fitted with cellars, racks and other requisite conveniences for curing 'white and red herrings'. Fishguard was famed for its herrings, *sgadan Abergwaun*: even its people were known by this by-name, and as a schoolboy attending the Fishguard County School, I was proud to wear a badge depicting a Fishguard herring between two curved leeks on my cap. The prosperity of the industry was enhanced by Samuel Fenton, who, on retiring from the Royal Navy, introduced a method of curing pilchards which he had observed in Spain and exported the fish to the Mediterranean countries and to the Baltic. On his death, in 1796, he bequeathed his estate to his nephew, Richard.

Richard Fenton was born at Rhosson, St David's, in 1747, and was educated at the cathedral school and at Magdalen College, Oxford. In 1777 he entered the Middle Temple and in 1783 was called to the Bar; then he went on circuit in Wales, during which time he resided near Machynlleth. While he was in London, he became friendly with David Garrick, to whom he addressed a number of his poems, and with Goldsmith, Johnson, Burke, Fox and Joshua Reynolds. He was said to have been 'of a fine poetical fancy, of a very cheerful disposition, of particularly gentlemanly and fascinating manners, and a person of the best information on almost every subject'. He was well versed in Greek, Latin and French and became increasingly interested in literary pursuits during the latter part of his life. His best-known work is his *Historical Tour through Pembrokeshire* published in 1810 at the suggestion of, and illustrated by, his friend Sir Richard Colt Hoare, but he also published *A Tour in Quest of Genealogy* (1811), *Memoirs of an Old Wig* (1815) and two volumes of poems.

One summer afternoon, Fenton and Goldsmith were strolling along a lane in Marylebone when they saw a party of ladies and an elderly gentleman taking tea in a garden. Fenton, at a glance, was struck by the beauty of one of the young ladies and said as much to his companion, who thereupon took him by the arm, led him into the garden and introduced him to the elderly gentleman as 'my friend, Mr Fenton, the celebrated Welsh poet'. They were invited to stay for tea, and on leaving Fenton asked Goldsmith who their host was. 'Never saw him before in my life,' answered Goldsmith, 'but I thought if ye wanted to flirt with a pretty girl, you should!' Fenton called again, and the young lady, Eloise, daughter of the Baron Pillet de Moudon, a Swiss aristocrat who had settled in England as Secretary to the Duke of Marlborough, became his wife.

After Samuel Fenton's death, Richard entered into the

business of managing the mercantile fleet that he had inherited. In 1799, when the local people suffered from bread shortage on account of the Napoleonic wars, he sent his ships to bring corn from Turkey and from Egypt, which he sold free of freight charge to the impoverished populace at cost price.

He built a fine residence for himself at Carn y Garth, in the valley above Lower Fishguard, which he called Plas Glynamel, and planted the grounds with exotic shrubs and trees. He held a consecration ceremony at the laying of the foundation stone and, as the vicar concluded the ceremony with a blessing, a woman rushed foward and screamed a curse upon the place, maintaining that Samuel Fenton had promised her a meadow and the cottage at Carn y Gath in return for her care of him during his old age. Richard made good the promise by granting her nominal ownership of the land and paying her an annual rental of £30 while, at the same time, providing her with a comfortable house and garden. He died, suddenly, at Glynamel in November 1821 and was buried at Manorowen church.

It was already getting dark on the evening of Wednesday 22 February 1797, 'a still night when all nature, earth and ocean wore an air of unusual serenity', as Richard Fenton remembered it, when an army of Frenchmen clambered up the cliffs and steep slopes at Carreg Wastad, on the Pencaer peninsula. They had sailed from Brest for Camaret, six days earlier, on the frigates *Résistance* and *Vengeance*, each mounted with twenty-eight eighteen-pounder, and twelve eight-pounder guns, the corvette *Constance*, twenty-four guns, and the lugger *Vautour*, fourteen guns. The troops were under the command of Colonel William Tate, an unknown veteran adventurer from South Carolina, as *chef de brigade*, with orders to burn and destroy Bristol, then the second city in Britain, and afterwards to plunder their way towards Chester and Liverpool so as 'to prepare and facilitate the way for a descent by distracting the attention of the English Government'. The force comprised six hundred regulars and eight hundred convicts released from French gaols, along with a hundred Royalist emigrés captured at Quiberon, and three officers of Irish origin. They wore uniforms which the British had left at Quiberon, that had been dyed a dark brown or black, from which the force was known as *La Légion Noire*, but they were well armed with long muskets and cutlasses. The squadron, which was commanded by Commodore Jean-Joseph Castagnier, left Camaret on 18 February and on the following day was spotted in the Bristol Channel flying the Russian flag so as to avoid recognition, but an easterly wind prevented them from making Bristol and so they sailed northward with a view to landing the troops on the coast of Cardigan Bay, whence they would march to Chester and Liverpool.

By noon on the 22nd, the squadron was sighted off the North Bishop Rock by Thomas Williams of Treleddyn, and although the four ships were flying the British colours, he, being a retired master mariner, suspected they were Frenchmen. His wife, Margaret Theodosia, who had spotted the crew of a Swedish vessel clinging to the Bishops through her telescope some years before and rescued them in her boat in the Grace Darling manner, confirmed his suspicions.

Mr Williams Treleddyn did know every tide
From England to Greenland without any guide.
Mrs Williams Treleddyn did take the spy-glass
And then she cried out: 'There they was!'

The squadron sailed on and anchored inshore off Carreg Wastad Point, except for the *Vautour* which ventured beyond Pen Anglas and received a blank from a nine-pounder at Fishguard Fort in salute to the British ensign she was flying. She rapidly returned and reported that Fishguard was defended. John Owen's sloop *Britannia*, carrying a cargo of culm from Hook, was stopped by *Vengeance*, and he was taken on board; when interrogated, he gave an exaggerated account of the port's defences. Whilst on board, he recognized James Bowen, a former farm servant at Trehowel Farm who had been sentenced to transportation for horse-stealing. Was it he who had guided the squadron to this inhospitable coast in the hope of gaining his freedom and returning to his family?

Led by Lieutenant Barry St Leger, one of the Irish officers, the *Légion Noire* landed in a remarkably short space of time and reached the top of the cliff with forty-seven barrels of gunpowder, twelve boxes of hand grenades, stores and two thousand stand of arms. Tate came ashore and made Trehowel his headquarters, undoubtedly led there by James Bowen, while his men camped near the landing-place and occupied a commanding position on Carn Wnda.

Castagnier weighed anchor on the Thursday afternoon and made for Dublin roads, and then for Brest, but lost the *Résistance* and the *Constance* to British frigates *en route*. The *Résistance* became part of the Royal Navy as HMS *Fisgard*.

John Mortimer of Trehowel had made preparations for his forthcoming wedding, and the French plundered his well-stocked larder to such an extent that he was to receive £133 from the Government in compensation. Foraging parties ravenously raided the surrounding farms and cottages, slaughtered poultry and drank wine taken from a smuggling vessel providentially wrecked on the coast a few days before. 'Gluttony was followed by intoxication,' commented Fenton, 'and here the finger of heaven was manifestly visible.' At Brestgarn, a fuddled Frenchman fired at a grandfather clock in the belief that someone was hiding in its case: the clock is still there, with a bullet hole in its case. Mary Williams of Caerlem attempted to escape and had a musket ball in her leg, but a woman lying in her bed with her new-born child at Cotts was spared.

Several French soldiers were captured by the country people. Jemima Nicholas, a Fishguard cobbler-woman, marched out to Llanwnda with a pitchfork in her hand, brought back a dozen prisoners and then went out for more. Her heroism is recorded on a monument beside the parish church at Fishguard.

Meanwhile, the military forces available were being hastily mobilized to repel the invader. The Pembrokeshire Militia was away on duty at Harwich, but the Cardiganshire Militia had taken its place and was on guard at the prison at Pembroke Dock. Otherwise there were the Yeomanry and the Fencibles.

The Pembroke Yeomanry was raised when king and country were outraged by the savagery of the French Revolution and by the fear of invasion. In March 1794 Lords Lieutenant were requested by the Prime Minister, William Pitt the Younger, to raise volunteer corps in order to supplement the Militia service, and in the following month Lord Milford, the Lord Lieutenant of Pembrokeshire, presided over a meeting of Pembrokeshire gentlemen, held in London, at which it was decided to form the Pembrokeshire Company of Gentlemen and Yeomanry Cavalry. John Campbell of Stackpole Court, later Lord Cawdor, lost no time in raising the Castlemartin Troop, and the Dungleddy Troop was commanded by Lord Milford, each troop comprising fifty officers and men. At the same time, the Pembroke Fencibles were being raised in south Pembrokeshire, and the Fishguard Fencibles in the north, numbering in all 235 rank and file.

On the evening of 22 February, the Castlemartin Troop had assembled at Haverfordwest in order to attend the funeral of a comrade the next day, and by the following morning the Pembroke Fencibles and the Cardiganshire Militia had arrived, together with fifty seamen from Milford Haven. At noon, the full complement of some 750 men, taking two nine-pounder guns from the revenue cutter *Speedwell* with them, set out towards Fishguard led by Lord Cawdor.

Colonel Thomas Knox commanded the Fishguard Fencibles, which had been formed at the expense of his father, William Knox of Llanstinan. Colonel Knox had been invited to a ball at Tregwynt, near St Nicholas, and as the company was sitting down to dinner at Mrs Harries's well-laden table, a Fencible galloped up to the door of the house with news of the French landing. Knox hurriedly rode to the Fishguard Fort and assembled the Fencibles, but when he heard of the strength of the enemy, he gave the order to retreat towards Haverfordwest. He met Cawdor's force at Treffgarne and, after some argument about command, turned about to form the rear of the column of route. On Thursday night the troops lay on their arms at Fishguard.

Tate, having been led to believe that the area was heavily defended, while his own undisciplined troops were mostly drunk and out of control, decided to seek terms of surrender. He sent two of his officers to Fishguard, where they delivered his conditional terms to Lord Cawdor at the guard-house which had been established at the house of Hugh Meyler, now the 'Royal Oak'. Cawdor demanded a complete surrender and, on the following morning, rode over to Trehowel. There Tate delivered up his sword to him and signed articles of capitulation, but no trace of this important military document, or of any 'treaty', has ever been found. Tate, despondent and frightened for his life, asked that he should be taken direct from Trehowel to Haverfordwest by way of Llangloffan and Camrose, and thus never set foot in Fishguard. His men were assembled on

Goodwick Sands, where they emptied their pans and laid down their arms, and then they marched through Fishguard to Haverfordwest, where they were lodged in the county gaol, in three churches and in storehouses. The 'great fiasco of the French invasion' was over, but the legends remained.

Lord Cawdor, it was said, seeing the women of Fishguard in their red flannel cloaks, had assembled them and marched them, as the noble Duke of York had done with his ten thousand men, up behind Bigney Hill and down in full view of the Frenchmen, who had mistaken them for grenadiers (who, incidentally, wore blue coats) and had decided to surrender. That there was some substance to this story is attested by statements in two letters, written at Narberth and at Haverfordwest three days after the surrender, referring to the presence, among those who had gathered on vantage points to witness the scene, of some four hundred women in red flannel cloaks whom the French mistook for troops of the line.

Two young women, Anne Beach and Eleanor Martin, who brought provisions to the Frenchmen who were later held at the Golden Prison in Pembroke, contrived the escape of some of them and accompanied the fugitives as they got away in a yacht that belonged to none other than Lord Cawdor.

The Castlemartin Troop was called to Fishguard again, in January 1827, to suppress a riot, and in December of that year the Government ordered that all Troops of Yeomanry Cavalry should be disbanded. The Castlemartin Troop ignored the order, however, and elected to continue to serve, without pay or allowances. During the Rebecca Riots, in the early 1840s, they were summoned on a great number of occasions to quell the rioters in various parts of west Wales. In 1853 Queen Victoria granted the Pembroke Yeomanry the right to wear 'Fishguard' on their standard and appointments, and this is the only battle honour ever awarded to any unit of the British Army for an action fought in Great Britain.

The Yeomanry saw action in Palestine and in France during the 1914-18 War, and in 1939-45 in the Western Desert, Italy, including Cassino, and France where, in Normandy in 1944, it became known as 'the Fishguard Express'. It is now part of the Royal Corps of Transport but its officers and men still proudly wear the word 'Fishguard' on their badges.

In 1844 Isambard Kingdom Brunel conducted a survey, on behalf of the South Wales Railway Company, to bring the railway westward into Pembrokeshire and to connect with a sea passage from Fishguard to Ireland. Work began in the following summer, and by August 1847 the line had been brought to within a few miles of Fishguard. The famine that followed the failure of the Irish potato crops and the 'Young Ireland' insurrection, however, prevented the construction of a connecting railway from Waterford to Dublin and to Cork, and work on the line to Fishguard had to be suspended. Fifty years were to pass before the first train steamed out of Fishguard harbour. Work began in 1899 on blasting rock to build a breakwater, a third of a mile long, and, at the same time, to provide a platform for a harbour and a railway terminus; the task was completed eleven years later. The Irish packet service was inaugurated, with the Great Western Railway steamers *St David, St Patrick* and *St George* sailing daily to Rosslare, but attempts to develop Fishguard as a transatlantic port were not so successful. The *Mauretania* called in 1909, followed by other ocean liners, including the ill-fated *Lusitania*, but they had to anchor in the bay and unload by tender.

The scattered hamlet of Goodwick developed rapidly with the establishment of the port and railway terminus. The mansion house where William Rogers, a merchant of Minehead, came and amassed a fortune as an enterprising smuggler, was rebuilt and called Wyncliff, and latter extended to become the Fishguard Bay Hotel.

The parish church of Llanwnda, with its double bellcote and sanctus, stands by a boulder-strewn common and looks down on a rugged coastline from Pencaer to Penanglas, with its pentagonal columnar rocks that are known locally as *torthe ceinioge*, penny loaves. Inside the church, a stone bench runs along the west wall of the nave and a roof beam has a rude boss of a tonsured priest of the fifteenth century. A be-shawled face on a stone in the outside wall, perhaps of the Virgin Mary, is eight centuries older. The church is dedicated to St Gwyndaf.

During the French landing the silver chalice was taken from the church and offered for sale at Carmarthen by a French officer who claimed unconvincingly that the inscription *'Poculum eclesie de Llanwnda'* proved that the vessel had come from La Vendée.

A chapel that stood on the cliff near Pencaer was built by St

Degan in gratitude for a safe landing, and on the rocks nearby are the hoof marks of the horse he rode out of the sea!

Pencaer peninsula is rich in megalithic remains and prehistoric sites. There are burial chambers at Penrhiw, Garnwen, Carnwnda and Carn Gyllwch, some of which have been erected against outcrops of rock. Garn Fawr has one of the finest Iron Age hill forts in the country, with multiple defensive walls connecting natural outcrops, and the remains of hut dwellings on its south-western slopes. An oval enclosure on the south side is called Ysgubor Gaer (granary fort), and on the west side is a cell with a corbelled roof that looks like an Irish *clochan*.

Pwllderi has been immortalized by the Welsh poet Dewi Emrys in a poem written in the local dialect. I once stood on its steep slopes with him as he recited his poem, the sea breeze tossing his ample grey hair, his falcon-like face and his eyes fixed on the distant horizon. Around us, 'the gorse was spilling its sovereigns, enough to make an old miser faint, or even die,' and below us lay 'the half-moon of sand' where no footprint was ever seen, save that of Dai Beca the wreck-gatherer. The noise from the seething cauldron that Pwllderi is on wild wintery nights, sounded like the screeching of witches and the baying of hounds echoing through the caverns, and made the poet think of the shipwrecked sailor crying to be saved, but no one there to hear him save the birds of the cliffs ... 'Such are the thoughts that come to you, as you sit above Pwllderi.'

I came again to Pwllderi when a stone pillar was erected to the poet's memory and on it inscribed:

DEWI EMRYS
1879-1952
A thinn'r meddylie sy'n dwad ichi
Pan fo'ch chi'n ishte uwchben Pwllderi

– such are the thoughts ...

Trefasser was the birthplace of Asser, confidant and adviser to King Alfred. Educated at St David's, where his uncle, Nobis, was bishop, he eventually succeeded to the see. His reputation for scholarship was such that it reached the ears of the King, who invited him to his court in 804. St David's had suffered considerably from attacks by Hyfaidd, King of Dyfed, and Asser felt that a close relationship with King Alfred, as Hyfaidd's overlord, would put an end to the harassment. Alfred found him indispensable and promoted him to various dignities to keep him from returning to St David's. He was eventually appointed Bishop of Sherborne and remained in that office until he died in 909.

When great storms scour the beach at Abermawr, there lie exposed the stumps of oaks that stood in a forest there some eight thousand years ago. The greatest of these storms, which struck the coasts of Wales in 1859, threw up the bank of shingle that dominates the beach today.

When the Irish famine led Isambard Kingdom Brunel to abandon Fishguard as the terminus of the South Wales Railway, he decided upon the remote and isolated bay of Abermawr as the site of a port for the Atlantic trade. Abutments for piers were laid from Pen Morfa and from Carregolchfa, and traces of the excavation for the railway line that was to wind down the valley are still visible in places. The work ceased in 1851, when Neyland was chosen as the terminus.

In 1883 a submarine telegraph cable was laid from Abermawr across the sea to Ireland, and a telegraph station was built there, which is now a private dwelling.

A cottage which is now a heap of rubble, beside the beach, was the birthplace of William Lewis, weaver of cloth, of carpets and of words that have lived on in many of our popular hymns. Perhaps he stood there on the shingle, looked out to sea and thought of the faraway places from which sailors he knew returned, when he wrote:

Pe meddwn aur Peru
A pherlau'r India bell,
Mae gronyn bach o ras fy Nuw
Yn drysor canmil gwell.

(Were I to possess the gold of Peru, and the pearls of distant India, a grain of my God's grace would be a treasure far greater.)

The village of St Nicholas is 'shaped rather like a capital T. Along the top stroke were the Squire's stone-built residence with its large garden and orchard, the two tiny cottages where a farm worker and the old school cleaner lived ... Along the down stroke lived a roadman, a middle aged dying consumptive, another rabbit trapper, the schoolmaster.' Or rather, so it was, some fifty years ago, as my friend Llewelyn Jones remembers it in his autobiographical book, *Schoolin's Log*. My memory is of loud rookeries in tall trees and of owls that hooted the night through when I stayed at the schoolin's house, which was his father's when we were boys at school together.

St Nicholas was one of the manors of the episcopal lordship of St David's: the village is referred to, in the thirteenth century, as *villa camerarii*, the chamberlain's settlement, but its Welsh name is Tremarchog, the knight's place, Knighton. The church is dedicated to St Nicholas, and within its walls are three stones commemorating Melus, Paanus and Tunccetace, the wife of Daarus, who lived in the fifth or sixth century.

There are two burial chambers in the vicinity, one at Ffynnon Dridian and the other, Ffyst Samson (Samson's flail), at Trellys-y-coed; in each the capstone rests on two orthostats only. Recent excavation at the standing stone at Rhos y Clegyrn has revealed that it stood outside the perimeter of a Bronze Age round barrow, possibly as the focus of ritual activity connected with cremated burials, while analysis of wheat pollen found on the site indicates an earlier settlement.

The wife of Cynwayw, a man of Daugleddau, had septuplets, all seven of them sons, whom the distraught father proceeded to drown, as he knew that he could never provide for them. But the good St Teilo came by as Cynwayw was about to perform the heinous act, baptized the children and took them with him. After a period under his tutelage and that of St Dyfrig, he sent them to Mathry, where they became known as 'the seven saints of Mathry'. And there, when they died, they were 'interred in coffins of stone'. The tale, which is told in *The Book of Llan Dav*, is an onomastic attempt at the derivation of the name of the village from the Latin word *martyrium*, martyrs. Its origin, however, is in the Welsh words *ma-thru*, 'the field of woe'.

Mathry, like the villages of the Land of Israel, is set on a hill, and all roads climb towards it. The parish church, dedicated to the Seven Saints, stands in a churchyard that is roughly circular in shape, which adds to the speculation that the original settlement dates back to the Iron Age. The squat belfry was formerly dignified by a steeple that served as a landmark for mariners. A stone pillar in the church porch bears a Latin memorial to Maccudicl, son of Caticuus, and has an indecipherable ogham inscription, on its reverse side, which may refer to another person, and also the vestige of a circle. There are two stones built into the churchyard wall, each incised with a linear ring-cross. The church's rich endowment of the great tithes caused Giraldus Cambrensis, who was appointed to the prebend, to refer to it as the Golden Prebend, and led to its plunder by Gwilym ap Gwrwared of Cemais in 1195.

Castlemorris takes its name from Maurice FitzGerald who was one of the knights that followed Richard de Clare, Earl of Pembroke, into Ireland in 1169 in support of Dermot, the deposed King of Leinster.

Sloops carried corn and butter from the little harbour of Abercastle to the port of Bristol, and returned with general merchandise which was sold at the local shop, called 'The Bristol Trader'. The coastal hamlet, which lies at the end of a drowned valley, had two limekilns, of which one remains, a water-mill and storehouses built of imported limestone, and a tavern and a shebeen – an illicit liquor house. The brick trade was sprinkled, it was rumoured, with a little smuggling.

The burial chamber at Longhouse, above Abercastle, has six orthostats, only three of which bear the massive capstone that was raised, according to legend, by Samson, using only his little finger, which he then lost and buried in Bedd Bys Samson, the grave of Samson's finger, on Ynys y Castell, an islet that may be an early Christian site. The burial chamber is a passage-grave of the type built by people who came along the Atlantic seaboard from Spain or western France and settled in Ireland, around the Boyne, before crossing to Wales about 2,500 BC.

Longhouse Farm was visited in 1743 by the Methodist triumvirate Howell Harris, Daniel Rowland and Howel Davies, 'the Apostle of Pembrokeshire', who preached there and attracted a vast congregation in the field outside the house.

The annual fair at Trefin lasted three days, beginning on the feast of St Martin, when *pasteoid Ffair Fartin*, traditional pies made with mutton, brown sugar, currants and sultanas, were eaten. In the good old days

> There were three taverns at Trefin,
> The Ship, the Swan, the Fiddler's Green.

Now, only the Ship remains to offer cheer to the traveller.

Trefin is laid out rather like an English village, except that in the place of a village green there is an upthrust of natural rock. It was once the centre of an important episcopal manor with its own *prepositus*, or mayor, and a court leet and view of frankpledge that was held up to the end of the last century. The bishop of St David's, as lord of the manor, had his own 'stone and wooden buildings there, and two water mills, and a boat with nets for herring fishing'. Tenants paid their rents in capons, gloves or needles, or in service 'by following the relics of St David to Garn Turne', or 'in sounding the horn when there was a wreck and guarding the goods there'.

Legend has it that a mermaid sat on a rock at Aberfelin, below Trefin, singing *'Medi yn Sir Benfro, chwynnu yn Sir Gaer'* – 'They're reaping in Pembrokeshire while they weed in Carmarthenshire.' And those who had the gifted sight saw *Ynysoedd y Gwynfyd*, the blessed isles, or *Gwerddonau Llion*, the green islands of enchantment, where 'the little people' lived, across the sea from Aberfelin.

The ruined manorial mill at Aberfelin, 'the mill among the rocks' of *The Black Book of St David's*, inspired the poet and archdruid Crwys to write one of the finest lyrics in the Welsh language. 'I had finished supper on a Sunday evening, in 1918,' he told me when we were together on one occasion, 'after preaching at the local chapel, and went for a walk as far as Aberfelin where I saw the old mill and the fallen millstone beside it. I went back to the house where I was staying – with a Mrs Owen whose husband had come down from Llanberis to work in the local quarries: the supper things were still on the table, so I pushed them to one side and began to write:

Nid yw'r felin heno'n malu
Yn Nhrefin ym min y môr ...

[The mill does not grind tonight, at Trefin beside the sea. ...] It all came very easy, with no effort at all, but the last four lines,' he pointed upwards, 'the last four lines came from above!

Ond 'does yma neb yn malu,
Namyn amser swrth a'r hin
Wrthi'n chwalu ut yn malu,
Malu'r felin yn Nhrefin.'

[But no one grinds here any more, save sullen time, strewing and grinding – grinding the mill at Trefin.]

Trefin was the birthplace of another archdruid, Edgar Phillips, who adopted the name of his native village as his bardic title. He was appointed Grand Sword-bearer of the Gorsedd of Bards of the Isle of Britain in 1947, and when I succeeded him in that office twelve years later, when he was appointed Archdruid, he consoled me by saying that he had been able to bear the great weight of the Grand Sword through carrying heavy shells during the World War. I had the pleasure of introducing him to the author Maxwell Fraser, whom he later married and who, in her book *Introducing West Wales*, writes lovingly of the village of Trefin, seemingly remote but 'more in touch with the far places of the earth than many an inland town ... through its sea-going men-folk', so that 'many a house could boast fine embroidered silks of far Cathay, or curios from Argentina.'

The Methodist leaders, the brothers Ebenezer and Thomas Richard were also born at Trefin. Ebenezer's son, Henry Richard, became Member of Parliament for Merthyr Tydfil: his statue stands on the square at Tregaron. Thomas persuaded his lady-love, Bridget Gwyn, to leap from her bedroom window at Manorowen and steal across the road to the little church, where a friendly priest was waiting at the altar to marry them.

The parish church at Llanrhian, half-hidden in a rookery, is dedicated to St Rheian. The tower is thirteenth century but the rest of the church was rebuilt in 1836 and harmoniously restored in 1891. A rare decagonal font has plain shields on each face, except for one which bears the arms of Thomas ap Rhys of Rickeston, a chevron between three ravens, indicating descent, illegitimate though it was, from Sir Rhys ap Thomas. There was a chapel-of-ease at Llannon that contained a stone whereon St Non 'had leaned with her hands' before she gave birth to the patron saint, and left her finger marks: a reference no doubt to the ogham writing on the stone.

Porthgain bears skeletal remains of stone and slate workings to delight the industrial archaeologist. Its geological resources began to be exploited in the middle of the last century. A tram road was laid around the headland of Barry Island to haul slates from Abereiddi, which were shaped and trimmed to various sizes known, as they are in the North Wales slate quarries, as

Duchesses, Countesses and Ladies, and when the slate workings became too deep for the tram road, a tunnel was constructed from the harbour, with a railway that also brought clay from which bricks were made and exported. But Porthgain's main export was fine granite stone which was used in the erection of public buildings in London, Liverpool and Dublin, and when road were macadamized, the streets of Barnstaple and Bristol and the highways of South Wales and beyond were coated with granite chips from Porthgain. In the summer of 1909, 12,897 tons of crushed stone were exported as far as Sussex and Kent. The harbour was built in the 1850s, and by the end of the century it had a fleet of fifty-two ketches and forty-three steamships. It was considerably improved in 1904 but trade never recovered after the Great War, and Porthgain Village Industries Ltd, which had been established in 1878, went into receivership in 1929 and ceased trading two years later.

In the bar of the Sloop Inn hangs the bulkhead of the *Carolina,* a Danish barque that sank off Porthgain in 1859.

Barry Island which, like Dinas Island, was insulated at one time, is believed to have been named after St Barre, or Finbarr, who sailed from here to establish his island retreat at Gouganebarra, near Cork.

Geese graze on the green sward at Abereiddi, and grey seals are born beneath the dark cliffs that contain the hairpin-like graptolites *Didymograptus bifidus* in the Ordovician shales of the Llanvirn series, so named from the farmhouse above the bay. A hollowed slate quarry, which closed in 1904, was made into a safe anchorage, known as the Blue Lagoon, when fishermen blasted a passage to the sea. The tower on Trwyncastell was a navigation beacon built during the last century.

Crocsgoch was the scene, they say, of a battle so gory that blood ran down the four roads that meet here: hence its name, 'the red cross'. The Baptist chapel, painted brightly in yellow and Venetian red, was built in 1859. The 'Atramont Arms' carries the name of the Atramont estate of the Le Hunte family in Ireland, where they owned lands before they became landowners in Pembrokeshire.

A roadside stone pillar, half buried in the hedge at Mesur-y-dorth, is inscribed with a ring-cross with intercrossing arms, probably of the eighth century: its hot-cross-bun appearance may account for the name, 'the measure of the loaf', although tradition states that it was here that pilgrims to St David's would break bread for the last time before reaching the shrine of the saint.

7

Around Treffgarne

Letard Littleking, the Fleming, was described as 'the enemy of God and St David' when he was killed by Anarawd ap Gruffydd in 1137. His pious son, Ivo, granted *'ecclesia villa Letardi'* to the Knights Commandery at Slebech, and the village, Letterston, has perpetuated his father's name. Letard's castle may have stood where there is a mound on the village green. At Pendre, a pair of Middle Bronze Age barrows have features which suggest that they were erected in the twelfth century BC, by people who came from an area where stone was not readily available, and along the prehistoric route that drovers from the St David's peninsula followed, and that crossed the main route to Fishguard, thus giving the village its crucial pattern.

The present church was built in 1881, in place of an earlier establishment that may have been sited at Hen Eglwys. It is dedicated to St Giles, and a well, Ffynnon San Shilin, also bears his name.

John Harries, who died at Priskilly in 1803, was the last surviving member of the Society of Sea Serjeants, a Jacobite club, founded about 1725, which met annually at Tenby and other sea-port towns in west Wales. Its members, drawn from the local gentry, wore a dolphin for a badge and drank, from glasses emblazoned with the badge, to 'the little gentleman in black velvet', a reference to the mole that raised the molehill against which the horse of William III had stumbled and caused his death.

The grass in the churchyard at St Edren's was 'in great esteem on account of its efficacy and wonderful effects in curing people, cattle, horses and sheep, and pigs, which have been bitten by mad dogs', and up to a century ago people came to gather grass, which they consumed in a bread and butter sandwich. The church, which was rebuilt in 1846, has three cross-incised stones of the tenth century, two of which bear abbreviated Greek monograms for 'the [Cross of] Alpha [and] Omega – Jesus Christ'.

*Barti ddu o Gasnewy' Bach
Y morwr tal a'r chwerthiniad iach –*

'Black Barti from Little Newcastle, the tall sailor with the wholesome laugh', was born John (he later assumed Bartholomew) Roberts, in 1682. He went to sea as a boy of thirteen and served throughout the long War of the Spanish Succession. In 1718 he was second mate on the galley *Princess* when it was captured by the Welsh pirate Howel Davis in the *Royal Rover*. Six weeks later Davis was killed and the crew elected Bartholomew Roberts to take his place. After capturing rich prizes off the Guinea Coast, Roberts headed for Brazil, where he sailed into a fleet of forty-two Portuguese men-of-war and took the prize ship, the *Sagrada Familia*, laden with sugar, tobacco and moidores of gold, away with him. By 1720 his reputation was such that the crews of twenty ships abandoned them as he entered the harbour at Trepanny in Newfoundland, and from the French who arrived at the port while he was there, he took a fine frigate and renamed it *Royal Fortune*; he gave the same name to another Frenchman which he captured off Guinea in the following year. In two years he took over four hundred prizes, with goods and bullion that today would be valued at many millions of pounds.

In January 1722, however, Captain Chaloner Ogle RN, in HMS *Swallow*, came upon Roberts unprepared, while breakfasting on 'a savoury dish of salmagundi', off Cape St Lopez. He was dressed conspicuously, as always, in his 'crimson damask waistcoat and breeches, a red feather in his hat', and the first broadside caught him. His body slid into the sea on 5 February 1722 – the boy from Little Newcastle who had become the most successful pirate of all time.

A gambit is a ploy in a game of chess, as every player knows, in which a pawn or piece is sacrificed for the sake of an advantage, but not every master, even, is familiar with Evans's Gambit. William Davies Evans was born at Musland Farm, near Wolfscastle, in 1790. He went to sea as a boy of fourteen, and by

1819 he had become master of the sailing packet *Auckland* plying between Milford Haven and Waterford. He learned to play chess to relieve the boredom of life at sea. He is believed to have invented his gambit in 1827, and in 1840 he retired from the sea in order to devote more time to the game. On his first visit to Lewis's Chess Room in St Martin's Lane, London, he defeated the Irish champion Alexander McDonnell with his gambit. In 1845 he was a member of the first team to play chess by electric telegraph. He died in Ostend in 1872, where his tombstone credits him with the invention of tri-coloured lights for shipping as well as of the gambit that has been described as 'a gift of the gods to a languishing chess world'.

The Sealyham Terrier was bred at Sealyham by Captain Jack Edwardes, Master of the Pembrokeshire Foxhounds, who wanted a dog of derring-do that would bolt a fox or an otter or dig out a badger. By careful cross-breeding he produced a short-legged, rough-haired terrier, but each dog had to prove its mettle. A live polecat was dragged across a field and placed in a covered pit, and any dog that went in after it without hesitation made the grade, but any that showed the slightest indecision was destroyed. On one occasion, its handler pleaded for such a craven to be spared and he was reluctantly allowed to do so on condition that he took it out of the squire's sight. It developed into such a game terrier, however, that Captain Edwardes eventually bought it back from the handler. The breed was first recognized at a show held at Haverfordwest in 1903, and within twenty years the Sealyham was one of the most highly prized, and priced, terriers in the western world.

Sealyham came to the Tucker family when Thomas Tucker of Halton, in Cheshire, having served in the army of Edward III, received a grant of land there. His descendant of the same name was a distinguished naval officer, promoted admiral, who is credited with having killed the pirate Bluebeard in the West Indies. By marriage, Sealyham passed to John Owen Edwardes of Little Trefgarn, whose son assumed the name Tucker at the request of his uncle, the admiral.

Embowered in trees and flowering rhododendrons, the church of St Dogwell's has a nave and chancel of the late thirteenth century, a south aisle of the fourteenth, and arches which are similar to those at Rudbaxton. A rough pillar stone that was found as a gatepost is inscribed HOGTIVIS FILI DEMETI in Latin and OGTENAS in ogham to commemorate Hogtivis, the son of Demetus, who lived in the sixth century.

A collapsed cromlech at Garn Turne is of the same type as Pentre Ifan cromlech except that its forecourt is more funnel-like. According to *The Black Book of St David's*, the tenants of St Nicholas and Trefin were obliged to follow the relics of St David as far as here. East of Garn Turne, 'lying flat on the ground' in the time of George Owen, is a boundary stone 'called the Three Lords, for that three lords may keep three several courts on the same, and every lord and tenants standing on his own lordship, viz. the Bishop of St David's for Dewsland, the lord of Cemais, and the lord of Daugleddau'.

Wolfscastle was the settlement of a family called Wolf whose motte-and-bailey is strategically placed at the confluence of the Western Cleddau and the Angof. Signs of an earlier occupation were provided by the discovery of Roman tiles and slates, and the remains of a hypocaust, at Ford, indicating that here was the site of a fortified Romano-British villa.

The 'father' of Welsh journalism was born at Wolfscastle in 1773. The son of a farm bailiff, Joseph Harris, who adopted the name 'Gomer', became a Methodist minister in Swansea where his chapel was rebuilt and called Capel Gomer. In 1814 he published the first all-Welsh weekly, *Seren Gomer*, in which he was assisted by his son, John Ryland Harris.

The stern crags of Maiden Castle and Poll Carn at Treffgarne are among the oldest of rocks: they are the rhyolitic lavas and tuffs of the Pre-Cambrian period that were laid down a thousand million years ago.

The Irish Sea Glacier came as far south as the north Pembrokeshire coast and, according to one theory, formed a barrier that blocked the outflow of the rivers Teifi, Nevern and Gwaun and dammed up temporary lakes in the valleys of those rivers. The lakes overspilled, one into the other, and flowed southward by cutting a gorge at Treffgarne. An alternative interpretation is that the gorge was cut sub-aerially by the rush of meltwater during the last stages of the glacial period.

Trwy Trawgarn pob lladron, 'through Treffgarne all robbers': the old saying remembers the days when the Welsh descended on the lusher pastures of the south, 'where herds of kine were drowsing', and brought home through the gorge the cattle and the fatter valley sheep.

A scattering of defensive settlements and hut circles among the outcrops bespeak considerable activity during the Iron Age.

Like the river, the road and the railway pass through the gorge. The railway came in 1906,. Brunel's interrupted dream, but the hard rocks of Treffgarne proved too much for the well-known London firm of contractors, Messrs J.T. Firbank & Co., and made them bankrupt.

The quarrying of stone has left scars on the valley but there is now no trace of the South Wales Gold Mining Company's short-lived effort to dig for gold in the 1860s.

Cistercian monks who came to establish their houses in Wales were enjoined to seek out the remote areas, where they became an important influence in agriculture. It was not unusual for them to move from their first foundation to another site: this happened at Margam, Grace Dieu, Cwmhir and Strata Florida, and it also happened at Treffgarne, where Bishop Bernard of St David's had given land to the monks in 1141, but ten years later they moved their house to Whitland, where they established an abbey. The abbey was granted the fisheries of Haverfordwest 'every Friday and Friday night'.

The persistent myth that Owain Glyn Dŵr was born at Treffgarne arises from his descent from Llywelyn ab Owen, who received the manor of Treffgarne on his marriage to Elen, daughter and heiress of Robert de Vale. Another descendant of that union, Thomas Newport of High Ercall, sheriff of Shropshire in 1542 and ancestor of the Earl of Bradford, was patron of the living of Treffgarne at the date of the *Valor Ecclesiasticus*, 1535.

One enters the parish church of St Mary at Ambleston through the Norman tower. Its font, which is also Norman, was sold by auction, during restoration in 1883, to a local farmer, who used its base as a cheese-press and the bowl as a trough to feed his pigs, but it was restored twenty years later when the chancel and nave were rebuilt.

An early reference to *villa Amelot* indicates that Ambleston, or Treamlod, was the settlement of Amolot, who was probably a Flemish settler.

Castle Flemish, or Fleming's Castle, has no Flemish

connection: the name is more likely to derive from a family called Fleming who held land at Ambleston in the fourteenth century. It is the *Ad Vigessimum* which puzzled historians for two centuries, until it was shown to be the invention of Charles Bertram, professor of English at Copenhagen, who fooled his friends, in 1757, by sending them copies of the *Itinerary* of one Richard of Cirencester, a fourteenth-century Benedictine monk. Richard, he claimed, had taken this itinerary from *Ab Aquis* (Bath) along the *Via Julia* through *Ad Vigessimum* to *Ad Menapia* (a Roman coastal station near St David's, probably at Whitesand) and thence to Ireland. The earthwork, which comprises an irregular quadrilateral defended by a rampart and ditch, was party excavated by Sir Mortimer Wheeler, who found traces of hypocausted buildings and fragments of Samian and other pottery, which showed that the site was occupied, possibly as a military post, during the second century AD. Local legend tells of a table of gold that lies buried there.

In a field at Scollock West Farm is a white marble monument with life-size statues of John and Martha Llewellin, dressed in their Sunday best, who 'by the blessing of God on their joint undertaking and thrift ... bought this farm and handed it down without encumbrance to their heirs'. Those who pass by are enjoined to 'endeavour to pull together as they did. Union is strength.'

The Evans brothers of North Court Farm invented the spare wheel for motor vehicles. The venture was financed by one of the Stepneys of Llanelli, and the wheel became known as the Stepney Wheel.

The chapel at Woodstock was the first Methodist chapel built in Pembrokeshire, and although the tablet on the wall gives the date 1754, it is likely that the original building was erected three years earlier. Here, for the first time, the Methodists celebrated the sacrament in an unconsecrated building, a practice that was not to become general until 1811. One of the founders of Woodstock was the Reverend Howel Davies who came as a curate to Llys-y-frân in 1741 but was already committed to Methodism. Among his followers he was known as 'the Apostle of Pembrokeshire'.

Woodstock was once an extensive manor owned by one Hugo Howel, a man of considerable power whose daughters were married to 'some of the most distinguished Norman leaders', according to Fenton. The daughter and heiress of his descendant, John Howell, married Sir Peter Perrott, and the estate eventually passed to their descendant Sir John Perrot among whose papers, on his attainder, there was a reference to three hives of bees in the custody of John Hire at the manor of Woodstock, and half a gallon of honey 'which cometh to her majesty for the half of two hives of bees lately killed there'.

The Wallis Factory is one of the last remaining woollen factories in Pembrokeshire, where there were over thirty at the beginning of the century.

The construction of Brunel's broad-gauge railway westward from Swansea was begun in 1847 but, owing to indecision in choosing a terminal that would also serve as a port, it got no further than Cross Inn, where a station was established and called Clarbeston Road. Here, eventually, the line divided, northward to Fishguard harbour and south to Haverfordwest and Neyland and, later, to Milford Haven.

In September 1572 John Wogan of Wiston wrote to Lord Burghley, the Lord High Treasurer, to inform him, as was his duty as High Sheriff, that 'a great quantity of treasure, gold and silver, contained in a certain crock of brass', had been unearthed at Spittal by three local men who had gained knowledge thereof from a priest in Carmarthenshire. The Sheriff feared that 'the truth of the matter will never be bolted out without that the priest be examined and the parties also menaced with some torture or extremity,' all which he remits to the Lord High Treasurer's 'further discretion'. The treasure is believed to have been found in the walls of the *hospitium*, from which Spittal takes its name and which was built by Bishop Bek of St David's about 1290 for pilgrims travelling to the shrine of the patron saint.

In the church porch is a stone bearing the Latin inscription EVALI FILI DENCVI CVNIOVENDE MATER EIVS which may be translated as '[the stone of] Evalus son Dencuus: Cuniovende his mother [erected it]'.

When John Wesley preached on the village green on 3 August 1781, James Higgon of Scolton was moved to join the Methodist Society and thus became the first lay preacher in Pembrokeshire. His grandson built Scolton in 1840, in late Georgian style, and it remained the home of the Higgon family until it was purchased by the County Council in 1974 and converted into a rural museum and country park.

One of the most impressive earthworks in Pembrokeshire is Rudbaxton Rath, standing above a bend of Cartlett Brook, near Crundale. The term *rath*, sometimes pronounced *wraith*, is employed to describe some forty earthworks of varying types in mid-Pembrokeshire, in contrast to its original use in Ireland to signify a circular enclosure defended by a bank and ditch. Rudbaxton Rath is a massive oval earthwork that may well have been an Iron Age hill fort which the Normans adapted to their own use. On its north-eastern slope stood a chapel, referred to as '*capella Sti Leonardi de castro Symonis*', and the earthwork is sometimes called St Leonard's Rath, and sometimes Simon's Castle. Rudbaxton Mount is a low motte beside Rudbaxton church.

Alexander de Rudepac, who gave his name to Rudbaxton, may have held the lordship of Wizo the Fleming, for it was he who held the advowson of Rudbaxton church, which he granted to the Knights Hospitallers of St John of Jerusalem at their Commandery at Slebech in the early part of the twelfth century. In the original grant the church is shown as dedicated to St Madog, and there is a holy well bearing his name in the field adjoining the churchyard, but the dedication was later changed to St Mary.

Along the east wall of the Lady Chapel is a rustic Baroque monument to five members of the Howard family of Flether Hill, all dressed in the colourful garments of the Restoration period. Above the monument are the arms of Howard, 'or a bend sable between three lioncels rampant gules', impaling the arms of Lloyd, 'sable a spearhead imbrued between three scaling ladders argent on a chief gules a castle triple towered of the second'. Four of the five Howards carry a skull as a grim reminder of the mortality of man. The one without, Joanna, erected the monument.

A brass plate in the chancel commemorates William Laud, Bishop of St David's from 1621 to 1626, who received the living of Rudbaxton to supplement his income from the see, which had been impoverished by his predecessor, Bishop Barlow. He became Archbishop of Canterbury in 1633 and was beheaded for treason on Tower Hill in January 1645.

Henry Owen, who died in 1919 and is remembered on a tablet in the Lady Chapel, was the author of *Gerald the Welshman* and *Old Pembrokeshire Families* and editor of George Owen's *Description of Penbrokshire* and of *A Calendar of Public Records relating to Pembrokeshire*.

Among memorials to several members of the Picton family of Poyston is a bust to General Sir Thomas Picton, who was born in 1758 at a house in Hill Street, Haverfordwest, now the Dragon Hotel. At the age of thirteen he was gazetted ensign in the 12th Regiment of Foot, commanded by his uncle, Lieutenant-Colonel William Picton. In 1778 he was promoted Captain in the Prince of Wales Regiment and was at the siege of Gibraltar. His regiment was disbanded at Bristol in 1783, and he personally quelled the mutinous riots that followed. He then retired on half-pay to Wales where he lived in obscurity for the next twelve years until Britain went to war with France, when he embarked, of his own accord, for the West Indies, was placed in command of a regiment and bore a distinguished part in the capture of St Lucia in 1796. He was present at the surrender of Trinidad in the following year and was appointed Military Governor. In 1801 he became Governor, with the powers of the previous Spanish Governor and the rank of a Brigadier General. Within two years he was charged, by those who did not understand the administration of Spanish law, with 'unlawfully inflicting torture on Luise Calderon', a loose woman who, with her paramour, had robbed her master. Picton resigned his post, returned to Britain and appeared before the Court of the King's Bench where, after a delay of six years, he was cleared of guilt. The influential people of Trinidad collected £4,000 towards his legal expenses, but he returned the money for the relief of those who had suffered from a disastrous fire in Port of Spain.

Meanwhile, Picton had been promoted Major-General and, after taking part in Flushing's siege and capture, was appointed its Governor. From 1810 onward he commanded the Third Division in Portugal and was entrusted by Wellington with the siege of Badajos, where he was wounded and invalided home. He returned to the Peninsula in 1813 and pursued the French as far as Toulouse and the abdication of Napoleon. Peerages were conferred on the other army commanders but Picton was awarded the Grand Cross of the Most Honourable Order of the Bath and a vote of thanks, the seventh, in the House of Commons. He retired, once again, to Wales and devoted himself to the improvement of his estate at Iscoed, near Ferryside, where his brother, the Reverend Edward Picton, also resided.

When Napoleon escaped from Elba, Wellington asked Picton to join him in the Netherlands. He spent his last night in Wales at Ewenny Priory with his eldest brother, Richard, who had assumed the name Turberville on inheriting the estate. He arrived at the Hôtel d'Angleterre in the Rue de Madeleine at Brussels on 15 June 1815, and while he was at breakfast the next morning, Colonel George Canning (later to be Prime Minister) came to inform him that Wellington wished to see him immediately. The Duke ordered him to take command of the advance troops, in support of the Prince of Orange, and Picton left without delay for Quatre Bras, where he was hit by a musket ball that fractured his ribs but continued to lead the charge. The next day he fell back on Waterloo, and on the morning of the 18th, although in great pain from his wound, he led his men on the left of the line at La Haye Sainte and, flourishing his sword, called on them to charge. He was struck on the head by a musket ball and fell back dead.

Picton was described in a contemporary account as 'a stern-looking, strong-built man, about the middle height. ... He generally wore a blue-black frock coat, very tightly buttoned up to the throat; a very large black silk neckcloth showing little or no shirt collar; dark trousers, boots and a round hat: it was in this very dress that he was attired at Quatre Bras, as he hurried off to the scene of action before his uniform arrived.' It can be assumed that his uniform had not arrived two days later, for at Waterloo he was dressed in a shabby great-coat and a beaver hat, which may be seen at the United Services Museum in Whitehall.

Picton's body was brought back to Britain for burial in the family vault in the cemetery of St George's, Hanover Square, London. In 1859 his remains were removed to St Paul's Cathedral where, by resolution of Parliament, a monument was raised to him in the north transept. A tall obelisk was raised as his memorial at Carmarthen by public subscription.

Although he never was married, it is said that he had two illegitimate sons, by a woman of Trinidad, who adopted their mother's name, Rose, as their surname, and that one of them came to Haverfordwest in the vain hope of inheriting some of his putative father's estate.

The General's brother, Major John Picton, challenged his own Commanding Officer, Colonel Henry Aston, to a duel over an argument relating to supplies for the Nizam of Hyderabad's army while preparing to eliminate Tipoo Sultan, 'the Tiger of Mysore', in 1798. Luckily Picton's pistol misfired and the Colonel fired in the air, and they shook hands, but Picton was placed under close arrest by Wellington and, soon after, he fell ill and died. General Picton, unjustly, blamed Wellington for his brother's death and never forgave him.

8

Dewsland

The St David's peninsula is a bare, windswept plateau from which rise the resistant monadnocks of Carn Llidi, Carn Lleithr and Penbiri, one-time islands in a receded sea. Its coastline is indented with bays and creeks, where the softer rocks have yielded to the persistent waves.

From Porth Melgan a path leads to Penmaen Dewi, St David's Head, to which Ptolemy refers in his *Geographia*, written in AD 140, as *Octopitarum promontorium*, 'the promontory of the eight perils', having in mind the dangerous offshore rocks and pinnacles known as the Bishop and his Clerks which, warned George Owen, 'preach deadly doctrine to their winter audience'. The tip of the promontory is cut off by a ditch and a drystone wall, *Clawdd y milwyr*, 'the warriors' dyke', to form an Iron Age fort with hut circles and rock shelters which, on excavation, have produced spindle whorls, stone rubbers and a flint scraper. Stone-walled field enclosures below Carn Llidi show that farming has been going on here for the last two thousand years.

An ancient trackway that brought men of the Bronze Age, a millennium and a half earlier still, from Wessex across the Presely Hills, ended at Traeth Mawr, or Whitesand, whence they crossed the sea to Ireland, lured by copper and gold in the Wicklow Hills.

St Patrick, they say, set sail for Ireland from Whitesand: the scanty foundations of a chapel dedicated to him lie beside the beach. Before going, he raised from the dead one Criumther, who had lain in his grave for forty years, and took him with him to Ireland and made him a bishop there.

St Justinian and St Dyfanog built themselves a cell each on Ynys Dyfanog, later called Ramsey by the Norse, in honour of Hrafn. Justinian prayed that the isthmus, then connecting with the mainland, should disappear, and only the dangerous reef known as 'the Bitches' remains. When Justinian died a violent death, he had to walk across the Sound, bearing his severed head in his arms, so that he might be buried at St Justinian's, where he also had a cell, upon which Bishop Vaughan built a chapel in the sixteenth century. Its stolen bells, sunk in the Sound, ring when the sea rages, they say.

The St David's Lifeboat Station was founded in 1868, but the lifeboat house and the slipway were not built until 1918, and a new motor lifeboat, the *General Farrell*, considered 'the best in the world', was launched in the following year. Its predecessor, the *Gem*, had met a sad fate.

On a fearful night in October 1910, the ketch *Democrat* of Barnstaple sought shelter in Ramsey Sound, but the wind swung to north-east and the vessel dragged its anchor. The *Gem*, rowing through tempestuous seas, managed to rescue the ship's crew of three, but itself ran onto the Bitches. The coxswain and two lifeboatmen were drowned, but the others, and the ketch's crew, managed to cling to the reef all night. At daybreak, eighteen-year-old Sidney Mortimer and two coastguards set out in an open boat from Porthclais, and the survivors were rescued. Mortimer was awarded the silver medal of the Royal National Lifeboat Institution, and when the new lifeboat arrived, he became its coxwain.

The caves and shingle beaches of Ramsey are breeding places of the grey seal in late autumn. The cow feeds her solitary calf, which rapidly gains weight on her rich milk, for about three weeks, and then mates again, but there is a delayed implantation, and pregnancy does not commence for three or more months. Little was known about the habits of the grey seal until a study was carried out, on behalf of the West Wales Naturalists' Trust, by R.M. Lockley, and for this purpose it was necessary to mark the seals by clipping a numbered ring on the 'engagement finger' of the fin. Young calves presented no great problem, although their teeth are razor sharp, but it was necessary often to capture adult seals by placing a rope net at the entrance to the caves they frequented. Marked seals, especially the young ones, were found to reach the coasts of Ireland, south-west England and Brittany in a short space of time, and one travelled, in a matter of a month, all the way to Santander in northern Spain.

When Henry II was making preparations for his voyage from

Milford Haven to Ireland in 1171, apart from making a pilgrimage to St David's he was also 'desirous of taking the diversion of hawking', according to Giraldus. He saw 'a noble falcon perched upon a rock. Going sideways round him, he let loose a fine Norway hawk which he carried on his left hand.' The native peregrine soared into the air, swooped upon Henry's goshawk and struck it so that it fell dead at his feet. 'From that time,' Giraldus adds, 'the King sent every year, about the breeding season, for the falcons of this country, which are produced on sea cliffs; nor can any better be found in any part of his dominions.' It has always been maintained that the king's falcons were obtained from Ramsey.

Porth Clais was the port of the monastic community at St David's. Here was brought, from Caerfai and Caerbwdy, plum-coloured stone to build the cathedral, and oak from Ireland for the roof of the nave. And it was here that Twrch Trwyth, the legendary wild boar, landed, having ravaged Ireland, followed by King Arthur, who chased it over the Presely Hills and lost many of his best men before the beast was run to earth in Cornwall.

St Non gave birth to her child David, or Dewi, during a violent thunderstorm, at the place where a chapel was later dedicated to her, at St Non's, somewhere around the year 520. The stone beneath the altar bore the marks of her fingers, where she clutched in the hour of her labour but, as at Llanrhian, it is more likely that these were traces of an ogham inscription.

David was descended of mixed Welsh and Irish princely stock. His father was Sant, son of Ceredig, eponymous lord of Ceredigion and son of Cunedda Wledig, Prince of Manaw Gododdin, the land to the south of the Firth of Forth with its capital at Edinburgh. His paternal grandmother was Meleri, daughter of the Irish lord Brychan Brycheiniog of Brecknock, and his mother, Non, could also trace her ancestry to the Irish aristocracy. He was baptized by St Ailbe of Munster, whose name survives in St Elvis, and one of the earliest references to him, in the *Catalogue of Irish Saints*, indicates that he was respected in Ireland before the end of the sixth century. *The Martyrology of Oengus the Culdee* describes him as David Cille Muine – that is, of the cell or church of Mynyw, or Menevia, and confirms that his feast day was the first day of March and that it was celebrated in Ireland during the eighth century.

After a lengthy period of education under Paulinus, David established his house in the shadow of Carn Llidi at Tŷ Gwyn, 'the white house' or 'holy house'. An early Breton chronicle refers to him as *Aquaticus*, which suggests that he was a member of a monastic set that rejoiced in the rigour of an ascetic life and were known as *aquatici*, the watermen. His influence may be gathered from the number of dedications to him – over sixty in south Wales, nine in south-west England and seven in Brittany. Before long, he came into conflict with Boia, the Irish chieftain and landowner commemorated at Clegyr Boia, over David's desire to remove his religious house from Tŷ Gwyn to the banks of the River Alun. Boia's wife sent her handmaidens to bathe in the nude in the river, as in Irish tales naked women were sent to confront the enemy, but David succeeded in persuading Boia to grant him the land on which the cathedral now stands in *Vallis Rosina*, 'the valley of the little thicket', which is the same meaning as the Irish *muine*, from which are derived 'Mynyw' and 'Menevia'.

David died on the first day of March in the year 589. In 1120 he was canonized by Pope Calixtus II, although Asser, in his life of King Alfred written in 893, refers to him as *'sancti Degui'*. An edict was promulgated by Archbishop Arundel of Canterbury in 1398 ordering the celebration of his feast-day throughout the province of Canterbury, while Archbishop Chicheley, in 1415, further ordered that it should be celebrated with a choir and nine lessons.

There is no trace of the rude building that housed the strict community of St David on the banks of the Alun. It was raided by the Norse in 795 and on nine other occasions between 982 and 1088, and in 999 they slew its bishop, Morgeneu, while Bishop Abraham was killed 'by the gentiles' in 1080.

William the Conqueror came to St David's in 1081 not so much to worship as to reach a compact with the powerful Rhys ap Tewdwr, Prince of Deheubarth. With the death of Rhys in 1093, the Normans lost no time in invading south and west Wales. On the death of Wilfred, the last of the Welsh bishops, in 1115, Bernard, the chancellor of Queen Matilda, was appointed in his place, and he and his successors concerned themselves with imposing a Norman pattern on the diocese and with rebuilding the cathedral.

Henry II came, on his way to Ireland in 1171, only months after the murder of Thomas à Becket, and brought gifts. He came again, on his return from Ireland the following Easter, 'habited like a pilgrim and leaning on a staff', only to be roundly cursed by an old Welsh woman.

The main structure of the present cathedral is the work of Peter de Leia, a Florentine monk and Prior of Wenlock before his appointment as bishop in 1176, and the nave as it is today is much as he left it, except that the roof came crashing down in 1240 and damaged the choir and transepts. Eight years later an earth tremor disturbed the foundations so that the arcade pillars in the nave lean outward, and there is still movement owing to the unstable nature of the site. The floor slopes upward and rises fourteen feet to the Lady Chapel.

Edward I came, with his queen, in 1284, ordered the carrying out of certain works and gave Bishop Bek 55 marks to meet the cost. Bishop David Martin (1296-1325) added the Lady Chapel, and his successor, Bishop Gower (1328-47) raised the aisles and the tower and built the splendid rood screen, beneath which he lies. Owen Pole, the cathedral Treasurer (1472-1509), was responsible for the unique and beautiful Irish oak roof of the nave, one of the glories of the cathedral. Bishop Vaughan (1509-22), the last of the great builders, raised the tower to its present height, vaulted the Lady Chapel and built the fine Perpendicular chapel dedicated to the Holy Trinity where, in the pilgrim's recess, is an oaken casket bearing the relics of the patron saint.

An attempt by Bishop Barlow (1536-68) to remove the see to Carmarthen was unsuccessful, although he managed to take the bishop's residence to Abergwili, where it has remained.

The neglect that followed the Reformation, when the roof of the Lady Chapel was stripped of its lead, contributed to the near ruin of the cathedral. The dilapidated west front was restored in 1793 to a design by John Nash, which proved disappointing, and in 1862 Sir Gilbert Scott was commissioned to undertake a general restoration, when the west front was rebuilt 'to the old design', the tower strengthened and the foundations drained. The cathedral stood in no greater splendour at any time in its long history than it does today.

In the north transept, over the shrine of St Caradoc, is a

Poll Carn rhyolite outcrop

Whitesand Bay from Carn Llidi

The Howards of Rudbaxton

Seasick voyager, misericord at St David's Cathedral

Bishop's Palace, St David's

St David's Cathedral

Trefrân colliery stack, St Bride's Bay

Haverfordwest Castle surrounded by the town with its medieval layout

Old warehouses, Haverfordwest

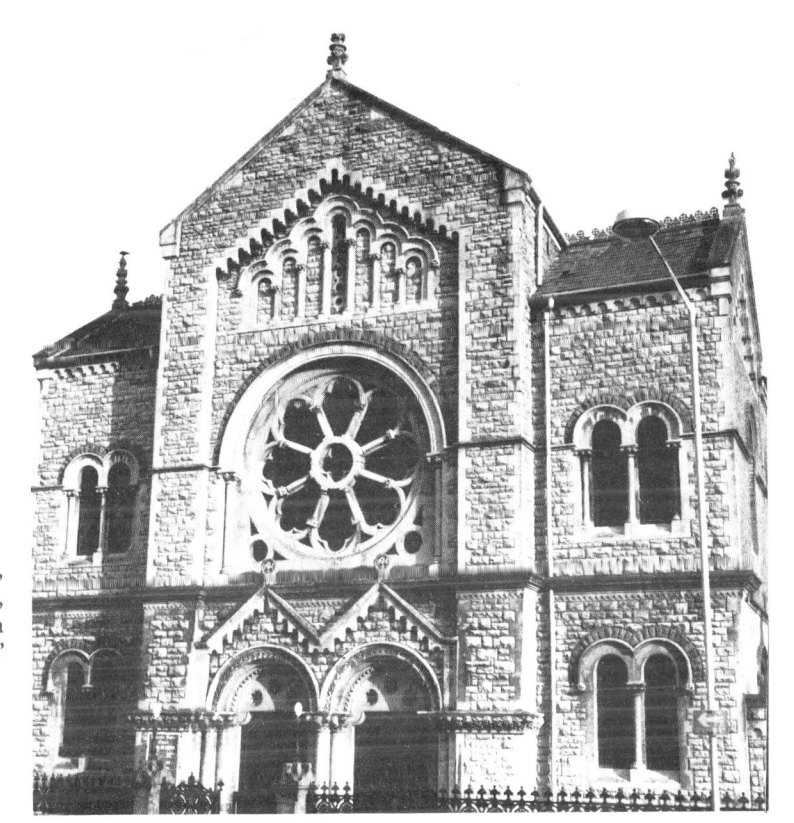

Bethesda Chapel, Haverfordwest, 'Welsh Romanesque'

Wiston, shell keep

Llawhaden, bishop's castle

Stack Rock Fort – the most complete of the 'Palmerston Follies' around the Haven

Friends' Meeting House, Milford

Oil tankers in Milford Haven

Milford Docks

memorial to Thomas Tomkins, son of Thomas Tomkins, 'Master of the Choristers and Organ-player' in the cathedral: he was born at St David's, became organist of Worcester Cathedral and one of the organists of the Chapel Royal, and left many anthems and madrigals, galliards and pavans. The chapel of St Andrew holds the County of Pembroke War Memorial to those who fell in the last war. Leading off it is the chapel of St Thomas à Becket.

Among the tombs in the south choir aisle are those ascribed to the Prince Rhys ap Gruffydd, known as the Lord Rhys, and Silvester, the physician whose 'dissolution showeth that medicine withstandeth not death', and Giraldus Cambrensis. The ornate alabaster tomb in St Edward's Chapel is that of the Viscountess Maidstone who restored the chapel in remembrance of her kinsman, Bishop Jenkinson, whose robes, worn at the coronation of Queen Victoria, are displayed in a wall case.

A portable altar stone, sunk into a table in the south transept, is said to have been brought by St David from Jerusalem. An inscribed stone commemorates the sons of Bishop Abraham, Hedd and Isaac.

The shrine of St David, in the presbytery, once had an ornamental wooden canopy with painted panels showing St David, St Patrick and St Denis. The relics were placed upon it in a reliquary that, if endangered, could be carried a day's journey from the cathedral. Behind the shrine are holes in which pilgrims left their offerings.

Before the high altar stands the tomb of Edmund Tudor, Earl of Richmond, the father of King Henry VII, removed to St David's from the Grey Friars at Carmarthen by command of his grandson, Henry VIII, at the dissolution of the monasteries.

The choir, beneath the high, painted roof of the Tower, has twenty-eight stalls with hinged seats, seven of which are modern.

The first cursal prebend was held by the Master of St Mary's College, and at the dissolution it passed to the Crown. There is no account of a sovereign occupying the prebendal stall until Her Majesty the Queen made a royal visit in 1955. She came again in 1982 to distribute the Maundy money, for the first time ever in this cathedral.

The misericords beneath the seats were carved, about 1500, by a craftsman who had keen observation and a great sense of humour. They portray a pig in a head-dress, a fox in a cowl, another fox eating a goose, a pig eating a fox, two dogs fighting over a bone, two men dancing (or are they suffering from sciatica?), a man asleep with his pint of ale, a man caulking a ship while his mate pauses for a drink, and four men in a boat with one being seasick. The coat-of-arms decorating the end of the treasurer's stall is that of Owen Pole, who ordered the roof of the nave to be done, and, very likely, the misericords.

The bishop's throne, with seats for his chaplains on either side, is fourteenth century, an exceptional piece of craftsmanship and one of the finest examples of its kind in the country.

Two chalices and a patten preserved in the cathedral are the only pre-Reformation church plate in Pembrokeshire. One chalice was found in the grave of Bishop Richard de Carew (1256-80): it was the custom to bury eucharistic vessels with a bishop or a priest, for which purpose churches had two chalices, one of silver for use at the Mass, and the other of pewter or latten for burial. The second coffin chalice and the patten were discovered in the tomb of Bishop Thomas Bek (1280-93). The silver counterparts of these vessels, along with the plate of other Pembrokeshire churches, were destroyed at the dissolution of the monasteries and the confiscation of all things 'idolatrous'.

St Mary's College was founded, in 1377, by Bishop Adam Houghton as a college of priests so as to ensure that divine offices should be properly sung, and connected to the cathedral by a cloister. Four men, working on a windlass to raise stones to the top of the cliff at Caerfai for the building of the College, received 6d. a day between them, but it cost another 4d. to supply them with ale. The sacristy and the domestic buildings have disappeared, but the chapel has been restored and is used as the cathedral hall.

Adam Houghton was born at Caerforiog, near Solva, and was educated at Oxford. He was appointed Bishop of St David's in 1361 and, through the influence of John of Gaunt, became Chancellor of England in 1377. A curious story relates that he was excommunicated by the anti-pope Clement VII whom he excommunicated in return, and the incident is alleged to have been represented in the windows of the collegiate chapel.

The cathedral close is bounded by a wall which was broken by four gates: Porth-y-tŵr, Porth Padrig below the Deanery, Porth Gwyn and Porth Boning. The walls were built by Bishop Bek who ordered, in 1287, that the canons' houses should be enclosed. Porth-y-tŵr, standing above the 'thirty-nine steps', is the only gate that remains. It has a thirteenth-century octagonal tower, now used as a bell tower, and a gateway of the fourteenth century flanked by a prison and a postern, with a portcullis chamber over.

The bishop's palace has three ranges of buildings around a rectangular courtyard. On entering the vaulted gateway, the bishop's chapel stands to the left and, beyond it, the bishop's solar and hall, and the kitchen. Facing is the great hall, which was large enough, it was claimed, for all the bishops of Europe to sit down and dine together. The range of buildings on the west side of the courtyard contained the guest chambers.

In contrast to the magnificence of the bishop's palace, nothing remains of the original bishop's castle, a motte-and-bailey, save a mound on the side of the valley leading down to Porth Clais.

The mayor of St David's was appointed by a steward acting on behalf of the bishop, who was lord of Dewsland and had to approve the appointment. Later on, and up to 1925, a mayor was selected by a jury of the lord's court.

Nun Street was formerly St Non Street: Ezekial Williams, the last dog-whipper at the cathedral, held land there in 1853. The figurehead of the good ship *Catherine*, that once adorned a granary in that street, gave its name to Catherine Street, while Quickwell is a corruption of the Welsh *cwcwll*, the cowl that covered a well on that hill. The Pebbles, leading to Porth-y-tŵr, used to be Pit Street until it was surfaced with rounded pebbles in 1856.

Tŵr-y-felin was erected as a windmill, in 1806, by a local wrecker of whom it was said that 'he got his money on the water and invested it on the wind.' It continued in operation as a mill until 1904, when the sails were dismantled and the tower was converted into a hotel. Another windmill, nearby, was dismantled by a purchaser who considered that there was not enough wind for the two.

It is sometimes claimed that King William IV used to spend weekends with his mistress, Mrs Jordan, at Treleddyn Farm, above Porthselau. Dorothea Jordan was born near Waterford in 1762, the daughter of Francis Bland, a stage-hand of Dublin, and his wife Grace, actress daughter of the Reverend David

Philipps, a Carmarthenshire vicar. After a period of acting in Dublin and Cork, and in Leeds, she reached Drury Lane in 1785. In 1790 she became the mistress of the Duke of Clarence, as William then was, having already given birth to five illegitimate children. She called herself Mrs Jordan when she first became pregnant. She bore the Duke ten children, who were given the surname FitzClarence and the precedence due to the sons and daughters of a marquess. One son became the Earl of Munster, and daughters married the Earl of Erroll, Viscount Falkland and Lord de L'Isle and Dudley. The relationship ended in 1811 and, after playing in London and the provinces for another three years, Mrs Jordan left for France and died, of a broken heart it was said, at St Cloud in 1816. Portraits of her hang in the Garrick Club, and William ordered a statue to be made by Chantrey.

Mrs Jordan came to Treleddyn to visit her mother's sister, Blanche Scudamore Philipps, who had married Thomas Williams in 1758. During those visits Major Samuel Harries of Trefacwn would send his carriage, the only one of its kind in the neighbourhood, to take her out for drives through the countryside. The aunt died in 1788, and three years later Thomas Williams married Margaret Theodosia Harries of Priskilly. He was sheriff in 1778 and is remembered as the man who spotted the invading French ships in 1797, while she was 'the Grace Darling of Pembrokeshire' who rowed a boat out to the Bishops to rescue the crew of a Swedish vessel.

Solva is like no other place. It has a uniqueness and charm that make it one of the most attractive coastal villages in Britain. Its name has long been the subject of speculation and has sometimes been given a Norse derivation, but its earliest known form is Saleuuach, or Salfach, which corresponds to its Welsh name, Solfach. There is a Porth Solfach on Bardsey.

The village lies in two parts, Upper and Lower, and is within the parish of Whitchurch where, according to legend, there are no snakes because St Patrick passed this way on his journey to Ireland. The parish church, which is away from the village, is dedicated to St David and has, in front of the churchyard gate, the stump of a cross known as Maen Dewi, 'St David's stone', which accounts for the Welsh name of the parish, Tregroes. Corpses were carried round the stone before interment. The church was restored in 1874, and some five years later another church was built in Upper Solva, dedicated to St Aidan. A Calvinistic Methodist chapel in Lower Solva has been converted into a nectarium that has beautiful butterflies from various parts of the world. The Wesleyan chapel in Upper Solva forms part of the Solva Memorial Hall that was built in memory of those who fell in the Great War: the memorial cross, on the hill, was designed by Sir John Lavery.

The Gribin, hung with the gold of gorse in summer, has an Early Iron Age promontory fort on its summit. The drowned valley that forms Solva harbour, despite an entrance made treacherous by dangerous rocks, provided the best 'creek for ballingers and fishing boats' in St Bride's Bay. Among many disasters was the wreck of the *Phoebe and Mary* bound from Philadelphia for Liverpool in 1773. Seven men of Solva went to her rescue, but on their return their boat struck Black Rock, and sixty lives were lost in all. The packet *Cradle*, sailing direct from Solva to New York in 1848, offered passage for £3, but passengers had to provide their own food and were warned that the voyage might last four months. In 1756 a local trading company built nine warehouses and acquired a fleet of sailing coasters. The limestone brought in by these vessels from south Pembrokeshire was burned in a dozen limekilns, four of which, on the beach, have been restored.

The first lighthouse to be erected on 'the Smalls' was assembled at Solva in 1775, and when a more substantial lighthouse was built in 1856, under the direction of Sir James Douglass, engineer-in-chief of Trinity House, steam tugs and barges brought 3,696 tons of granite from the De Lank quarries, near Bodmin, to Solva. Each stone was trimmed and numbered before being shipped out from Trinity Quay, which had been built for the purpose. A reading-room was built in the village for the use of the workmen, and on Sundays they and their families were assembled there for divine worship in a service conducted by Sir James. The workmen's more pressing needs were provided for by a dozen inns, three of which remain.

The lifeboat house on Trinity Quay was built in 1869, and a lifeboat provided, from money given by Mrs Charles Egerton of Pangbourne in memory of her husband, a naval captain. The lifeboat was sold, however, when it was found that it could not be launched at low tide.

Efforts were made to mine silver in the early part of the seventeenth century, near Dinas Mawr, and copper mining was carried out along the coast until 1885. The steps that led to the copper mine near Porth-y-rhaw are known as the Smugglers' Steps, and the houses in the village, at one time, had hidden cupboards to conceal smuggled goods. The people of Llanunwas Farm had 'the reputation of hanging out false lights to decoy the wandering mariner', and it is significant that a cave below the house is known as Ogof Tobacco.

The little hamlet of Caerfarchell bears the name of Marchell, the daughter of Tewdrig, who is said to have embarked at Whitesand for Ireland where she married Anlach and by him became the mother of Brychan Brycheiniog, the eponymous lord of Brecknock.

At very low tides, after violent storms, stumps of trees in a sunken forest that was drowned in post-glacial times are laid bare on Newgale. When Henry II passed by in 1171, he saw a sight that looked 'like a grove cut down perhaps at the time of the deluge', Giraldus records, and in each stump 'the wood was like ebony'. A storm in 1795 exposed the paved causeway of the old Welsh Way that led to St David's.

The two-mile stretch of sand is backed by a spectacular pebble ridge formed during the great storm of 1859. An old man told me how he remembered yet another storm, 'when the pub was washed away and the old lady who kept it was only able to grab twenty sovereigns from the till before the whole place was overwhelmed by the sea.' The 'pub' that vanished was on the seaward side of the road and was visited by the then Duke of Edinburgh on his way to the shrine of St David in 1882.

When St Caradog the hermit died in 1124 and his body was borne for burial at St David's, the bearers had to seek shelter from a heavy shower of rain near Bathesland Water. When they emerged, they found the silken pall that covered the bier perfectly dry. A chapel was built, of large pebble stones and mortar, to mark the site of the miraculous happening.

The *Resolution* laden with coal and other cargo and sailing from Milford Haven to Poole in Dorset, on 2 March 1690, was blown ashore at Newgale. Her master later complained to the Great Sessions that he was 'almost totally robbed and deprived of what the merciless waves had reduced him unto, by the more unmerciful people of that neighbourhood'.

Brawdy Brook, marked 'Brandy' on the OS maps, is at its western end the linguistic divide between the Welshry of north Pembrokeshire and Little England beyond Wales.

'Brawdy' is a corruption of 'Breudeth', the Welsh for Brigid or St Bride, but the parish church is dedicated to St David. Inside the church porch are three inscribed stones remembering Briacus, Vendagnus and the son of Qagte, who lived in the fifth and sixth centuries. Another stone, found in the farmyard next to the church in 1936, is now at the National Museum of Wales. It commemorates Macutrenus, son of Catomaglus, whose son Trenegussus may be the subject of the inscription on the stone in Cilgerran churchyard.

A Royal Air Force station was established at Brawdy in 1944; it was transferred to the Royal Navy two years later and commissioned as HMS *Goldcrest* in 1952. In 1971 the station reverted to the Royal Air Force; in addition to its training programme, it provides a valuable rescue service through its helicopters, which stand by to answer calls for help from those who are in danger on land or sea.

The motte-and-bailey at Pointz Castle was the stronghold of Ponce, a tenant-in-chief of the Bishop of St David's.

'Take me anywhere,' appealed a traveller of long ago, 'as long as I don't see Roch Castle.' Unlike William Morris, who ate his sandwiches on top of the Eiffel Tower because that was the only place where he didn't 'have to look at the confounded thing', the traveller only meant that he wished to go further afield, for Roch commands, and can be seen from, a wide field. It stands on a Pre-Cambrian rhyolitic crag, the oldest rock there is, and John Wesley, when he passed that way, asked the local squire whether the castle was 'natural or artificial'. 'Artificial, to be sure,' answered the ribald squire, 'I imported it myself from Ireland,' a reply which Wesley later quoted as an example of answering a fool according to his folly.

Adam de la Roche, who lived in the twelfth century, is the first recorded lord of Roch. He had a presentiment that he would die of the bite of a serpent, and so he built himself a castle on a rock, where he felt he was safe. But one day a servant brought in a bundle of firewood, out of which sprang a venomous viper, and Adam met his dreaded fate.

David de la Roche accompanied Strongbow to Ireland in 1169. He obtained land in Wexford which is still known as Rochesland, and founded Selskar Abbey, where the first Anglo-Irish treaty was signed when Wexford was surrendered to Robert FitzStephen. From him are descended Lord Fermoy and the Princess of Wales.

Thomas, the last of the de la Roches, left two daughters, one of whom married Lord Ferrers of Chartley, and the other became the wife of Sir George Longueville of Wolverton. During the reign of Queen Elizabeth I, Roch is recorded as the joint possession of the earls of Essex, by descent from Ferrers, and the Longuevilles.

In 1601 the manor and castle of Roch were purchased by William Walter, whose grandfather, John Walter, a native of Essex, had been appointed approver of the King's lordships in Pembrokeshire and had married Alson Mendus of Fishguard. William's grandson, another William, was married to a niece of the first Earl of Carbery, commander of the Royalist forces in west Wales during the Civil War, who garrisoned Roch Castle until it was seized by General Rowland Laugharne for the Cromwellians in 1644, only to be retaken by the King's men four months later. William Walter claimed that his property, and his stock of five hundred cattle and two thousand sheep, had suffered great damage and plunder during these exchanges and submitted a claim for £3,000 in compensation. He maintained that he was already impoverished by the demands of his 'disloyal and malignant wife' whom he had deserted because he had 'more than a suspicion of her incontinency'. Claims and counter-claims were considered by the House or Lords over a period of six years before judgement was given, in February 1647, by which Walter should have charge of his children, who had hitherto spent most of their time with their mother in London.

Their daughter, Lucy Walter, was seventeen years of age at the time, and in the following year she was taken to Holland by her aunt, Margaret Gosfright, who had married a Dutchman, though it is also held that she went to The Hague as the mistress of Colonel Robert Sydney and captivated Charles Stuart, later Charles II, there. On 9 April 1649, at Rotterdam, Lucy gave birth to a son, James, who was to become Duke of Monmouth. She was with Charles in Paris and St Germain in July and August of that year, but when he left for Scotland in 1650, she became involved with the future Earl of Arlington, by whom she had a daughter, Mary. When Lucy returned to England in 1656 she was arrested as a spy and clapped in the Tower, but discharged a month later, when Parliament decided to deport 'Charles Stuart's lady of pleasure and the young heir'. She was sent back to the Netherlands and found her way to Paris, where she died a wretched death in 1658.

The diarist John Evelyn travelled in the same coach as Lucy from Paris to St Germain in 1649 and wrote of her as 'a brown, beautiful, bold but insipid creature'.

Charles recognized Lucy's son as the eldest of his illegitimate children, gave him the dukedom of Monmouth with precedence over all dukes not of the blood royal and heaped honours upon him, including the Order of the Garter, so that Samuel Pepys observed that the King 'did doat' upon his son. In April 1663 he was married to the wealthy Countess of Buccleuch in the King's chamber, and they were thereupon created Duke and Duchess of Buccleuch: their present descendants include the Duke of Gloucester and the Princess of Wales.

During the agitation of the Exclusion Bill, between 1673 and 1680, a rumour was spread by the Country party that Charles and Lucy had been legally married, but this was denied by him on three occasions.

Keeston Castle is a prehistoric earthwork with three concentric banks defending an enclosure, and a small enclosure oddly placed on the outer bank to the south of the main earthwork. The old name, Keatingston, is derived from the Keating family, one of whom followed Strongbow to Ireland. Their house, at Keeston, was converted into a hospice for pilgrims travelling to St David's.

Recent excavations at Walesland rath, nearby, reveal that it was originally an oval enclosure, with bank and ditch, erected in the fourth or third century BC, with two or three circular huts and a range of timber buildings along the bank. The site was later enlarged and improved, and was occupied throughout the Roman period. A ploughshare tip and the remains of buildings that were probably granaries provide evidence of arable cultivation.

Camrose Castle is no more than a low mound, for the motte has been eroded by cultivation, and the bailey is considerably obscured. The church is dedicated to St Ismael, the son of Budoc, King of Cornouaille in Brittany, who appears to have been popular in this area, for there are dedications to him also at Lambston, Uzmaston, Rosemarket and St Ishmael's.

The Causeway, crossing the parish of Camrose, has been regarded as the linguistic 'lansker' in western Pembrokeshire but this, in fact, more closely coincides with the northern boundary of the parish, and then follows Brawdy Brook to the sea at Newgale bridge. The divide has remained unchanged for the last four hundred years, at least, but the number of people speaking Welsh has, sadly, declined.

Llywelyn the Great, after ravaging the Gower peninsula in 1217, set out for Pembrokeshire and forded the Western Cleddau below Wolfsdale in order to launch an attack at Haverfordwest. At Wolfsdale he was met by Iorwerth, Bishop of St David's, who persuaded the Prince to proceed no further.

John Mathias Berry, born at Upper House, Wolfsdale, the son of James Berry, a farm worker, and his wife Rebecca Mathias of Wolfsdale, became an estate agent at Merthyr Tydfil. By his wife, Anne, daughter of Thomas Rowe of Pembroke Dock, he had three sons: Henry Seymour Berry, who became Lord Buckland of Bwlch; William Ewert who, as Viscount Camrose, was chairman and editor-in-chief of the *Daily Telegraph* and Amalgamated Press, and James Gomer, Viscount Kemsley, chairman of Kemsley Newspapers and editor-in-chief of the *Sunday Times*.

The western end of the Pembrokeshire coalfield meets the coast between Newgale and Little Haven and stretches beyond under the sea. The rich seam of anthracite was dug in bell pits during the late medieval period, but by the eighteenth century the workings had shafts ventilated by beam engines, with the attendant sheds and spoil-heaps and tramways. A solitary stack still stands on the edge of St Bride's Bay to mark the site of the colliery at Trefrân, and there are traces of tram-roads along which the coal was drawn by horses, and later by traction engine, to the beach at Nolton Haven for export. The Folkestone Colliery Company was established in 1769 by Abel Hicks, who was the owner of coastal vessels, such as the *Industrious Bee*, that were employed in the export trade. The small quay and a pier built at Nolton Haven have vanished, but the Counting House, now a private residence, still stands overlooking the beach.

Nolton stone was easily chiselled into tombstones and troughs and was much in demand for making grindstones and mustard-mills.

The parish church is in the village, up a bosky valley, and is described in the charter of its endowment to Pill Priory as *'ecclesia de S Madoci de Veteri Villa'*, 'the church of St Madoc [who is said to have arrived from Ireland at Madoc's Haven] in the old town'; the 'old town' with time became 'Nolton'. In the church is a mutilated effigy of a knight, weathered by long use as a gatepost. The old manor house, which stood on the north side of the churchyard, was at one time in the possession of the City of London.

There is no evidence that druids ever worshipped in oak groves, or cut mistletoe with their golden sickles, at Druidston. Local people, more correctly, call it Drewson, for it was the settlement of someone called Drew, whose stronghold may have been the castle-ring at Druidston Cross. Druidston Haven has a fine stretch of sand, approached by a footpath, and at its southern end is Druidston Chins to which there is reference in a long contemporary poem describing the invasion of Ireland by the Pembrokeshire knights, called *The Song of Dermot and the Earl*. When Henry II was faced with rebellion, both at home and in France, in 1173, Strongbow and his men had orders to return to the aid of the King and, according to the poem, they landed at 'Druidson Chinn'.

The Scarborough vessel *Increase*, laden with a cargo of gunpowder and Government ordnance, ran ashore at Druidston Haven on her way from St Kitt's in 1791. The pillagers of the neighbourhood lost no time in plundering the ship, and in so doing, they scattered quantities of gunpowder on the beach. A metal object, thrown onto the rocks, caused a spark which ignited the gunpowder, and eight people were killed in the ensuing explosion. Women in their long skirts were enveloped in flames, and many of the sixty people who were injured bore burn scars on their faces for the rest of their lives.

9

Town and County of Haverfordwest

Haverfordwest is still 'the county town', thriving and vigorous. It still has the air of a border town, perhaps most noticeable on mart and market days when farmers from Welsh Pembrokeshire and Little England meet to strike their bargains with a spit and a handshake, as their forbears have done for nigh on a thousand years. It has no great industries but a profusion of banks and finance offices indicate its importance as a market town and centre of a prosperous agricultural area and of the tourist industry in Pembrokeshire.

'Haverfordwest is the handsomest, the largest, and the genteelest town in South Wales,' wrote Mary Morgan, the wife of a Cambridgeshire clergyman, in her *Tour to Milford Haven in 1791*. Among others who have sung the praises of the town was the eighteenth-century travelling entertainer Charles Dibdin, who composed verses beginning:

> Oh! Haverfordwest is a mighty fine place
> Where Welsh hospitality shines in each face ...

In those days, the fashionable town was known as 'the Bath of the west', and in it the gentry of the surrounding countryside had their town houses: the gentlemen had their carriages and the ladies their sedan chairs to convey them to take tea with their equals and to attend banquets and balls. The houses remain as reminders of the elegant Regency and early Victorian period: Foley House, designed by Nash but disfigured by its renovators, Hermon's Hill with its Regency double bow front, houses with elaborate cast-iron balconies and railings in Spring Gardens, eighteenth-century Hill Street where the first flagstone pavements in Wales were laid, and High Street, which is surely one of the most attractive streets in the Principality.

TOWN AND COUNTY OF HAVERFORDWEST

Nothing is known of Haverfordwest until the Normans came and built a castle there, perhaps on the site of an earlier settlement. As its name indicates, it stands on a ford, the lowest fording point of the Western Cleddau. Dr B.G. Charles, the authority on non-Celtic place-names in Wales, derives the first part of the name from the Old English *haefr*, meaning a buck, or male goat. The terminal was added about 1400 to distinguish Haverford from Hereford and Hertford, which Shakespeare, even, found necessary in his *Richard III*, where Lord Stanley asks: 'Where is the princely Richmond now?' – and is told: 'At Pembroke or at Ha'rford-west in Wales.' Its people call it 'Harford' and refer to themselves as 'Honey Harfats'. The Welsh name Hwlffordd is a corruption of the English.

Haverfordwest stood also on the tidal limit for navigation, and vessels of two-hundred tons could reach its quays at high water. Furthermore, it was situated at the heart of the peninsula, 'whither men may at all seasons repair', for which reason it was chosen, in place of Pembroke, in 1542, as the county town.

The castle was built, on a spur overlooking the river, possibly by Gilbert de Clare, lord of Pembroke, early in the twelfth century. It first appears in history when Giraldus Cambrensis was welcomed there, in 1188, by Richard, the son of Tancred, a Flemish settler, who may also have been its builder. In 1213 the castle was granted, by King John who had expelled Richard's son, to William Marshal, Earl of Pembroke, and it remained in that earldom until 1289 when it was given by Edward I to his wife, Eleanor, and then, in 1301, to his son Edward, when he was created Prince of Wales. Among its many holders were the Black Prince, Jasper Tudor and Anne Boleyn, as the Marquess of Pembroke. It survived an attack by Llywelyn the Great in 1220, and the assault of the French mercenaries which had landed at Milford Haven to support Owain Glyn Dŵr, though they ravaged the town, in 1405.

It was garrisoned by trained bands for the Parliament at the outbreak of the Civil War in 1642, even though the Member of Parliament for the Haverfordwest borough, Sir John Stepney, was an ardent Royalist. In September 1643 the Earl of Carbery occupied the town for the King to the ringing of bells, and the Common Council signed a declaration of loyalty to His Majesty, but in the following February Major-General Rowland Laugharne, commander of the Parliamentary forces in Pembrokeshire, came and was equally warmly welcomed. The King's men returned in April 1645, under Colonel Sir Charles Gerard, and the Mayor gave him 10 shillings in gold 'to avoid his fury', but on 2 August, the day after 'the rout of Colby Moor', Laugharne entered the town and stormed the castle. In 1648 Cromwell, writing from Pembroke, ordered the Mayor to summon 'ye inhabitants of the towne and country of Haverfordwest, and that they forthwith demolish the workes, walls and towers of the said Castle, soe as that the said Castle may not be possesst by the enemy, to the endangering of the peace of these parts,' and he added that he expected 'an account of your proceedings with effect in this business by Saturday, being the 15th day of July instant'. The mayor, John Prynne, replied to say that he and his Common Council had 'this daye putt some workmen aboute it, but we finde the worke too difficult to be brought aboute without powder to blow it up. ... Wherefore, we become suitors to your Honor that there may a competent quantyty of powder be spared out of the shypps for the speedy effectynge the worke, and the county paying for the same.' The hundreds of Cemais, Cilgerran, Dewsland and Rhos had, in fact, to meet the bulk of the cost of demolition, amounting to £130, of which the inhabitants of the town of Haverfordwest had to find £20. The mayor, one assumes with great deliberation, carried out his task with the utmost inefficiency, for much of the castle still stands, square and sentinel above the town.

The gatehouse and drawbridge stood at the present approach and led from the Castle-town into the outer ward, or Castle Green. A square tower projected from the north curtain wall, and adjoining it were the stables. The inner ward comprises a round tower near its entrance, a large rectangular tower which contained the Great Chamber and, next to it, the solar and the chapel, whose arched east window overlooks the town. Next to the solar stood the Great Hall, adjoining which was the buttery and the kitchen, and beneath it was a large room 'called the coyning house, out of which goeth a stayer into a walke called the Queen's Arbour'. A well, in the inner ward, was cut through the rock, over a hundred feet, down to the water table.

A gaol was built in the inner ward in 1779, but from 1822 it was used as an asylum, the second to be established in Wales. The asylum was roundly condemned for its primitive condition but it remained open until 1866, when the inmates were transferred to Carmarthen. Meanwhile a three-storeyed prison building had been erected in the outer ward, which later became the headquarters of the Pembrokeshire Constabulary and in 1963 was converted to accommodate the County Museum and County Record Office.

The town was greatly impoverished as a result of military occupation during the Civil War, and it suffered further, in 1652, from a severe outbreak of a pestilence, from which over three hundred of its inhabitants died, so much so that prayers were said in some London churches for 'the stricken folk of Haverfordwest'.

Haverfordwest's earliest extant charter was granted by Henry II, and in 1479 Edward, Prince of Wales and Lord of Haverford, by the mandate of his father, Edward IV, incorporated the town and decreed that it should be governed by a mayor, sheriff and bailiffs together with 'twenty-four of the honestest men of the town'. The mayor was also to be a Justice of the Peace, Coroner, Admiral of the Port and Clerk of the Market. In 1543 Haverfordwest became a county with its own assizes, and two years later it was given the right to have a *Custos Rotulorum* and to elect a Member of Parliament; in 1761 it was able to appoint its own Lord Lieutenant. Though it ceased to be a Parliamentary constituency in 1885, it retained its Lord Lieutenant and *Custos Rotulorum* until the 1930s.

The port of Haverfordwest flourished from Tudor times to the early part of this century, exporting wool, friezes, hides, corn, malt and coal, while its imports included salt, iron and wine from France and Spain. There was a weekly packet to Bristol and to Waterford, and a passenger vessel once a month to London. The town was hung with banners and bunting to welcome the arrival of the first train, at the railway station built by the South Wales Railway at Cartlett, on 28 December 1853, little realizing that its coming would bring an abrupt end to the waterborne traffic and mark the beginning of the decline of the port.

As a port, Haverfordwest was at one time the haunt of pirates, the most wanted of whom, during the sixteenth century, was John Callice, born at Tintern and skipper of a ship belonging to Sir John Berkeley until he took to piracy, operating from Lulworth and Poole along the Cornish and Pembrokeshire coasts. In January 1577 the Privy Council sent an indignant letter to Sir John Perrot, as Vice-Admiral of Pembrokeshire, stating that 'their Lordships are given to understand that one John Callice, a notable pirate frequenting that country and arriving lately at Milford, was lodged and housed at Haverfordwest, and being there known was suffered to escape, their lordships do not a little marvel at the negligence of such as are Justices in those parts.' Sir John made enquiry of the Mayor who said that he was not aware that Mr Callice had paid the town a visit.

Adjoining Freemen's Way are the ruins of the Augustinian Priory of St Mary and St Thomas the Martyr founded by Robert, son of Richard FitzTancred, or Robert de Hwlffordd as he was sometimes known, who died in 1213. When the Order of Canons Regular of the Lateran was instituted by Pope Alexander II in 1061, the canons adopted the rule of St Augustine and were known as Augustinians, and also, from their dark-coloured habits, as Black Canons. They first appeared in Wales at Llanthony in 1108, and by 1140 a cell of the abbey of St Augustine at Bristol had been established at Carmarthen. Unlike the Benedictines, the Augustinians identified themselves with the Welsh way of life and thereby gained the affection and trust of the Welsh people. The cloisters and the frater of the priory have long vanished but the ruins of the cruciform church which had a central tower on four pointed arches are now preserved at the instigation of the Gild of Freemen of Haverfordwest.

The Dominicans, or Black Friars, also had a house at Haverfordwest, situated in Bridge Street. At the dissolution of the monasteries it was recorded that it had 'no substance of lead' save some small gutters, and that its bell had been taken to Bristol.

St Mary's Church is of cathedral proportions: its Early English arcades, its Perpendicular clerestory and its fifteenth-century oak roof combine to mark it out as one of the finest churches in Wales. There are traces of an earlier structure, but the main fabric is of the thirteenth century, possibly a reconstruction following the sacking of the town by Llewelyn the Great, and extensive alterations were made during the Tudor period. The panelled roof springs from corbels bearing the carved figures and heads of men on the south side, and of women on the north: it was originally gilded and coloured. The grotesquerie on the capitals of the arcade pillars includes a pig playing a fiddle and an ape on the harp. The scallops on the scrip of a mutilated recumbent figure near the south-west corner of the nave indicate that he had made the pilgrimage to the shrine of St James at Compostela during the fifteenth century. In the chancel a brass commemorates the mayor of 1642, John Davids, and his wife Sage, and a lengthy epitaph proclaims the virtues of 'the lovely Hessy Jones' who 'finish'd her task at 16, full of Grace and ripe for Glory' in 1771. There are monuments and hatchments of the Philipps family of Picton Castle, and a floor-slab marks the grave of Sir John Pryce, fifth baronet of Newtown Hall, Montgomery, whose third wife insisted, before she would enter his bed, that the embalmed corpses of her two predecessors be removed from the bedroom. The elaborately carved bench-end of a two-seater pew reserved for the mayor and the sheriff shows a knight slaying a dragon, which may be symbolic, and is surmounted by a poppy-head bearing the royal arms of England and France.

A spire of timber and lead was removed in 1801 when it was in danger of tumbling. On the south porch gable end is a square sundial set there in 1656. A peal of five bells was recast as six by Thomas Bayley of Bridgewater in 1765 when two new ones were added, one inscribed: 'I do my best for Haverfordwest.' The clock, set in the tower in 1887 as a memorial to the town's benefactor Sir John Perrot, was made by Joyce of Whitchurch with a gravity escapement of the type invented by Lord Brimthorpe who designed Big Ben.

St Martin's proudly claims a more ancient ancestry:

St Martin's bell rang many a knell
When St Mary's was a furzy dell.

It is often described as 'the castle church' because of its proximity to the castle, in accordance with Norman custom. The tower has a stone spire, and the south chapel and porch were added in the fourteenth century.

Apart from its tower, the church of St Thomas is early Victorian. A broken monumental slab resting against the interior west wall bears a cross fleury and a palm branch and is inscribed with the name of Richard the Palmer, who had made the pilgrimage to the Holy Land.

Religious reform was slow in taking root in rural Wales until the translation of the New Testament and Prayer Book in 1567, and the appearance of the Welsh Bible in 1588, made the doctrines of the Reformation intelligible. The Welsh had no difficulty, therefore, in accepting the return to Catholicism ordered by Queen Mary, and there were only three Protestant martyrs in Wales. One was William Nichol, 'an honest good simple poor man', who was burned at the stake in the High Street on Saturday 9 April 1558. The 'martyr stone' was removed to Dale Castle when the road was widened, and a Balmoral red granite column was erected in its place in 1912.

When William Laud, a former Bishop of St David's, became Archbishop of Canterbury in 1633, a persecution of the clergy in this diocese who were not strict conformists began, and many of them held meetings in private houses. A house on St Thomas Green, used for such a purpose from about 1638, became known as 'the Green Meeting', and a small chapel was built on the adjoining site in 1651. The Reverend Stephen Love, rector of St Thomas and vicar of St Mary's, was listed among its members, and so was the Reverend Peregrine Phillips, vicar of Llangwm and Freystrop until deprived under the Act of Uniformity of 1662. In 1665 he became the first pastor of the Green Meeting, which is regarded as the mother-church of Nonconformity in Pembrokeshire. The chapel was restored in 1841 and was named Albany Independent Chapel, possibly after Albion Terrace, a row of white-painted houses in Hill Street which the entrance to the chapel then faced.

Those who considered that the ministry at Albany was insufficiently evangelical eventually established the Tabernacle Congregational Church at the bottom of City Road.

John Wesley preached at Haverfordwest when he paid the first of his fourteen visits to Pembrokeshire in 1763. In the following year, as no one knew of his coming, he 'walked up towards the Castle and began singing a hymn. The people presently ran together from all quarters.' In 1771 he 'preached in St Martin's Church-yard to a numerous and deeply attentive congregation', and in that year the Pembrokeshire Circuit was established. A year later he preached at the opening of 'a new house at

Haverfordwest, far the neatest in Wales'. The entrance to the 'Wesley Room', as it was known, was through St Martin's churchyard, and on the site of the 'room' was built the Wesleyan Chapel. On his last visit to Haverfordwest, in August 1790 and only eight months before he died in his eighty-seventh year, Wesley mounted a horse-block outside the Blue Boar Inn and used the broad shoulders of John Green, one of the founder members of the Wesley Room, as a lectern. A plaque marking the spot, and now on a plinth outside the Library, was unveiled in 1956 by the mayor, Colonel John Green, a direct descendant.

A Baptist college was opened in Bridge Street in 1839 and was later moved to 'The Grove', on St Thomas Green, but in 1894 it was transferred to Aberystwyth before being absorbed by the colleges at Cardiff and Bangor. Bethesda Baptist Chapel was built in 1878 on an earlier site in a style that has been described as Welsh Romanesque.

The Quakers established themselves at Haverfordwest soon after 1650, and in 1662 a number of Quakers and Dissenters were committed after being taken 'at an unlawful meeting, pretence of Religious worship and evil principles in great disobedience to His Majesties government'. A Friends' meeting-house stood at the bottom of High Street until the Shire Hall was built on the site in 1835, when they moved to a building adjoining the storehouses on the Old Quay. Their burial ground, enclosed by a stone wall, is at Sutton outside the town.

The first Welshman to join the Moravian Brethren was William Holland, a native of Haverfordwest who had a house painting business in London. When *Unitas Fratrum*, the United Brethren, as the Moravians called themselves, established their official congregation in Fetter Lane, in 1742, his name stood first on the list of its members, and in the following year he was appointed their correspondent for Wales and came on a mission to Pembrokeshire. At the same time, John Gambold, born in Puncheston, who through his friendship with Charles Wesley while at Oxford had joined the Oxford Methodists, resigned his living at Stanton Harcourt after he had met Count von Zinzendorf, the founder of the Moravian movement, and returned to Pembrokeshire to keep a school in Market Street at Haverfordwest. He joined the Brethren and became a Moravian bishop in 1753. Several other early

Methodists in the town, who had converted a large malthouse on the Quay into a Society Room, had leanings towards Moravianism, and in 1755 they formed a Moravian Society and held meetings in an adjoining warehouse before establishing a chapel on St Thomas's Green ten years later, and another at Portfield Gate in 1816. The movement survived until 1956, and in 1961 the chapel on St Thomas's Green was demolished to make way for a block of flats for the elderly.

Of the fifteen paper mills in Wales at the end of the eighteenth century, two were situated at Haverfordwest, the Hartsmore Mill and the Haverfordwest Mill. They were operated by Thomas Lloyd, who in 1815 went into partnership with John Phillips, but by 1830 the mills were owned by Benjamin Harvey. In 1842 a third mill, the Millbank mill, was opened by Harvey, who sold the three mills to Samuel Read & Co, a company that described itself as 'the manufacturers of rope browns and manilla papers'. Before the end of the century, however, the paper mills had ceased to function.

Somewhere around the middle of the eighteenth century, two brothers, Samuel and Moses Levi, came to Haverfordwest and were befriended by a man called Phillips, whose surname they adopted. The register of St Mary's Church shows that on 23 June 1755 'a Jew called Moses Phillips, aged about two and twenty years, was baptised'; Samuel became a Christian about the same time, and from him some families who became prominent in Welsh life are descended. He founded the Haverfordwest Bank, which was carried on by his son, Nathaniel Phillips, but which, along with all the other banks in Pembrokeshire, became insolvent during the financial crisis of 1826.

Higgon's Well provided a cure for rheumatism, until the mineral properties of its water were realized and a mineral water factory was built, which provided 'pop' in egg-shaped bottles that, when emptied, were often used as rustic barometers.

An outcrop of Silurian mudstones near the gasworks has suffered badly from the hammers of fossil-collecting geologists. Brachiopods from the site were exhibited in the geological museum at Moscow and labelled 'Mudstoneski Gasworksi Haverfordwestski', I was once told.

Fortune's Frolic, a riverside walk along the Cleddau, was the scene of a duel fought on a fine afternoon in September 1799 between Samuel Fortune, a member of a well-known Haverfordwest family, and his fiancée's brother, John James of Pantsaeson, near Moylegrove, with whom he had had a trivial quarrel while attending a hunt ball at Tenby. Fortune fired his pistol into the air but James took aim and delivered a shot that proved fatal for Fortune. He was buried in St Thomas's churchyard, and his betrothed, who died of a broken heart, was laid in the same grave. James fled to the Continent but returned ten years later and became Colonel of the Pembrokeshire Militia.

The Old Bridge was raised across the Cleddau in 1726, and on its north parapet is a memorial which commemorates its crossing by George IV on his way to Ireland in 1821.

A race-course was laid out on Portfield Common in 1727, and provision was made for the road across it to be closed when races were held. The name Portfield indicates 'open land belonging to the town', and the Freemen of Haverfordwest had the right to pasture their horses, cattle and sheep on the common, which covered some six hundred acres. Most of the land was parcelled, however, under the Portfield Inclosure Act of 1840, leaving an area as 'a place of recreation and exercise for the neighbouring population at their free will and pleasure ... and to be depastured by sheep, but by sheep only, at all times of the year except at such times as public races shall be held'.

George de la Poer Beresford was enrolled among the peers of Great Britain as Baron Tyrone of Haverfordwest in the county of Pembroke in 1786, and three years later he was created Marquess of Waterford in the peerage of Ireland. The present Marquess sits in the House of Lords as Lord Tyrone.

When John Lort Stokes was carrying out a survey of the coast of New Zealand in 1848, he felt at home on the Cleddau river that empties into Milford Sound, and at Dale Point, St Ann's Point and Mount Pembroke. These places had been so named by Captain Peter Williams of Milford Haven a quarter of a century earlier because he considered that the coast resembled that of Pembrokeshire, but Stokes felt that he could have 'retained but an imperfect recollection of the celebrated haven of his native land, after which he thought proper to name it'. Stokes was born at Scotchwell, Haverfordwest, in 1812. He went to sea as a boy and served as a lieutenant on HMS *Beagle*, the survey ship that carried Charles Darwin as its naturalist from 1831 to 1836. In

1843 Stokes returned to Britain, after being speared by an Australian aborigine, and settled down to write his *Discoveries in Australia with an Account of the Coasts and Rivers explored and surveyed during the Voyage of the Beagle 1837-1843*. Lort River in Western Australia commemorates his name. He was promoted Captain in 1846, and in the following year he left on HMS *Acheron* to carry out a four-year survey of New Zealand. He died, an Admiral, in 1885.

Australia's 'national poet' is George Essex Evans, whose father, John Evans of Foley House, was Member of Parliament for Haverfordwest borough from 1847 to 1852. George emigrated to Australia in 1871, and each year, on the anniversary of his birth, his admirers gather at his memorial at Toowooba in Queensland.

Maurice de Prendergast was among the Pembrokeshire knights who landed at Bannow, near Wexford, in May 1169, in response to a request from Dermot, the dethroned King of Leinster. The Prendergast family settled on a hill to the north of Haverfordwest where a village that runs into the town bears their name, but their descendants are mostly to be found in Ireland.

In the sixteenth century Prendergast was the residence of Henry Catharne, Recorder of Courts for the bishopric of St David's. His son, Thomas Catharne, who was sheriff of Pembrokeshire in 1568, died without male issue, and his daughter, Margaret, married Alban Stepney, who had been appointed Receiver-General of the diocese and was later Member of Parliament. The Stepneys had originated at Stebenhithe in Essex, now Stepney in London. Sir John Stepney, the fourth baronet, married the daughter of the painter van Dyck. The seventh baronet's daughter became the wife of John Gulston, Member of Parliament for Poole in Dorset, from whom the Stepney-Gulston family of Llanelli derives.

George Stepney, grandson of Sir Thomas Stepney of Prendergast, acquired a reputation as a writer of Latin verse at Trinity College, Cambridge, but his poems had no great merit and he was regarded as 'a very licentious translator' who did not 'recompense his neglect of the author by beauties of his own'. His success was as a diplomat in various German electorates and as an envoy to The Hague. He was a member of the Kitcat Club and appears among the Kitcat portraits by Sir Godfrey Kneller. He died unmarried in Chelsea in 1707, and his pall was carried by two dukes, two earls and two barons to his resting-place in the south aisle of Westminster Abbey, where an elaborate monument was erected to his memory.

Howell Davies, the Methodist leader who is often referred to as 'the Apostle of Pembrokeshire', married, for his second wife, Elizabeth White of Prendergast, and lies buried beside the porch of St David's Church.

The church was appropriated to the Knight Hospitallers of Slebech by Wizo the Fleming. Apart from its tower, it was rebuilt in 1867.

There were no pheasants in Pembrokeshire until the latter part of the sixteenth century when Sir Thomas Perrot, according to George Owen, 'procured certain hens and cocks to be transported out of Ireland which he, purposing to endenize in a pleasant grove of his own planting adjoining to his house of Haroldston, gave them liberty therein'. Only the ruin remains of the Tudor mansion that was once 'surrounded by a pleasaunce and walled gardens', and the faint traces of a cockpit in a field nearby.

Here was born, in 1527, the celebrated John Perrot, said to have been the natural son of King Henry VIII by Mary Berkeley, a royal lady-in-waiting who 'was of the king's familiarity' and the wife of Thomas Perrot of Haroldston, son of Sir Owen Perrot, the only Pembrokeshire man ever to be created a Knight of the Holy Sepulchre. After being educated at St David's, young John entered the household of the Marquis of Winchester, Lord Treasurer of England, and little is known of his life for the next twenty years. In 1562 he was made Vice-Admiral of South Wales, and in the following year he became Member of Parliament for Pembrokeshire. He was three times mayor of Haverfordwest and became the town's greatest benefactor, leaving property to benefit the poor which is still administered by the Perrot's Trustees. He became President of Munster and later Lord Deputy of Ireland, but in 1592 he was arraigned at Westminster and found guilty of treason, for his indiscreet references to Queen Elizabeth, whose canopy he had carried at her coronation. He was sentenced to death but died of natural causes in the Tower of London.

His forfeited estates were shortly afterwards restored to his heir, Sir Thomas Perrot, but Haroldston passed to his illegitimate son, Sir James Perrot, Member of Parliament for Haverfordwest borough and for Pembrokeshire, author of *Discovery of Discontented Minds*, published in 1596 with the object of restraining malcontents who had 'settled in foreign countries, especially under the umbrage of the King of Spain, to negociate conspiracies and invasions'. On his death, in 1637, Haroldston was acquired by a distant kinsman, Sir Herbert Perrot of Hereford. Sir Herbert entertained his friend Joseph Addison at Haroldston with 'a masque conducted with great expense and classical taste' at which, it is claimed, the essayist met his future wife, Charlotte, Countess of Warwick. Sir Herbert's only child, Hester, married Sir John Pakington, Bart, who is reputed to have been Addison's inspiration for his Sir Roger de Coverley, 'a gentleman of Worcestershire of ancient descent, a baronet ... a gentleman that is very singular in his behaviour'.

Among the pages of a book of prayers at the British Museum is a fourteenth-century calendar, with an illustration for each month showing peasants following their seasonal tasks. The calendar is associated with Haroldston House and is known as the Haroldston Calendar.

Merlin's Bridge was at one time called Maudlens Bridge and is known locally as Marlan's Bridge, but its original name was derived from St Magdalene's Chapel, the north wall of which forms part of a cottage and was recently exposed to reveal three lancet windows.

10

The Rout of Colby Moor

Wizo the Fleming was granted the lordship of Daugleddau by Henry I and was settled there by 1108, having established his stronghold, comprising a motte and a bean-shaped bailey, at Wiston. In 1147 the castle was attacked and taken by the sons of Gruffydd ap Rhys ap Tewdwr but was soon recovered. Hywel Sais captured it in 1193 but was able to hold it for only two years before it was back in Flemish hands. Then, in 1220, Llywelyn the Great came and caused such damage that the King, Henry III, called on the knights and free tenants of the surrounding lordships to assist William Marshal, Earl of Pembroke, to rebuild the castle. The shell-keep that surmounts the motte is the only one in Pembrokeshire.

Wiston was a borough with its own market and a fair held on the feast of St Simon and St Jude, which is 28 October, and in 1718 the House of Commons resolved that its mayor and burgesses should have the right to vote in the parliamentary election for the Pembroke borough.

When the parish church was being restored in 1864, three cartloads of human bones were found buried under the pews and taken away. It was believed that these were the remains of those who had been slain at the disastrous battle of Colby Moor, a mile away to the south. On 29 July 1645 Major-General Rowland Laugharne arranged a rendezvous at Canaston Wood and, having set out on 1 August, met the Royalist army, which had marched from Haverfordwest, at Colby Moor. The Royalists lost 150 men killed and 700 taken prisoner, with all their arms. A scene of utter confusion is still referred to locally as 'a Colby Moor rout'.

Colby was the residence of John Barlow, whose daughter, Catherine, became the first wife of Sir William Hamilton and brought him extensive properties including the manors of Hubberston and Pill, in which the town of Milford Haven was established.

'It was recently stated in a daily newspaper that if a schoolmaster, wishing to give a particular boy permission to leave the school, were rash enough to call out from his desk, "Jones, you can go home," the school house would at once be entirely emptied. Similarly in the case of the Wogans. ....' So wrote the scholarly genealogist Francis Green in his treatise on *The Wogans of Pembrokeshire*, a family that played an important part in the life of Pembrokeshire from the thirteenth century onward and produced ten sheriffs of the county, two justiciaries of Ireland and a regicide.

The Wogans claimed descent from Gwrgan ap Bleddyn ap Maenarch, lord of Brecon, who flourished towards the end of the eleventh century, but the first Wogan of whom there is record was Sir John, who may have been a grandson of the eponymous Gwrgan and whose mother may have been Gwenllian, the daughter of Philip, son of Wizo.

Colonel Thomas Wogan of Wiston was one of the judges who sat at the trial of King Charles I and signed the warrant for his execution. His property was sequestered at the Restoration, and in 1664 he was arrested and imprisoned in the Tower of London. He managed to escape, however, and appears to have fled to Holland, but local tradition has it that he was later seen, a melancholy and dejected figure, in the neighbourhood of Walwyn's Castle, though when asked his name, he said it was Drinkwater. He was eventually found dead in the church porch.

Thomas Wogan, the last of the line of Wiston, died while taking the waters at the Hotwells at Bristol, and the manor and other properties were sold, in 1794, to John Campbell of Stackpole, later Earl Cawdor, for £38,000.

The village of Llawhaden stands on a lofty ridge that commands a wide prospect of the valley of the Eastern Cleddau and is dominated by a bishop's castle. The castle was built by Bernard, the first Norman bishop of St David's, who was elected to the see in 1115. Giraldus Cambrensis received some of his early education here from his uncle, David FitzGerald, who succeeded Bernard as bishop in 1147. He states that Bernard had built a ringwork, the encircling ditch of which may still be traced, in order to protect his possessions within the episcopal lordship of Llawhaden. The castle was captured by the Lord Rhys in 1192, and in the following year he razed its defences. In the thirteenth century the curtain wall was erected, flanked by projecting round towers; early in the fourteenth the castle was rebuilt by Bishop David Martin and transformed into a great fortified residence, with quarters for a permanent garrison and comfortable accommodation for visitors, and so it remained until it was dismantled by Bishop Barlow in 1540.

Bishop Morgan, during his episcopacy in the sixteenth century, seized a lady of easy virtue, named Tanglost, who lived in the village, and incarcerated her at the castle, but Thomas Wyrriott of Orielton came along with his mounted troops and released her. Tanglost persisted in her wicked ways, however, and the bishop imprisoned her again. Thomas Wyrriott came once more, but this time to seek the bishop's pardon, for both Tanglost and himself, which he obtained. The young lady then removed herself to Bristol and there decided to avenge herself on the bishop. She got a witch in that town to stick pins in a waxen image of him, which caused him to suffer considerably until he appealed to the mayor of Bristol to intercede on his behalf, offering Tanglost forgiveness for all her transgressions.

The church, which lies deep in the valley, is dedicated to St Aidan of Ferns, from whom the village derived its name, Llanaedan, later corrupted to Llawhaden. It was built in the fourteenth century on a site that overlaps that of an earlier church so that a section of the original tower clings to the later one. A mutilated effigy of a priest lying in a recess in the chancel aisle is said to be of St. Hugh, a hermit who lived in a cave at Rock Hill. For the first twelve days of each year he would sit and contemplate a pool of water at the entrance to the cave and was then able to forecast the weather for the rest of the year, and he would provide testimony of his forecasts, written on birch bark, to local farmers for a suitable fee. A grotesque on a capital shows a man biting the tail of a human-faced beast, and a stone pillar bearing a wheel-cross and shaft, dating from the tenth century, is built into the external east wall of the church. The Elizabethan chalice is inscribed '*Poculum eclesye de Lanychaden*', and a plate used as a credence paten, dated 1715, was 'the gift of William Meares' and bears his arms, a three-masted ship, and his crest, a mermaid combing her hair, like the siren on the Lorelei.

A *hospitium* 'for the poor and needy' was built by Bishop Bek in 1287 and dedicated to St Mary, St Thomas the Martyr and St Edward the King. Only a stone vaulted chamber remains.

Leland states that the castle had 'a forest of red deer called Llwydarth', and the stone wall that borders a part of the village street may have been the boundary of a deer park.

St Kennox farmhouse stands on the site of the Chancellor's House that was built in 1334. The Reverend Rhys Prichard, author of *Cannwyll y Cymry* (*The Welshmen's Candle*) and known throughout Wales as Vicar Prichard, lived here when he was made Chancellor of St David's in 1626. He was also vicar of Llawhaden, and his popularity as a preacher was such that he had to preach from a rocky eminence, later used as a winnowing bank, near his house, to an audience that no church could contain.

When Nelson visited Milford Haven in 1802, he came to Ridgeway House to visit his friend Admiral Sir Thomas Foley, who had led the British line at the Battle of the Nile. Foley was descended from John Fawley, architect to the Bishop of St David's and Constable of Llawhaden Castle, who was granted land at Llawhaden by Bishop Adam Houghton in 1383. He entered the navy in 1770 and was with Nelson at Cape St Vincent and Copenhagen but was prevented by illness from taking part at Trafalgar. He was knighted in 1815 and appointed admiral ten years later, and was commander-in-chief Portsmouth when he died in 1833.

Apart from the hill forts and promontory forts scattered over Pembrokeshire, there are numerous enclosures that appear to have been fortified farmsteads, defended by a bank and ditch, occupied during the Iron Age and later. In the Llawhaden area, such enclosures have been identified at Drim Castle, Drim Camp, Gelli, Bodringallt, Woodside, Dan-y-coed, Broadway, Pilcornswell and Holgan. Excavation at the Drim Camp has revealed a horseshoe bank and ditch within which was a round timber house with a gate tower at the entrance, and outbuildings, and evidence of a later occupation was yielded by medieval pottery and a small penannular brooch.

John Herbert (Jimmy) James of Sodston learnt to fly an

aeroplane at Hendon in 1912, and he and his brother, Howell, returned home the following year having bought the skeleton of a Caudron biplane which they rebuilt and were able to fly over the startled neighbourhood. After the 1914-18 War, in which they both served, Jimmy James won the Air Derby two years running.

The village of Robeston Wathen is described in the thirteenth century as *villa Roberti*, but from the sixteenth century onward the additional personal name of Wathen, found in Llangwadden nearby, was added, perhaps to distinguish it from Robeston West.

When the Duke of Beaufort, Lord President of the Council and Lord Warden of the Marches, made his progress through Pembrokeshire to inspect the militia forces in August 1684, his secretary, Mr Dineley, recorded that, as they approached Robeston Wathen, accompanied by 'a fair cavalcade of the capital gentry', the villagers 'not only exercised their three (church) bells but complemented His Grace at noon-day, and a very warm time, with a fire of joy in the road near the church, called a *bonefire* after their own interpretation being part wood and part bones which, by reason of the bright shining of the sun thereon, became more obvious to the smell than sight'.

Thomas Roscoe, travelling through Pembrokeshire in 1820, arrived at Robeston Wathen one afternoon, as the rain was beginning to fall, and came across 'a roadside hostelrie' in which there were 'more appliances of comfort' than he had expected to find. Moreover, he met, 'in the inn's best room, an agreeable and intellectual companion – one whose profession was connected with all that is refined and liberal'. He was an artist who had travelled over much the same route as Roscoe, and they spent the evening together convivially discussing their travels – 'an evening in my changeful life that I shall long remember'.

Llanddewi Velfrey, 'the church of St David in (the commot of) Efelfre' had strong Quaker connections during the seventeenth century. Richard Davies of Cloddiau Cochion, near Welshpool, on his way from Bristol in 1665, called 'at the house of our Friend Lewis David' at Llanddewi, who loaned him a horse so that his own could rest while Davies went on to Redstone, a farm on the main road, north of Narberth, to a Quaker meeting which had to be held out of doors as there was no house or building 'that could contain the multitude of people'. At the end of the meeting, he aeroplane at Hendon in 1912, and he and his brother, Howell, returned home the following year having bought the skeleton of a Caudron biplane which they rebuilt and were able to fly over the startled neighbourhood. After the 1914-18 War, in which they both served, Jimmy James won the Air Derby two years running.

The village of Robeston Wathen is described in the thirteenth century as *villa Roberti*, but from the sixteenth century onward the additional personal name of Wathen, found in Llangwadden nearby, was added, perhaps to distinguish it from Robeston West.

When the Duke of Beaufort, Lord President of the Council and Lord Warden of the Marches, made his progress through Pembrokeshire to inspect the militia forces in August 1684, his secretary, Mr Dineley, recorded that, as they approached Robeston Wathen, accompanied by 'a fair cavalcade of the capital gentry', the villagers 'not only exercised their three (church) bells but complemented His Grace at noon-day, and a very warm time, with a fire of joy in the road near the church, called a *bonefire* after their own interpretation being part wood and part bones which, by reason of the bright shining of the sun thereon, became more obvious to the smell than sight'.

Thomas Roscoe, travelling through Pembrokeshire in 1820, arrived at Robeston Wathen one afternoon, as the rain was beginning to fall, and came across 'a roadside hostelrie' in which there were 'more appliances of comfort' than he had expected to find. Moreover, he met, 'in the inn's best room, an agreeable and intellectual companion – one whose profession was connected with all that is refined and liberal'. He was an artist who had travelled over much the same route as Roscoe, and they spent the evening together convivially discussing their travels – 'an evening in my changeful life that I shall long remember'.

Llanddewi Velfrey, 'the church of St David in (the commot of) Efelfre' had strong Quaker connections during the seventeenth century. Richard Davies of Cloddiau Cochion, near Welshpool, on his way from Bristol in 1665, called 'at the house of our Friend Lewis David' at Llanddewi, who loaned him a horse so that his own could rest while Davies went on to Redstone, a farm on the main road, north of Narberth, to a Quaker meeting which had to be held out of doors as there was no house or building 'that could contain the multitude of people'. At the end of the meeting, he

Henry Lewis named his Pennsylvanian homestead after his old home, Redstone, and this became the name of the township that grew up around it. But when a murder was committed there, the inhabitants felt so disgraced that they changed the name, strangely, to Narberth. When I went to Philadelphia in search of Narberth, now a suburb of that city, I had difficulty in finding it, and I remembered W.C. Fields' cruel quip: 'I went to Philadelphia and it was closed.' I eventually came across a brick building which bore the sign 'Narberth Post Office', and a pleasant counter clerk smiled knowingly when he saw that I was sending a postcard to a friend in the old Narberth. When I came out of the post office, I saw a string of pale blue cars with white doors marked 'Narberth Cabs'. Haverford, nearby, so named by an emigrant from Haverfordwest, is likewise lost in the suburbia of 'the city of brotherly love'.

David Lewis of Llanddewi Velfrey, a friend of Alexander Pope and Dr Samuel Johnson, was headmaster of Westminster School and the author of *Philip of Macedon*, a play in blank verse, which was performed at Lincoln's Inn Fields in 1727 and later at Drury Lane.

The square, hip-roofed Ffynnon chapel is named from the roadside well at its gate, *Ffynnon well na buwch*, 'a well that is better than a cow'. In the graveyard, strewn with primroses in springtime, the tomb of Evan Thomas, buried in 1871, is inscribed in angular bardic script.

On the high ground above Llanddewi Velfrey church stand two Iron Age forts overlooking the valley of the Marlais. Llanddewi Gaer is a fine promontory fort with a triple line of ramparts, while Caerau Gaer, a circular enclosure in a commanding position, many have been an annex to it, or possibly used for herding cattle.

' "Give me Narberth on a wet Saturday afternoon!" was the reply made by a local squire on returning from a tour in Italy, when he was asked how he had enjoyed himself on his continental trip,' recorded H.M. Vaughan in his *South Wales Squires*. The town has a Georgian atmosphere, and the little town hall in the middle of the street, with its display of the royal arms, is reminiscent of an English village.

Narberth has the distinction of being the first place mentioned in *The Mabinogion*, the oldest recorded Welsh tales, which begins: 'Pwyll prince of Dyfed was lord over the seven cantrefs of Dyfed, and once upon a time he was at Arberth, a chief court of his.'

One day, he arose from a feast and 'made for the top of a mound which was above the court and called Gorsedd Arberth', and as he sat there, a maiden came riding by 'on a big fine pale white horse, with a garment of shining gold brocaded silk upon her'. Pwyll mounted his horse and followed her, but the faster he rode, the further she was from him, until he called on her to stay, which she did gladly. She said her name was Rhiannon and that she had come to seek his love. A year and a day later, they feasted at Arberth and became man and wife.

Gorsedd Arberth has been identified as Sentence Castle at Templeton, where the Normans later built a castle-ring.

During his rebellion against the Normans and the Flemings, Gryffydd ap Rhys ap Tewdwr destroyed Narberth Castle in 1116, and it was taken by Llywelyn the Great in 1215 and 1220, and by Llywelyn the Last in 1257. The stone castle on the present site was built by Sir Andrew Perrot in 1246, and the lordship was held in turn by William Marshal, Earl of Pembroke, the Mortimers, the Perrots, Bishop Gower of St David's, Thomas de Carew, the Prince of Wales (later Edward V) and Henry, Duke of Buckingham. John Leland referred to the castle as the 'little pretty pile of old Sir Rhys (ap Thomas) given unto him by King Henry the VIII. ... Gruffydd ap Nicholas, grandfather to Sir Rhys, bought it off the Duke of York but after lost (it).' On the attainder of Sir Rhys's grandson, Sir Rhys ap Gruffydd, in 1531, his estates, including Narberth, became forfeit to the Crown. A survey of 1539 provides a detailed description of the castle, but fifty years later it was reported to be 'decayed and wasted'.

The church, dedicated to St Andrew, was completely rebuilt in 1879, except for the tower which was erected in the thirteenth century by Sir Andrew Perrot. A pedigree dedicated to his descendant, 'the most noble and puissant prince Sir James Perrot', by his 'poor but most faithful servant, Owen Griffiths, who was wounded by his side in Carew Castle in 1650', grandiloquently describes Sir James as the 'Marquis of Narberth'.

Lampeter Velfrey, 'the church of St Peter in Efelfre', stands in a circular churchyard and has a seventeenth-century tomb to the

Phillips family. Nun Morgan Harry, born at Lampeter Velfrey, became minister of New Broad Street Independent Chapel in London and joint secretary of the Peace society and editor of its journal, *The Herald of Peace*. Thomas Phillips, another native, emigrated to South Africa and established a settlement which he named Lampeter but was later called New Bristol.

Tavernspite was originally a *hospitium* of Whitland Abbey, for pilgrims to rest on their way to the shrine of the patron saint at St David's. A coaching inn was built when the road was turnpiked in the eighteenth century.

'Red Roses' is a corruption, by English surveyors when the road to Pembroke Dock was built in 1830, of the name of the neighbouring farm Rhos Goch, 'the red moor'.

Blaengwyddno, 'the source of the Gwyddno', is shown on the Ordnance Map as Blaen Gwaith Noah, indicating an old belief that Noah's Ark came to rest here, rather than on Mount Ararat. It was a grange of the Cistercian abbey at Whitland from the twelfth century until the dissolution of the monasteries. There are several prehistoric sites in the neighbourhood, including a promontory fort at Blaengwyddno and a significant earthwork at Castell Meherin. Castell Cynon, near the parish church, was a Norman ring-castle, and there are the remains of a motte at Green Castle on Clun Pattel farm.

A round barrow at Crug-y-swllt is said to have been the site of a gibbet, and there are other barrows at the crossroads near Newhouse farm.

The church at Ludchurch, dedicated to St Elidyr, stands on a limestone rock left by quarrymen who dug all round it. In the churchyard is the grave of Commander John Martin who served as second in command to Captain Cook on his voyage of discovery to Australia in 1770.

A tale in *The Mabinogion* tells that Manawydan the son of Llyr brought with him a burden of wheat from England, where he had sojourned, and scattered it over three crofts near Narberth. No wheat in the world sprouted better, and when harvest time came, he set out to reap the first croft. But when he got to it, in the grey dawn, he found nothing but bare stalks. The next morning he found the second croft equally devastated. And so he kept watch over the third croft and, in the night, saw 'the mightiest host of mice in all the world' descend upon it and destroy the crop, but when he gave chase they all escaped save one pregnant mouse. He placed it in his glove and went to Gorsedd Arberth, and as he was setting up a crossbeam on two forked sticks, from which to hang the miscreant, a scholar came by and offered him a pound to release the mouse, which he refused. Then a priest, who was passing, offered him £3 but again he refused. Then came a bishop and offered him anything and everything that he could desire if he would only set the mouse free, including the removal of the spell that had lain over Dyfed. The bishop announced that he was Llwyd, the son of Cilcoed, and that it was he who had cast the spell over the seven cantrefs of Dyfed and had transformed his people, including his pregnant wife, into mice, in order to avenge a wrong wrought upon a friend. He removed the spell, struck the pregnant mouse with his magic wand and 'changed her back into the fairest young woman that any one had seen'. It is claimed that Llwyd's residence was Blaen Cilcoed in Eglwys Lwyd, or Ludchurch.

Cat's pies were a delicacy at Templeton Fair, held on the day after Martinmas. The pies contained mutton and flavouring ingredients and used to be made at the Poyer's Arms, a house with a bold outside chimney and a mantel beam on which is carved the date 1672, but which is no longer an inn. Their origin is obscure but they may come from London. Christopher (Kit) Catt, a pastry cook in Shire Lane, where the Law Courts now stand, was renowned for his pies, and the Whigs of the day, who enjoyed Catt's pies, or kitcats as they became known, formed a literary club, which they called the Kitcat Club. Its members included Sir Robert Walpole, the Duke of Marlborough, the Duke of Somerset, Sir John Vanbrugh, Sir Christopher Wren, Joseph Addison and Richard Steele; their portraits, in the National Portrait Gallery, were painted by Kneller at three-quarter length to fit their low-ceilinged clubroom, hence the 'kitcat portrait'. Could it be that some Whig gentleman brought the recipe to Templeton?

Templeton, *villa Templarii* in 1282, takes its name from the Knights Templars who established a hospice here; when the Templars were suppressed in 1308, their property was transferred to the Knights Hospitallers at Slebech. The modern church of St John was built on the site of an earlier building which, for a time, was used as a Unitarian meeting-house.

The village consisted of thirteen farms, each with its burgage of about an acre, while the rest of its lands are a mile or more away.

11

Milford Haven

There are as many Hooks in Pembrokeshire as there are brambles, someone said: East Hook, West Hook, Bullhook, Honey Hook, Welsh Hook, White Hook, Nattshook, Farthing's Hook, to name a few. The name signified a spur of land in a bend of a river and, sometimes, a stretch of sloping land.

The village of Hook stands on a bend of the Western Cleddau and lies within the anthracite coalfield. The coal seams are irregular and heavily faulted by overthrusts from the south that occurred during the Armorican earth movements; the coalfield is consequently divided into narrow belts by the faults, and the seams vary in thickness and quality on account of the pressures brought upon them. In 1786 almost the whole of the output of 5,800 tons, produced by 78 colliers receiving 9d. a day, was exported from Hook Quay. The introduction of deeper mining during the nineteenth century led to the opening of a number of pits, bearing such names as Old Aurora and Amen, that yielded some 20,000 tons, and as much as 42,000 tons in 1934 when 250 men were employed. Most of the coal was conveyed on the Hook Colliery railway built in 1929 to join the main line at Johnston, but there was some shipments from Hook Quay up to 1936. Malting coal was sent to Ireland and East Anglia, and small quantities were exported to a jute factory on St Helena, and to Singapore for tin smelting. The colliery was taken over by the National Coal Board in 1947, and a serious flooding of the Hook West Drift in the following year led to the closure of the last colliery in the Pembrokeshire coalfield.

The colliery had survived until then through the persistence of its last owner, T. Harcourt Roberts, who devoted himself to the promotion of rural industry and, at the same time, the conservation of nature. I found him one day very excited at having found Touch-me-not Balsam (*Impatiens noli-tangere*) growing near his home. 'You will find it,' he told me, 'up by Brigham Young's cottage.' I found the flower but was never able to trace any connection between the area and the man from Vermont who led the Mormons to Utah.

Llangwm, at one time, depended largely on its oyster fishery. Although the oyster was small and 'the least estimable of the different sorts which Milford Haven produced', it found a ready market at 6d. a hundred, and quantities were pickled and shipped in barrels and earthen jugs to Bristol and elsewhere. The women of Llangwm, dressed in full woollen skirts and shawls, with their hats tied under their chins, would gather the oysters, as well as cockles and shrimps, and walk to the markets of Haverfordwest and Tenby, and even to Carmarthen, carrying their heavy creels.

A few fishermen still pursue the ancient method of compass-netting on the Western Cleddau. A man will stand in his black-tarred boat and dip a net fixed to two long poles into the river on a rising tide and lever up the poles when he senses a salmon in the net.

When Fenton entered the church at Llangwm and enquired who lay in a canopied tomb in the north transeptal chapel, he was told: 'Whay, 'a bee one Dolly Roch, sir, thay zay.' Thus folk memory has preserved the name of de la Roche, lords of Roch and of Benton. The effigy lies in armour, with sword and shield, his feet clad in curiously interwoven mail and resting on a fierce lion, the tail of which has been mistaken for the viper that caused the death of Adam de la Roche in his castle at Roch. There is a female effigy in a finely folded robe, and a pillared piscina beneath a canopied niche surmounted by a finial, built of Nolton stone and ornamented with unblazoned escutcheons. The church has a bellcote, but no tower, and is dedicated to St Jerome.

In the courtyard of Great Nash, where stood the fourteenth-century mansion house of Robert de Esse, is a domed dovecote, of the sixteenth century, with some two hundred pigeonholes.

Benton Castle rises from the oak woods, like an ivory tower, above the River Cleddau, along which it commands a wide prospect. It was built by Bishop Bek of St David's during the latter part of the thirteenth century, and later came into the possession of the de la Roche family. By the sixteenth century it is described as one of the manors belonging to Sir John Perrot of Haroldston. A description of the castle in 1865 states that it comprised a small round tower of three floors surmounted by an octagonal battlement of a later date. The tower had no fireplace or stairs, and its arched entrance bore no evidence of a portcullis. Attached to it, on its western side, was a square building which had garderobes on its second and third floors. In front of the main entrance to the castle was an upthrust of volcanic trap, forming a natural barbican, from which the geologist Roderick Murchison named the local rock Benton Trap. The castle was a ruin for several centuries until 1932, when Dr Ernest Pegge began to rebuild it, with his own hands, and over the entrance placed his own mask in concrete. It is now a private residence.

The Hanging Stone at Burton is a polygonal burial chamber, with a massive capstone supported by three orthostats, standing in a hedgerow between two fields near the village. The Burton parish church, unnoticed down a lane, has no dedication, but the south aisle is dedicated to St Andrew and may form part of an earlier church. A sixteenth-century altar tomb commemorates a member of the Wogan family of Boulston.

When the foundations for the caissons for the Cleddau Bridge were being excavated, a number of human skeletons were found close to the shore. The bodies had been wrapped in canvas and appeared to have been buried in some haste, probably during the seventeenth century. Work on the bridge began in 1968, at an estimated cost of £3 million, but in June 1970 a section of the box girder structure collapsed and work was suspended pending an investigation by the government into such structures. The bridge was eventually completed in 1975, by which time the cost had increased to £18 million, and as the loans to meet the cost were raised over a comparatively short term, the toll charges are high.

Neyland was a small fishing village until Isambard Kingdom Brunel's plan for a railway terminus and harbour at Fishguard was dashed by the Irish potato famine. In 1853, however, the broad seven-foot gauge was extended from Carmarthen to Haverfordwest, and Brunel chose Neyland as the site for a terminus to connect with the Irish packet service and, he hoped, the Atlantic passenger liners, despite the pleas of the merchants of Milford. The railway line was completed in 1856, and Brunel built a railway yard, a floating pontoon and streets that still bear commemorative names, like Brunel Avenue and Great Eastern Terrace. Brunel's *Great Eastern* of 22,000 tons, then the largest vessel ever built, anchored there in 1860 and returned to lie up in Milford Haven for the next three winters. Neyland was re-named Milford Haven by the South Wales Railway Company, which caused considerable confusion, and it did little to ease the chagrin of the inhabitants of the town of Milford when it was changed again to New Milford, by which name it continued to be known until the packet service to Waterford and Cork was transferred to Fishguard in 1906. There was little Atlantic trade, and the extension of the railway line to Milford in 1863 and to Pembroke Dock the following year provided more competition than Neyland could stand. Furthermore, the fishing industry that boomed briefly, and the waggon-works, the shipbuilding and the ice factory that complemented the development, began to decline, but Neyland remained a railway terminus until 1955, and there was a busy car ferry service to Hobbs Point until the Cleddau Bridge was opened.

The vicar of Llanstadwell, Thomas Balymore, received 40 shillings for accommodating King Richard II at his vicarage in 1394, on the monarch's passage to Ireland. The church, dedicated to St Tudwal, was appropriated to the priory of St Thomas at Haverfordwest and after the dissolution was leased to Sir Henry Jones, 'of the king's household'.

Scoveston fort, completed in 1865 at a cost of £45,000, was the only fortress built to provide protection from an attack upon Milford Haven from the north. Scoveston point-to-point races are an annual event in Pembrokeshire's racing calendar. John Scovyn held land here in the fifteenth century.

Rosemarket takes its name from the hundred of Rhos. Its market was held, in the twelfth century, by the Knights Hospitallers of the Commandery of Slebech, to whom Richard FitzTancred had also granted the church, a mill and land in the village. The church was formerly dedicated to St Leonard, and St Leonard's Well is nearby. The Rath, in the field adjoining the church, may be the site of 'the castle of Ros', the stronghold of the early settlers.

Zachariah Williams, medical practitioner and inventor, was born at Rosemarket in 1673. He was convinced that he had discovered the means of ascertaining 'the Longitude at Sea by an exact Theory of the variation of the Magnetic Needle' and set out for London in 1727 believing that his fortune was made. Instead, he was admitted to the Charterhouse two years later, as a 'poor brother pensioner', where he spent twenty unhappy years. He also invented a machine for making sea-water drinkable, which brought him no recognition, and he died a disappointed man, after much suffering, in 1755. Dr Samuel Johnson, who had tried to interest the authorities in his inventions, wrote of him in an obituary notice: 'He was a man of industry indefatigable, of conversation inoffensive, patient of adversity and disease, eminently sober, temperate and pious; and worthy to have ended his life with better fortune.'

Johnson befriended his daughter, Anna, who had gone to London with her father and who was 'possessed of more than ordinary talents and literature' and educated to a degree of proficiency in French and Italian. She helped Stephen Gray, also a pensioner at the Charterhouse, who was the first to 'observe and notify the emission of an electrical spark from a human body'. Her *Miscellanies in Prose and Verse* was published in 1766, with a preface by Dr Johnson, and her wit and conversation brought Goldsmith and Garrick among others to take tea with her. She became blind and moved into Johnson's house in Bolt Court, off Fleet Street, where she remained until her death in 1783, when the great doctor wrote to a friend: 'Thirty years and more she has been my companion, and her death has left me desolate.'

Johnston was the manorial settlement of John de la Roche, after whom it may have been named, in the twelfth century. His son, Thomas, is believed to have built the church and to have conveyed it to Pill Priory, founded by his ancestor Adam de la Roche. The monks of Pill held land at Monkton Farm. Arnold Butler of Johnston, a Gentleman Pensioner of Henry VIII, was sheriff in 1558, and his descendant Thomas Butler, the sheriff of 1645, served King Charles II and followed him into exile. Johnston Hall was the seat of Lord Kensington, 'a mighty hunter' who was able to leap into the saddle and follow the chase until he was eighty-six. He represented Haverfordwest in ten successive Parliaments.

At a sale at Bulford Farm in 1865 a small boy, swinging on the farm gate, stoutly resisted the taking away of goods purchased there. When he came again to the area, he was the most notable statesman of his time, David Lloyd George. His father, William George, had been born at Trecoed, near Fishguard, and had kept a private school at Llysyronnen, St Nicholas, and in Upper Market Street, Haverfordwest, where one of his pupils was Edwin John, father of Augustus John. William married a lady from Haverfordwest but she died shortly afterwards, and he moved to North Wales, where he met Margaret Lloyd of Caernarfon, who became his second wife. He then became a college tutor at Manchester, where David was born, and later returned to Pembrokeshire, on the advice of his doctor, and took a lease of Bulford Farm. Within two years, he died and was buried at Jordanston and, after the farm sale, his widow and three children returned to Caernarfon.

The Royalist owner of Bolton Hill shot dead a Roundhead soldier who had tried to grab his child, and then travelled to Haverfordwest to inform Cromwell of his action, only to be told: 'You have saved me the trouble of having the rascal executed.'

William James was born in 1722, the son of the miller at Beacon Hill. When it was found that he was no good at helping at the mill, he was sent to be apprenticed to a Bristol merchant, but he escaped to sea on an Indiaman. He later married the landlady of the Red Cow at Wapping and became the commander-in-chief of the East India Company's marine forces. The Company, and the Mahrattas, had for half a century endeavoured to capture the formidable pirate Angria, but without success, until James came along and stormed the corsair's stronghold at Severndroog. He was created a baronet in 1778 and became an Elder Brother and deputy-master of Trinity House. At his death, in 1784, his widow erected a memorial to him on the top of Shooter's Hill which became known as the Severndroog Tower or, less reverently, as Lady James's Folly.

During the restoration of the Steynton parish church in 1882, a human thigh bone was found under each pillar of the arcade, and beneath the chancel steps a human skull and the skulls of three horses. An inscribed stone, now in the church but formerly in the churchyard, commemorates, in Latin and in ogham writing, one Gendilus who lived in the fifth, or sixth, century. A wheel-cross was added about five centuries later, and the stone was used again in 1876 as a tombstone. The tower of the church was garrisoned during the Civil War with twenty musketeers in order to cut off communication between Pill Fort and Haverfordwest.

From the time the Normans built their castles, little effort was made to defend the Haven against an invader, although its vulnerability, and its value, had been demonstrated time and again. It was from here that the Pembrokeshire knights set out, in 1169 and 1170, to conquer Ireland. Henry II assembled a fleet here to follow them and assert his claim to the kingdom promised by Dermot of Leinster to Strongbow, Earl of Pembroke. His son John sailed from here twice, in 1185 and 1210, in an effort to subdue the Irish. Richard II set sail, in 1394, with an army to quell the defiant Anglo-Irish settlers, and again in 1399, only to find, on his return, that he had been deposed by the Lancastrian Henry IV. In 1405 a force of 2,500 French mercenaries landed in Milford Haven, sent by Charles VI of France to assist Owain Glyn Dŵr in his revolt. Eighty years later, Welsh hopes were fulfilled when Henry Tudor landed at Mill Bay and set off for Bosworth.

It was not until 1539 that Thomas Cromwell drew the attention of the Council of the Marches of Wales to the need for defence, and forty years afterwards the West Blockhouse, on the Dale Peninsula, and the East Blockhouse, on the headland behind Rat Island, were built as part of a scheme of fortification.

An examination of possible landing-places in the haven was made with the prospect of an invasion by the Spanish Armada, and in 1595 George Owen, the Pembrokeshire historian and lord of Cemais, who was a deputy lieutenant and deputy vice-admiral of the county, recommended the building of a triangle of forts, at Dale Point, Thorn Island and Stack Rock, but no action was taken. Despite the unhampered activities of pirates – the Queen's Remembrancer's Roll of 1562 reported that 'Milforde is ye grete resort and sucoure of all piratts' – and the insurrection in Ireland and the lessons of the Civil War, no attempt was made to provide any defence, except for the construction of a fort at the entrance to Castle Pill. The Privy Council discussed the matter in 1689, and in 1748 the Board of the Admiralty, alarmed at the number of shipwrecks, commissioned a survey of the coasts of St George's Channel. The survey was carried out by Lewis Morris, one of the erudite Morris brothers of Anglesey, who, despite his gout and melancholy and scorn of light verse, wrote *The Fishing*

Lass of Hakin, 'a new sea song in the sea style set to a new sea tune sung at sea by a seafaring man over a can of sea liquor called Phlip'.

The start of the Seven Years War, in 1756, brought fears of a French invasion, and the Government sent the Director of Engineers, Lieutenant-Colonel Bastide, to make another survey of the haven and to advise on methods of fortification. He recommended that forts should be constructed at Dale Point, Great Castle Head, West Angle Point, Popton Point, Paterchurch and Neyland, and a floating battery near Chapel Bay. Parliament considered the proposals to be too costly and adopted a more modest scheme, with forts at Paterchurch, Llanion and Neyland. Work on Paterchurch was begun in 1759 but suspended when the French fleet was defeated later that year at Quiberon Bay. When a French invasion did take place, the small fleet of four ships sailed past Milford Haven and dropped anchor off the inhospitable coast of Strumble Head.

With the development of the town of Milford and the establishment of a naval dockyard, batteries were constructed on either side of the town, and when the dockyard was transferred to Pembroke dock, proposals were made for its defence. The Pater Fort was replaced by the Pater Battery, and this was renovated in 1855 in accordance with plans prepared by Lieutenant Charles George Gordon RE, later General Gordon, Governor of the Sudan, who fell at the siege of Khartoum. Two 'martello' towers were built, one each side of the dockyard, in 1857, and the Defensible Barracks erected to accommodate a garrison of five hundred men. A reappraisal of the wider needs of the haven led to the completion of the batteries at Dale Point, West Blockhouse and Thorn Island. These were built as a first line of defence, and in 1858 Parliament decided to establish a second line, at a reinforced Stack Rock and at Chapel Bay and South Hook; a third line, at Popton Point and Hubberston, was completed in 1865. There were also to be nine forts for defence against any attack from landward, but only Scoveston was built. Outside the haven, it was proposed that suitable defences should be constructed at Caldey and along the south coast, but none was built except the fort on St Catherine's island at Tenby.

When the fortifications were all completed, they were out of date and deserving to be known as 'Palmerston's follies'. Yet they were garrisoned during the First World War, and some of them even during the Second, when they carried anti-aircraft batteries that were used against German air-raids. They remain interesting and, in some ways, unique examples of military architecture, and some have been converted to useful purposes. Dale Fort is a Field Studies Centre, and the fort on Thorn Island was converted into a small hotel. The BP Angle Bay Ocean Terminal has its administrative quarters at Popton Point, while Southook was used by the Esso refinery.

Where the town of Milford stands was open country two centuries ago, save for a farm called Summer Hill and a few cottages. On the east lay the hamlet of Pill, overlooking Castle Pill; to the west, another pill ran up to the priory, branched to Hubberston and passed out to sea beneath the village of Hakin. At the dissolution of the monasteries, the manor of Hubberston and Pill was acquired by Roger and Thomas Barlow of Slebech.

John Barlow of Colby, second son of Sir John Barlow of Slebech, was Member of Parliament for Pembrokeshire from 1710 to 1715. In 1708 he married Anne, the daughter of Sir Simon Harcourt, afterwards Lord Harcourt of Stanton Harcourt, the Lord Chancellor, and under the marriage settlement, certain manors and lands, including the manor Hubberston and Pill, were conveyed to his use. By his second marriage, to Anne, daughter of Richard Skrine of Wansley in Somerset, he had an only child, Catherine, 'a poor nervous creature' but, with an income of £8,000 a year, a desirable heiress. In 1758 she married William Hamilton, grandson of the third Duke of Hamilton, and brought with her an estate which included the manor of Hubberston and Pill, where Hamilton had the idea to build a town and a harbour.

In 1764 he was appointed Envoy Extraordinary to the Court at Naples, and it was hoped that the climate there would benefit his wife's weak health. She died in 1782 and her body was brought home for burial in Slebech old church. She left all her property to her husband, and when he returned to his duties at Naples, he appointed his nephew, Charles Greville, as his agent to promote the project at Milford.

Charles Francis Greville was born in 1749, the second son of the Earl of Warwick. He was Member of Parliament for the borough of Warwick for ten years from 1774 and held minor offices as a Lord of the Admiralty and a Treasurer of the Household. He was a man of wide interests, with considerable knowledge of geology, astronomy and botany. He was a Fellow of the Royal Society and a close friend of its President, Sir Joseph Banks, with whom he corresponded on botanical matters. In the garden of his home at Paddington Green he introduced plants that had never been grown in Britain before, specimens of which were used to prepare drawings for Curtis's *Botanical Magazine* and *The Botanists' Repository for New and Rare Plants* published by H. Andrews in 1797. The genus *Grevillea*, which includes the Silky Oak, was named after him, and he was one of the founders of the Royal Horticultural Society at a meeting held at Hatchard's bookshop in Piccadilly in March 1804.

During a shooting weekend at Up Park, the home of Sir Harry Featherstonhaugh on the South Downs, Greville met Amy Lyon, who was to become his mistress and, later, his aunt by marriage. Amy was born at Ness, on the Wirral Peninsula, in 1765. Her father, Henry Lyon, a blacksmith, died shortly after she was born, and his widow, Mary, returned, with her baby, to Hawarden where her mother had a cottage and a horse and cart, with which she made a living as a carrier between Hawarden and Chester. In 1779 Mary and her daughter moved to London and assumed new names: Mary Lyon became Mrs Cadogan, and Amy Lyon began to call herself Emma Hart. Their movements, for a time, remain a mystery, but there is reason to believe that Emma posed in the tableaux, and maybe sang, at Dr James Graham's Temple of Aesculapius in the Royal Terrace, Adelphi, and that it was there that Sir Harry Featherstonhaugh found her and took her home, to Up Park, as his mistress. Within a year, however, she had to leave as she was six months pregnant, and she received from Sir Harry nothing more than her fare home to Hawarden. From there she wrote to Charles Greville, who offered 'to dry up the tears of my lovely Emma and to give her comfort' by taking her and her mother into his house at Paddington Green in 1782.

Sir William Hamilton, by now a widower, visited his nephew at Paddington Green whenever he returned home from Naples, and he became very attached to Emma, as she now called herself. When Greville became anxious to settle down, with a lady of breeding and good fortune as his wife, he offered to place

Emma at Sir William's disposal, though he did not know 'how to part with what I am not tired with'. It was arranged that she, with her mother, should go to Naples while Greville was engaged on business, and she arrived there in March 1786 quite unaware of the plans that had been made for her future.

In September 1791 Sir William and Amy Lyons, for so she signed the register, were married quietly at St Marylebone parish church, and they returned to Naples two days later.

In September 1793 Captain Horatio Nelson sailed into the Bay of Naples in command of HMS *Agamemnon* with dispatches for Sir William and was entertained by the Hamiltons. When he came again, in 1798, it was as Admiral on HMS *Vanguard* to evacuate the Neapolitan royal family and the Hamiltons when the city was being threatened by Bonaparte. From now on, Nelson spent as much time as possible with the Hamiltons: '*tria juncta in uno*', Emma would say, quoting the motto of the Most Honourable Order of the Bath, which both men wore. When Nelson moved into Merton Place in October 1801, it was agreed that Sir William would bear half the expenses of the house while he and Emma resided there with him.

Meanwhile plans for the development of Milford were proceeding under Greville's direction. Sir William had obtained an Act of Parliament in 1790 which enabled him, his heirs and assigns 'to make and provide Quays, Docks, Piers and other erections and to establish a Market, with proper Roads and Avenues thereto respectively, within the Manor or Lordship of Hubberston and Pill in the County of Pembroke', and Greville lost no time in providing the necessary facilities for sheltering ships and in building a well-appointed inn to accommodate passengers taking the packet to Waterford. He offered favourable terms to some Quaker families from Nantucket Island, who had suffered during the War of American Independence on account of their desire to preserve their neutrality and wished to leave on the conclusion of the war, some of whom had already settled at Dartmouth but were unhappy there. They came in 1793, seven families, some fifty souls in all, with additional men to crew the brigantines so as to pursue their calling as whalers, led by Samuel Starbuck. Their aim was to provide spermaceti oil to light the lamps of London, but Murdoch's invention of coal-gas lighting stood in the way of their prosperity. The whalers became traders, bakers and brewers, and one of their number, Benjamin Rotch, became the most prominent businessman in town. But they are remembered by street names and in the Quakers' Yard where they lie under tombstones that bear no more than initials and a date.

Greville persuaded the Navy Board, in 1796, to build ships of war, and a contract was signed to construct the *Milford*, of seventy-eight guns, and the *Lavinia*, forty-eight guns. The proposal to establish a dockyard, and to develop the town on a gridiron pattern, had come from Jean-Louis Barrallier, a native of Toulon, who had come to Britain during the French Revolution and had been appointed assistant to the Inspector-General of Naval Construction.

In an attempt to relieve the tension that was mounting at Merton Place, and at the same time to provide publicity for the Milford project, Greville conceived the idea of inviting Nelson and the Hamiltons to visit the developing town. The party set out on 20 July 1802, and as the expenses of the journey, which amounted to £481, were shared by the two men, a detailed account was kept by Nelson.

Their arrival at Milford coincided with the anniversary of the Battle of the Nile, and celebrations arranged by Greville included a fair, a cattle show and, more appropriately, a regatta and boat race. At a sumptuous banquet attended by the leading gentry of the shire at the new hotel, Nelson made a speech in which he praised the project and all who were concerned with it, and proclaimed that Milford Haven and Trincomalee were the finest harbours he had ever seen. Sir William presented the landlord, Peter Cross, with a full length portrait of the admiral, painted by Guzzardi at Palermo, and the inn has been known ever after as the Lord Nelson Hotel.

The freedom of Haverfordwest was conferred upon Nelson, and the party was taken by boat from Milford to be entertained by Lord Milford at Picton Castle. The company then drove to Ridgeway where, as they arrived after nightfall, the driveway was lit with lanterns. Captain, later Admiral Sir, Thomas Foley, born here in 1757, who had served with Nelson at Cape St Vincent and Copenhagen, was delighted to welcome him, but his wife, Lady Lucy, daughter of the Duke of Leinster, was only civil to Lady Hamilton. The next day they left for Stackpole Court, to be well received by Lord Cawdor, and then moved on to Tenby where ships of the Royal Navy, dressed overall, fired a salute on their arrival and the citizens of the town took the horses out of their carriage and pulled it through the streets. They attended a performance of *The Mock Doctor* by Molière at the local theatre, and on the next evening they were entertained to dinner by Lord Kensington at the Lion Inn, followed by a ball 'attended by all the fashion of the town'.

Hamilton died in the following April and was buried in the vault of Slebech church beside his first wife. He left Charles Greville £7,000 in his will and a life interest in his estates in Pembrokeshire. Emma died in poverty in Calais and left her name to history, and fifty portraits by Romney commemorate her beauty. Greville died, a bachelor, in 1809, and in the sale of his works of art conducted by Christie's after his death, there were three portraits of Emma.

Charles was succeeded as life tenant by his brother Robert Fulke Greville, equerry to George III, who did not have the same interest in the development of Milford. The Navy Board transferred the dockyard to Paterchurch, which now became Pembroke Dock, in 1814, and Benjamin Rotch, the wealthiest inhabitant, removed to London five years later and sold his residence, Castle Hall, to Greville.

Castle Hall, built in the 1770s, became the home of John Zephaniah Holwell, a former Governor of Bengal who claimed to have been one of the few survivors of the Black Hole of Calcutta. It had been purchased by Benjamin Rotch in 1804, and Greville had bought it as a residence for his son, Robert Fulke Murray Greville, who engaged architects to rebuild the house in the style of the Italian Renaissance. In 1911 it was occupied by Benedictine nuns from Malling Abbey in Kent, but they left rather hurriedly in 1917 when they were suspected of signalling messages to German submarines. Castle Hall then became the residence of Sir Hugh Thomas, estate agent and landowner from Haverfordwest, and in 1934 it was absorbed into the Royal Naval Armaments Depot at Newton Noyes, when the house was demolished.

Robert Greville the younger fought an election against the sitting Member of Parliament, Sir John Owen of Orielton, in 1831, which cost him rather dearly. His bill for free food and beer for his supporters at 'The Mariners' at Haverfordwest, alone, amounted to £1,878, and harsh words led to a duel which he fought with John Jones of Ystrad, the member for Carmarthen, at Tavernspite. He had to flee the country to avoid his creditors and did not return for twenty years. He then became deeply involved in the development of the Haven and spent so much of his own money on improvements, including the building of a pier and the extension of the railway from Johnston, that he had to mortgage his estate and to sell Castle Hall.

A proposal to build a railway between Manchester and Milford was put forward in 1845 but abandoned when the South Wales Railway was extended from Haverfordwest.

The development of Milford as a port was given a fillip in 1874 with the formation of the Milford Docks Company, although the docks were not completed for another fourteen years. Even then, the ocean liner *City of Rome* had to anchor six miles away to discharge Phineas Barnum and his travelling menagerie in 1889. Attempts to capture the transatlantic trade met with little success, despite the impressive presence of Brunel's *Great Eastern* in the harbour. Milford had to 'give up its dreams of becoming an ocean port', a local newspaper commented, 'and be content with the more commonplace though no less useful role of a Welsh Grimsby'. The docks were adapted to the requirements of the fishing industry; ice factories, a fish market and smoke-houses were built, and Milford grew to be one of the chief fishing ports of Britain. The landing of sixty thousand tons of fish in 1946 was the highest recorded, but from then onward the industry has steadily declined. The closure of the Suez Canal and the consequent building of giant oil-tankers capable of carrying large loads round the Cape of Good Hope, led to a search for suitable port facilities. Someone remembered Milford Haven, with its deep-water channel, and in 1957 it was decided that it should be developed as a major oil port. The Esso oil refinery was opened in 1960, the second largest refinery in the British Isles, covering seven hundred acres between Gelliswick Bay and Sandy Haven. Few among those present at the opening ceremony, performed by Her Majesty the Queen, would have thought that in a little over twenty years' time the refinery would be closed.

The BP Ocean Terminal, with its administrative centre cleverly concealed within the old Popton Fort, began pumping oil by pipeline to the refinery at Llandarcy, near Swansea, in 1961. Three years later, the Texaco refinery started up on an adjoining site. The Gulf Oil refinery was opened in 1968 on the east side of Milford, and in 1973 the Amoco refinery, unable to find a suitable site on the Haven, established itself a little inland, near Robeston West. The deep-water channel was made deeper to allow tankers of a quarter of a million tons to enter the Haven and tie up alongside the refinery jetties. George Owen's 'finest port in Christendom' had become the leading oil port in Britain and the second largest in Europe.

The Pembroke Power Station, on Pennar Gut, was opened in 1973, at a cost of £100 million, to provide power for the national grid along power lines carrying 400,000 volts on massive pylons that march in pairs across the countryside towards Bristol and the Midlands.

Among Charles Greville's ambitions for Milford was a plan to 'found a College limited to Classes of Mathematicks and their application to Meckanicks, Military and Naval and Civil Engineering, Construction of Ships, Navigation and Survey and drawing', which he proposed to call 'The College of King George III founded at Milford'. The proposal was to build an observatory with a number of rooms adjoining, but the project was never completed and only the skeleton of the observatory remains.

The Benedictine priory of Pill was established, as a subordinate house to St Dogmael's Abbey, by Adam de la Roche and dedicated to St Budoc and St Mary. The priory comprised a quadrangle surrounded by buildings, but there remain only fragments of walls and a well-proportioned chancel arch. At the dissolution of the monasteries, the priory was granted to Sir Thomas Jones of Abermarlais, and of Haroldston in right of his wife Mary, the widow of Sir Thomas Perrot. Sir John Perrot later exchanged Pill Priory with the Barlows of Slebech for lands at the Priory of Haverfordwest which adjoined his demesne at Haroldston.

The suggestion that a church should be built at Milford came from William Price, master of St Katherine's Hospital in the Tower Hamlets, and in recognition of his generosity the church was dedicated to that saint. Greville laid the foundations in the autumn of 1802 but the building was not completed for another six years. His proposal to use a porphyry urn, brought from

Egypt by the Bishop of Meath, as a font, met with the disapproval of the Bishop of St David's, as did the idea of placing beside it the truck of the mainmast of the French ship *L'Orient* which had been blown up at the Battle of the Nile. The urn has remained in the church but the truck was removed to the Royal United Services Institute in Whitehall.

12

Dale and the Isles

Hubberston appears among the possessions of Pill Priory in 1291 as *villa Huberti*, the settlement of an Anglo-Norman named Hubert, but local folklore insists that it took its name from Hubba, a Viking who wintered his fleet in the Haven in 877.

A small chapel that formerly stood north of the village was dedicated to the Welsh saint Budoc who, in association with St Mawes, established monasteries in Cornwall and in Brittany. He became known, in the vernacular of south Pembrokeshire, as St Buttock, which was 'not considered euphonious', and when a house was built near the site of the chapel, it was considered more seemly to call it St Botolph's.

A much-worn effigy in Herbrandston church is probably that of a knight of the fourteenth century. In the churchyard is the tomb of Lieutenant Philip Carrol Walker, of the Royal Artillery, who was murdered, it was alleged, at Hubberston Fort by the staff surgeon, Sydney Alder, on 21 May 1875. Alder stood trial at the Assizes at Haverfordwest before the Lord Chief Justice, Sir Alexander Cockburn, and was defended by Mr Harding Giffard QC, who later, as Lord Halsbury, became Lord Chancellor. From the evidence it appeared that the two officers had dined together in the mess on the evening in question and had afterwards got into an argument over a small gambling debt, during which Walker was stabbed with a knife. The jury, having retired for an hour and a half after hearing the evidence, returned with a verdict of 'not guilty', and Alder was discharged. On the tombstone on Walker's grave, the mysterious outline of a hand and a dagger may be traced in the natural veins of the white marble.

The honorial barony of Walwyn's Castle was independent of the lordship of Haverfordwest and had its own subordinate castles at Benton and Dale. Legend has associated the place with Gwalchmai, or Gawayne, the shining knight of Arthur's Round Table, to the extent of claiming that his body, of gigantic stature, had been found in Walwyn's Castle 'in the time of William the Conqueror'.

The massive earthwork, south of the church, appears to have been a promontory fort, upon which the Normans established a castle-ring which may have carried a stone tower. In 1307, when the barony was held by Sir Guy de Brian, lord of Laugharne, it was reported that 'the habitable house' was in ruins.

There are similar earthworks commanding the valley leading down to Sandyhaven Pill: Syke Rath and Capeston Rath, with Rickeston Rath confronting it across the valley, and nearby is Roman's (properly Reymer's) Castle, a double-banked pentagonal earthwork, while the promontory forts at South Hook and Great Castle Head protect the entrance to the pill.

Under a gravestone in Hasguard churchyard 'lieth the bodie of Katherine Barrett', daughter of Owen Barrett of Gelliswick and Hasguard, and wife of Dr Rowland Meyrick, Bishop of Bangor. Their eldest son, Gelly, on his father's death when he was nine years old, entered the service of Sir George Devereux at Lamphey and later attended Devereux's nephew, the second Earl of Essex, in the Low Countries before becoming steward of the Earl's household and, in time, Essex's right-hand man. Through the Earl's influence he obtained extensive lands from the Queen, including Wigmore Castle, and in 1596 he was knighted on the Cadiz expedition, but by his devotion to Essex he was charged with treason and executed in 1601. His brother, Francis, who was with him during Essex's campaign in Ireland, commanding the west Wales contingents, was knighted in 1599. Sir Francis's son, Sir Gelly Meyrick, became adjutant-general of Essex's army during the Civil War. His descendants settled at Bush, now incorporated in the Bush Secondary School at Pembroke.

On the lawn at Great Hoaten Farm is an enormous anchor, over seventeen feet in length and with flukes measuring fourteen feet across, which is locally held to be a relic of the Spanish Armada but is eighteenth century. It was found on the beach at St Bride's Haven, though no one can say how it got there, and was dragged by teams of horses to its present site.

When St Caradog was driven from his island retreat by Norse

pirates, the Bishop of St David's gave him 'a place of residence in the monastery of St Ishmael, situated on the edge of the sea'. There is no trace of the monastery, but the inlet below the village of St Ishmael's is known as Monk Haven, and at one time the Haverfordwest Priory held land there. A dozen early Christian burials were recently found in Monk's Field near the church and may be associated with an early foundation at St Ishmael's, which was listed as one of the seven bishop's houses of Dyfed. The parish church, dedicated to St Ishmael, lies deep in the valley, sunk among trees, below Goose Green, its churchyard divided by a stream. Within its dark interior are a cross-incised stone and a broken slab bearing the foot of a cross flanked by ribbon plait work from around the tenth century.

St Ishmael's Tump is a fine example of a Norman motte which rises fifteen feet out of a ditch in a field on the outskirts of the village.

Dale appears in early documents as *Villa de Vale* and also as *le Dale*, and it is uncertain whether the name derives from the Norse *dalr* or the early English *dael*, both meaning a valley. The valley, which stretches from Dale beach to Westdale Bay, is a continuation of the Ritec Fault that runs the length of Milford Haven to the valley of the Ritec at Tenby, and beyond. The sea once flowed through it so that the Dale peninsula was an off-shore island.

The lord of the manor of Dale in 1150 was Richard de Vale, whose son Robert FitzRichard followed Strongbow into Ireland and founded a nunnery at Timolin in County Kildare. The last of the line, Sir Robert de Vale, obtained a charter in 1293 to hold a weekly market and a fair at Dale on the feast of St Crucis, which is 14 September. He left only daughters, among whom Elen, who received the manor of Treffgarne as her inheritance, married Llywelyn ab Owen, a descendant of the Lord Rhys, Prince of Deheubarth; their grand-daughter, also Elen, became the mother of Owain Glyn Dŵr. Another daughter, Margaret, married firstly William de la Pole, from which union are descended the earls of Bradford, and secondly Tudur ap Gronw of Penmynydd, by whom she had Maredudd ap Tudur, the father of Owen Tudor. From the de Vales of Dale, therefore, were descended Owain Glyn Dŵr, who established a Welsh parliament at Machynlleth and assumed the title Prince of

Wales, and Henry Tudor, who returned to Dale on his way to Bosworth to establish the Tudor dynasty.

In 1601 William Walter of Roch Castle purchased a fourth share of the lordship of Dale which his great-grandson, Richard Walter, sold in 1669 to David Paynter. Richard left behind him, at Dale Castle, a portrait of his sister Lucy, the mistress of King Charles II. Paynter's daughter and heiress married William Allen of Gelliswick, who was sheriff in 1693, and from the Allens, Dale Castle passed by marriage, in 1776, to John Lloyd of Ffosybleiddiaid and Mabws, in Cardiganshire. The family changed its name to Lloyd-Philipps in 1823 and remains in possession of the castle.

The church was granted to the priory of St Thomas, and on the dissolution it reverted to the Crown. Several restorations have robbed it of its original features. The font and the stone altar table were brought from Italy in 1818.

Those who came to settle at Dale Point somewhere around 300 BC threw a bank across the neck of the promontory for defensive purposes. Others, who arrived two hundred years later, built two curved banks at Great Castle Head. What were thought to be two concentric stone circles near Brunt Farm have proved to be erratic boulders brought by ice from northern Britain that had been dragged into one place so as to clear a field for farming purposes.

Dale was a flourishing port in the sixteenth century but by 1801 its population had dwindled and the village was 'ruinous and deserted'. 'The Griffin' alone remains of its eighteen inns, in one of which resided 'loose women ... who were suspected of murdering Portuguese sailors'. There was also a brewery, owned by a family named Runawae, that exported good Dale ale to Bristol and Liverpool.

St Ann's Head should be seen from the sea for its Neapolitan-cake rock strata, and the sharp folding of Cobbler's Hole, to be appreciated. Here was the southern limit of the last glaciation, and erratic boulders brought by the Irish Sea glacier from Cumbria and the Hebrides were carried this far south. When the ice melted, it drowned the pre-glacial valley of the Daugleddau, so that salt water flows as far as Haverfordwest on the Western Cleddau and Canaston Bridge on the Eastern. The drowned valley, or ria, became the deep-water channel of

Milford Haven. 'Tell me how Wales was made so happy to inherit such a haven?' Imogen asks in *Cymbeline*.

Along its shores were floated the bluestones of Presely *en route* for Stonehenge: two pillars may have slipped off the rafts and replacements been hurriedly found, which is why the Altar Stone comes from Llangwm. Promontory forts indicate an Iron Age population, and although there is no evidence, Roman galleys may well have sought refuge in the haven. Norsemen wintered here, and the Normans came to stay, and some of them set out from here to conquer Ireland. An army of French mercenaries landed in 1405, and Henry Tudor returned here from his exile in France to begin the long march to Bosworth.

A little before sunset on Sunday 7 August 1485 Henry, 'accompanyed with our ancient enemyes of Fraunce and othre straunge nacions', as Richard III was able to write from Beskwood Lodge near Nottingham only four days later, landed at Mill Bay, beneath St Ann's Head. Local tradition points to Harry's Carthouse as the precise landing-place, and maintains that Henry's complaint that the cliff-path was 'brunt', meaning steep, gave its name to the farm above the bay.

The contemporary historian Polydore Vergil states that Henry took Dale without delay as he had heard that his adversaries were gathered there to prevent his progress. Early next morning he crossed Mullock Bridge, where, according to another fanciful tradition, Sir Rhys ap Thomas was hiding under an arch in order to absolve himself from an oath he had sworn to King Richard that he would be faithful to him 'until the enemy doth step over my body'. In fact, Sir Rhys, whatever vows he may have made, joined Henry at Welshpool five days later.

The Welsh bards had long proclaimed Henry's just cause, and when he landed with his mixed army of two thousand men, Welsh, English, Breton and French, he attracted a great following along his route across Wales. He marched through Haverfordwest and across the Presely Hills, where he is said to have spent the night at Fagwyr Lwyd, near Cilgwyn, and then on to Cardigan, Machynlleth, Shrewsbury and Lichfield to Bosworth, which he reached on 21 August, and waged battle victoriously the next day.

'In the place where he first landed in Milford,' according to George Owen, Henry 'builded a chapel ... three flight shoots west of the haven's mouth.' But by 1600, when Owen was writing, it was 'owlde and decayed, having a rownde towre like a windmyle or pigion-howse'. The chapel, dedicated to St Ann, was demolished a century later and used as the site for a lighthouse. An illegal attempt to establish a lighthouse there had been made in the 1660s, but by 1713 there were two authorized coal-lights, one on a tower that could have belonged to the destroyed chapel and the other on a specially built tower. In 1800 two lighthouses were erected, lit by oil-lamps with hollow wicks invented sixteen years earlier by Ami Argand.

'A long, straggling, poor looking village, still poorer in appearance on account of the cottages being all ill thatched with straw': Fenton's description, in 1810, is far from applicable to the village of Marloes today, with neat and bright colour-washed cottages and houses. The grey double-bellcote church, dedicated to St Peter, has a baptistry sunk in the floor at its west end, alongside a Norman font. There is a tradition that an earlier church 'near the beach' was washed away by the sea, along with the glebe land, during a storm. The village clock tower was built in 1904 in memory of William Edwardes, Lord Kensington, the Liberal Member of Parliament for Haverfordwest, from money donated by the Pembrokeshire Liberal Association. Of him it was said that 'he observed at all times a remarkable punctuality, and those with whom he made appointments knew the penalty for non-observance of this sound rule.' The clock was therefore regarded as a suitable memorial.

Medicinal leeches were gathered in Marloes Mere for the doctors of Harley Street, but the mere was drained during the eighteenth century and is now a wetland where grows the rare tubular water-dropwort.

A lane beside the church leads to the mile-long stretch of Great Marloes Sands, where the tall cliffs, of Silurian rock, stand on end at the Three Chimneys.

Gatholm, named 'goat island' by the Norse, may have been an early Christian settlement: there are some 130 hut sites, which could have been monastic cells, and eight enclosures, on its undulating surface.

Martin's Haven provided a landing-place for those who came and built the great Iron Age fort, the largest in west Wales, on the promontory above and threw a bank across its neck. A century ago Lord Kensington built a wall along the bank to establish a deer park to complement the house he had built at St Bride's, but there is no evidence that deer ever grazed the bleak headland. The lord of Walwyn's Castle had a free fishery at Martin's Haven, and for centuries it was the way to the sea for the fishermen of Marloes, and landfall for those who lived on Skomer and Skokholm. The fishermen's boats that were hauled up on the shingly beach have vanished, and Martin's Haven is now the embarkation point for people wishing to visit the island nature reserves of Skomer and Skokholm.

There is no more turbulent stretch of water around the coast of Wales than Jack Sound, lying between Wooltack Point and Midland Island, where the tide runs at six knots at high and low water. The Celtic saints wisely avoided such tide-races, but centuries earlier the residents of Skomer had to negotiate the treacherous waters in their fragile craft. The terrifying experience of such a crossing came upon me when the author-naturalist R.M. Lockley and I, and our families, crossed the Sound in an Irish curragh.

Among the many ships wrecked in Jack Sound was the SS *Moseley*, which struck Midland early one evening in November 1929 with thirty-six people on board, when the British Broadcasting Corporation for the first time sent out an SOS appeal for help for a stricken vessel. Twenty-eight lives were saved by the Angle lifeboat, and a Maltese fireman, believed lost, was found the next day, having slept throughout the period of the rescue. The *Lucy* went aground on a rock in the Sound on St Valentine's Day 1967, and as its cargo of calcium carbide was in danger of conversion into explosive acetylene gas on contact with water, the crew quickly abandoned the vessel. When the tide rose, the ship was carried off the rock, and it sailed unmanned northward and vanished into the night until it sank to the north of Skomer. The packet *Albion* struck a rock in the Sound in April 1837, carrying fifty passengers from Dublin and a cargo of livestock including 180 pigs. The captain managed to run the ship onto a beach, known since as Albion Sands. The pigs swam ashore and were met by the villagers of Marloes, who soon converted them into bacon.

Middleholm, now named Midland Isle by map-makers, has traces of early settlement and a stone wall dividing its twenty-one acres. It was farmed for rabbits from the beginning of the fourteenth century.

Skomer Island is a national nature reserve and one of the most important breeding-places for sea-birds in all Europe. Puffins and Manx shearwaters nest in burrows and take advantage of the thousands of rabbit-holes on the island, while guillemots balance their tapered eggs on cliff ledges, and razorbills lay theirs in rocky fissures. Lesser black-backed gulls breed in large colonies among the bluebells; kittiwakes nest at Kittiwake Cove and cormorants on the Mew Stone. In all, some forty species of birds breed on the island, including fulmars, choughs, buzzards, wheatears, stonechats and short-eared owls. Among passing migrants are golden oriole, icterine warbler and scarlet grosbeak.

In springtime and early summer, there are great carpets of bluebell and pink thrift, red campion and white sea campion, in addition to quieter displays of primrose, wild thyme and heather, and the more flamboyant foxglove, purple loosestrife and meadow sweet.

Atlantic grey seals breed in caves and on open beaches, and bask on the rocks at low tide. The only land mammals are the rabbit, common and pygmy shrews, field mouse and Skomer vole, *Clethrionomys skomerensis*, which is larger in size and lighter in colour than the mainland bank vole and, by its tameness, would appear to have no fear of man.

The rabbits were introduced during the Norman period and provide the earliest glimpses of the island's recorded history. The *inquisitio post mortem* of Aymer de Valence, Earl of Pembroke, in 1324 values the pasturage of Skomer, Skokholm and Middleholm at £2.15.0 and the profits from the rabbits at £14.5.0. In the winter of 1387-8 two rabbit-catchers accounted for 3,120 rabbits on the islands, 540 of which they consumed themselves while 262 were eaten by their dog and two ferrets. The remaining carcases were sold to John Williams of Haverfordwest for £3.17.3½ and the skins for £8. The expenses of the trappers during their five-month stay on the islands amounted to £1.8.2 and included barley for bread, salt for salting rabbits and a shovel for digging them out, hire of cooking utensils, repairs to the houses on Skomer and Skokholm, and the purchase of three new oars. The profit to the landlord was therefore considerable, but it was not always so. The skins of the previous winter, sold at Haverfordwest for £11.9.2, had been badly stored at Tenby and during passage to Bristol, so that they 'had become rotten and were of no value'. The men came off the islands at the end of January, when the rabbit breeding season began and the shearwaters returned to the burrows.

An archaeological survey of Skomer, conducted by Professor W.F. Grimes, revealed that ancient fields of early settlers, during the Iron Age, once covered the island's 722 acres, but their stone walls have disappeared in the central area through more recent cultivation. Their round stone-built huts occur singly and in groups, sometimes in the shelter of the dark grey igneous outcrops.

The Norse came and called the island Skalmey, 'the cloven island', from its shape, but it has been known as Skomer from the eighteenth century onward. With the coming of the Normans, the offshore islands became part of the lordship of Pembroke, but from time to time they reverted to the Crown, when they were leased to tenants, including Sir John Perrot who increased the rents to such an extent in 1588 that the islands became 'uninhabited save for herdsmen' looking after Perrot's own stock of horses, cattle and sheep. The farmhouse and outbuildings were built about 1700 and considerably renovated in 1843.

Skomer was in the possession of William Philipps of Sandyhaven in 1713, and it then passed, through the distaff side, to Gilbert Harries of Llanunwas who sold it to Lord Kensington in 1897. It was purchased by Major W.F. Sturt in 1922, and by Leonard Lee of Coventry in 1949. Ten years later it was acquired by the West Wales Naturalists' Trust and sold, by agreement, to the Nature Conservancy Council, which leased it to the Trust and declared the island a national nature reserve that is open to visitors on payment of a landing fee.

Skokholm is separated from Skomer by Broad Sound, where the tides meet to form the Wild Goose Race. Unlike dark volcanic Skomer, its rocks are the burnt sienna of the Old Red Sandstone, and there are no signs of prehistoric occupation although some flints have been found on its surface. The earliest reference to the island is found in a grant by William Marshal the Younger, Earl of Pembroke, before 1230, to Gilbert de Vale of Dale, of lands in Ireland in exchange for properties in

Pembrokeshire that included Skokholm. The island passed, by marriage, to Humphrey de Bohun, Earl of Hereford, but the de Vales continued to receive the revenues until 1276 when Edward I ordered Nicholas FitzMartin, lord of Cemais and 'keeper of the island of Scugholm', to cause the island to be restored to Humphrey's son, as his right and inheritance. By 1324 it was again in the hands of the earls of Pembroke, and so remained except that it sometimes reverted to the Crown. In 1533 Henry VIII gave the rents of Skokholm and Skomer to his queen, Anne Boleyn, in her right as the Marquess of Pembroke, but the two islands were acquired in 1558 by Thomas Heburne, a 'Yeoman of Their Majesties' Bodyguard', for £75. In 1714 they belonged to William Philipps of Sandyhaven, who then released Skokholm, 'being a mortgage for £300' to William Allen the Younger of Gelliswick, whose son, William Allen of Dale Castle, succeeded to the property. His son, John Allen, placed some deer on the island which provided 'remarkably fine flavoured' venison. The deer were replenished by Allen's son-in-law, John Lloyd, but when he rented out the island, his tenant complained that they caused him damage and they were destroyed. The island was farmed until the outbreak of the Great War, the tenant paying the rent with the rabbits he caught, and thereafter it was left to the rabbit-catchers in winter, and in summer to fishermen who came with long nets to catch cocklollies, or shearwaters, and sea-parrots, or puffins, with which to bait their lobster pots.

In 1927 R.M. Lockley came to live on Skokholm, having 'read Thoreau very thoroughly'. Like Henry Thoreau, in his cabin on the shores of Walden Pond, he took notes in the field and later recorded his thoughts and observations in books. When I visited Walden, I felt that Thoreau would have envied Lockley his island.

The house on Skokholm had been 'built after a whimsical manner', with its steep roof brought down to within five feet of the ground so as to make it wind-resistant. It was now largely roofless and occupied by a pair of nesting blackbirds, and the barn was ruinous. Lockley was helped in his restoration work by the wreck of the *Alice Williams*, a 132 ton topsail schooner built at Llanelli in 1854, which had been abandoned by its crew when it sprang a leak and had been blown, with full sails set, onto the rocks at Skokholm. He bought the vessel for £5 and used its timbers to repair the buildings, and he was able to salvage fifty tons of its cargo of coal. The ship's brass-bound wheel was fixed over the hearth in the barn, which had been converted into a refectory, and its carved name-plate on a beam and the fog-bell hung over the door. The serene and proud figurehead of the schooner, the 'Alice Williams' herself, dressed in the fashion of the 1850s, with bright blue eyes and hair neatly coiled, was placed over South Haven to greet all who came to the island.

In 1933 Lockley established a bird observatory, the first in Britain, on Skokholm. The island is leased by the West Wales Naturalists' Trust from the Dale Castle estate and is open to visitors.

Bendigeidfran, King of Britain, having avenged the insults heaped on his sister Branwen during her marriage to the Irish chieftain Matholwch, ordered that his head be struck off and carried to the White Mount in London, for burial, by the seven survivors of the bitter battles he had fought in Ireland. They crossed the sea, bearing the royal head, and landed at Harlech, where they tarried and feasted for seven years, and 'at the end of the seventh year they set out for Gwales in Penfro', which is Grassholm. 'And there was for them a fair royal palace overlooking the sea and a great hall.' The hall had three doors, and they had been warned that the door facing Cornwall should never be opened, but after they had been there eighty years in merriment and enjoyment, one of their number could resist the temptation no longer. He threw open the forbidden portal, and in consequence all the sorrows in the world descended upon them. There are the scanty remains of a building on the island which one would like to imagine to have been the 'fair royal palace', but they are more likely to be all that is left of a small medieval farmhouse.

In 1890 there were half a million puffins on Grassholm but they have all but disappeared. A hundred years ago there were twenty gannets' nests on the island: by today, their number has increased to twenty thousand, and the population of up to a hundred thousand gannets makes Grassholm the third largest colony in the British Isles.

Out beyond Grassholm, and the perilous shoals and reefs of the Hats and Barrels, lies the most westerly morsel of Wales, a cluster of barren rocks known as 'the Smalls'. After they had been a perilous hazard for sailors for centuries, the idea of placing a light on the rocks came, in 1765, to John Phillips, a Cardiganshire man who had become a dockmaster at Liverpool. Having obtained a licence to do so, he engaged young Henry Whiteside, a Liverpudlian already known as a maker of spinets and harpsichords, to design a suitable lighthouse, which was assembled at Solva in 1775. It consisted of a lantern and quarters mounted on iron columns, but the columns turned out to be too rigid and they were replaced by pillars of oak, the petrified stumps of which are still implanted in the rock, to support a 'Malay-looking baracoon of a building'. Whiteside decided to put his creation to the test and joined the lighthouse keepers in January 1777, but they soon found themselves in difficulties, and on 1 February Whiteside sent three messages in bottles encased in casks addressed to Thomas Williams of Treleddyn. One came ashore in Galway Bay, another at Newgale and the third, providentially, at Porthselau, below Treleddyn. The message read: 'Being now in a most dangerous and distressed condition upon the Smalls ... our water near all gone, our fire all gone, and our house in a most melancholy manner, I doubt not but that you will fetch us from here as soon as possible,' which Williams succeeded in doing.

The lighthouse was manned during the stormy winter of 1801 by two keepers, Thomas Howell and Thomas Griffiths. Griffiths was taken ill and died and Howell, fearing that he might be suspected of foul play, as there had been bad blood between them, made a rough coffin for the corpse and lashed it to the lantern rail. His relief was delayed by rough weather, and when it came, Howell was half starved and all but demented. From that time forth, lighthouses were manned by three keepers.

Trinity House purchased the lease of the Smalls in 1836 from the Reverend A.B. Buchanan, grandson of John Phillips, and his co-lessee Thomas Clarke, for which the Elder Brethren had to pay £170,468, based on an income of £11,000 a year. By 1852, despite a reduction in dues, the income was doubled, thus making the Smalls the most lucrative lighthouse in Britain, if not the world.

The present red and white banded lighthouse was built, in 1861, of granite brought from Bodmin to Solva. In order to enter its front door, one has to climb rungs consisting of bends of brass jutting from the outer wall, twenty feet above the base rock, and when I first climbed them, I felt that I would sooner spend the rest of my life in the lighthouse rather than climb down again.

A shipwrecked man, the story goes, was washed ashore in St Bride's Haven and was found on the beach, with little life left in him, by the daughter and heiress of Sir John de St Bride's. She took him home to her father's house, now but an ivy-mantled ruin beside the church but then well appointed and surrounded by gardens with fishponds and a bowling green. She nursed him back to health, fell in love with him and married him, and so was founded the famous family of Laugharne of Orlandon. A less romantic record gives the marriage of Thomas Laugharne, early in the fifteenth century, to Jane, daughter and heiress of Philip de Crabhole. The Laugharnes, it was said, were like the Hapsburgs 'fortunate in their nuptials' and became one of the leading county families.

Gelly Laugharne purchased an ounce of tobacco from Richard Bateman, mercer of Haverfordwest, in 1603 and is said to have been the first person in Pembrokeshire to smoke tobacco for pleasure, not very long after Sir Walter Raleigh had introduced the habit to Elizabethan courtiers.

Rowland Laugharne, in his youth, was page to Robert Devereux, third Earl of Essex, and later became commander-in-chief of the Parliamentary forces during the Civil War. When the Royalists, under the Earl of Carbery, captured Haverfordwest and Tenby, Laugharne took the offensive and eventually defeated and routed the Cavaliers at the battle of Colby Moor on 1 August 1645, and entered Haverfordwest the next day. In the following year he was appointed commander-in-chief of South Wales, but in 1647 he turned against the Parliamentarians and took refuge in Pembroke Castle, where he surrendered to Cromwell and was sentenced to death but reprieved. At the Restoration he was elected Member of Parliament for Pembroke borough. He died in 1676, and when the Laugharnes came to end in the male line in 1715, the estate passed by marriage to Charles Philipps of Sandyhaven. His grandson built a commodious residence, which became known as Hill, on the slope above the church, with a deer park between it and the sea. The estate was later acquired by Lord Kensington, who rebuilt the house in grand style as a castellated mansion.

Lord Kensington was descended from William Edwardes, son

View from look-out at Abereiddi

Nab Head, mesolithic site

Carew Castle

St Govan's chapel

Pembroke Castle, Great Keep

Tudor Merchant's House, Tenby

Tenby harbour and castle

Five Arches, Tenby

St Mary's Church, Tenby

Two of the magnificent tombs at St Mary's, Tenby: (above) Margaret ap Rhys of Scotsborough; Thomas White and son

Begelly Church watch-tower

How many miles...?

of Francis Edwardes of Haylett, near Haverfordwest, and his wife, Elizabeth Rich, daughter of Robert Rich, Earl of Holland and Warwick. The title was originally granted, in 1622, to Henry Rich, who had married Isabel, daughter of Sir Walter Cope, Chamberlain of the Exchequer and Keeper of Hyde Park, and through that marriage Rich had acquired the manor of Kensington, in London, and the beautifully ornate Holland House, built by Sir Walter in 1605.

St Bride's Haven was once renowned for its herring fishery. A little chapel, built beside the sea, was used, when it became ruinous, to store salt for curing the fish, but –

When St Bride's chapel a salt-house was made,
St Bride's lost the herring trade.

The remains of the chapel have long been swept away, and the stone-lined graves of those who were buried beside it are constantly being claimed by the sea.

One of the mutilated effigies in the north transept of the church nearby is reputed to commemorate St Bride, or St Brigid of Kildare, who has more dedications in Wales than any other Irish saint although she never left her native Ireland. Her cult may well belong to the areas that were settled by Irish immigrants during the fifth and sixth centuries.

Nab Head was a clifftop settlement of the people who combined hunting with coastal food-gathering during the mesolithic period. In addition to small flint implements fashioned from flints gathered on local beaches, they left elongated tools that may have been used for knocking limpets off the rocks, and also a narrow wood-cutting stone axe indicating a connection with the Maglemosian culture of the forest people of the North Sea area, for Britain was still joined to the Continent at that time. The variety of finds suggest that coastal dwellers bearing more than one culture occupied this settlement. Tower Point Rath is a multivallate promontory fort of the Iron Age.

The bell in the bellcote of the remote church of Talbenny is inscribed *Sancti Martoine ora pro nobis* and was brought thither from 'the friars' church of St Martin' in Haverfordwest.

In Goultrop Roads, ships used to seek shelter during stormy weather, and a lifeboat station stood at the foot of the oak-hung cliffs. In 1597 a Spanish vessel was 'forced into the creek called

Galtop', and Hugh Butler, who commanded the local trained bands, prepared to board it, but the Spaniards put up a flag of truce and offered to send their cockboat ashore, whereupon John Wogan, 'a gentleman of those parts', stole a march on Butler, boarded the ship and rifled it, wounding Butler in three places in the process.

A sea-smoothed stone, three feet high, stands in Walton West church bearing a wheel-cross and decorated with a strapwork design and the four sacred monograms 'A ω IHC XPC' – 'the cross of Alpha and Omega: Jesus Christ'. It was found while digging a grave in the churchyard and dates from the tenth or eleventh century. The church also has a mutilated effigy.

Little Haven is not unlike a Cornish holiday village, with its houses clinging to the cliff slope and clustered deep in the valley. In summer, the sheltered beach is strewn with pleasure craft, in place of coastal smacks that loaded coal dug from pits in the surrounding area. Strawberry Hill, above the village, has a Bronze Age barrow which produced an urn burial on excavation a few years ago.

Broad Haven had become a favourite resort for bathing as early as 1800; 'many little villas were scattered about for that purpose', and there were 'bathing machines on the fine hard sands'. There were sailing boats that were used for pleasure and for fishing for turbot, sole and dory, the surplus being sold on landing at 6d. a pound. The Broad Haven National Park Information Centre provides information on a wide range of subjects, especially relating to marine life, and adjoining it is a youth hostel which has facilities for the disabled.

13

Canaston to Carew

Below Haverfordwest the two rivers, the Eastern and Western Cleddau, meet, 'becoming both a salt sea of a mile broad and sixteen miles longer before they forsake their native country, and then by course of nature yield themselves to the sea, the ending of all rivers, where, not forgetting the natural love of native country, twice every day return, as it were, with loving care to see and salute their ancient offspring'. (George Owen, *Description of Penbrokshire*, 1603.)

Much of the *entre deux rivières* is the park land of Picton Castle and Slebech Hall, and the rest is taken up by the parishes of Uzmaston and Boulston. Uzmaston takes its name from one Osmund who settled there. Its church, dedicated to St Ismael, was largely restored in 1870, but it retains its Norman tower, with an external staircase, parts of its walls and a cushion-type font.

The ancient manor house of Boulston stood so close to the river that the tide washed its walls. It was the residence of a branch of the ubiquitous Wogan family for four hundred years, until it was bought by Colonel Dudley Ackland of Philadelphia, who built the present house on higher ground in 1798. Boulston woods were believed to harbour a basilisk, a fabulous monster which fell dead on being observed. A Wogan, aware of this singularity, placed himself in a barrel and was rolled into the thick of the wood where, through a hole in the cask, he was able to set eyes on the basilisk before it could see him, and cause it to perish instantly.

Boulston church, now a ruin, was a peculiar, that is to say that it was exempt from diocesan jurisdiction. Fenton found 'amongst the lumber in a corner of the church ... a small *basso relievo* of the boy Bishop', but the small effigy was more likely to have been a decorative feature of a lost tomb. Genealogical inscriptions commemorate various Wogans and include Lewis Wogan, who died in 1692, and his wife Katherine, daughter of 'the Matchless Orinda', of Cardigan Priory, who had buried fifteen children during their lifetime and left a daughter and sole heiress, Anne Wogan, who married John Laugharne of St Bride's in 1698 and 'caused this monument to be erected'.

Sir John Wogan, Justiciary of Ireland, was described in 1302 as 'lord of Pykton', and he it was who built Picton Castle, on a site to the west of an earlier motte that is said to have been the work of William de Picton. The castle comprised a rectangular block with drum towers of unequal size at each angle, a plan which may have been inspired by thirteenth-century castles in Ireland, with which Sir John would have been familiar. A square block of four storeys was added on the west side by Sir Richard Philipps, the first Lord Milford, in about 1800. The original entrance was at basement level, but when the forecourt was raised, the present entrance was built between the two eastern towers. The castle, which remains in the Philipps family, has been extensively restored by the present owners.

A range of buildings on the north side of the castle has been converted into a gallery to house a collection of paintings by Graham Sutherland and presented by the artist in recognition of the inspiration he found in Pembrokeshire from the time of his first visit in 1934, when, captivated by its 'exultant strangeness', he 'began to learn painting'.

The last of the Wogans of Picton, John Wogan, was dead by 1420, and his daughter and heiress, Katherine, married Owen Dwnn of Muddlescomb, Kidwelly. Their son, Henry Dwnn, was killed on the eve of the battle of Banbury, in 1469, and Picton passed to his daughter and heiress, Joan, who married Thomas ap Philip of Cilsant. Thomas took a hundred men, on two occasions, to fight in France, and became Squire of the Body to King Henry VII. He was knighted in 1512 and died nine years later.

His descendant Sir John Philipps, a renowned patron of learning, was created a baronet in 1621. The fourth baronet devoted his talent and his wealth to relieve the lot of the poor and was deservedly known as 'the Good Sir John'. He was Member of Parliament for the Pembroke boroughs from 1695 to

1700, and for the town and county of Haverfordwest from 1718 to 1722. He was one of the earliest members of the Society for Promoting Christian Knowledge and was active in building some fifty churches in London and in establishing over a hundred charity schools in west Wales. His son, Sir John, the sixth baronet, whom his cousin Horace Walpole described as 'a notorious Jacobite', was a leading member of the Society of Sea Serjeants and high in the confidence of the Young Pretender. His son, Sir Richard Philipps, was Lord Lieutenant both for the town and county of Haverfordwest and for the county of Pembroke and in 1776 was created Baron Milford in the peerage of Ireland. The twelfth baronet was vicar of Warminster; his eldest son became Viscount St David's, another was elevated to the peerage as Lord Kylsant, and another as Lord Milford, of a third creation, while another was General Sir Ivor Philipps, who restored Pembroke Castle.

When the Seljuk Turks seized Jerusalem in 1076, the whole of Christendom became incensed and called for the redemption of the Holy Sepulchre from the hands of the infidel. Thus came about the First Crusade and the recapture of Jerusalem in 1099. The Knights of St John of Jerusalem won fame in that Crusade by their care for the wounded, from which they became known as the Hospitallers, and when the Crusade was over, some of them settled in Pembrokeshire, established a Commandery at Slebech and obtained grants of lands at Minwear, Rosemarket, Letterston, Newport and elsewhere.

Following the dissolution of the monasteries, Roger Barlow and his brother, Thomas, purchased the lordship of Slebech, the Commandery, the priory of Pill, the manor of Minwear and the Augustine priory and the house of the Black Friars at Haverfordwest, for £705.

Roger Barlow was a man of considerable experience before he came to Slebech. He had sailed in the flagship of Sebastian Cabot on the expedition to Brazil in 1526 and, had not the death of Henry VIII intervened, he would have set out from Milford Haven on a voyage to seek a northern passage to the East Indies. He had presented the King with the project in his *Brief Summe of Geographie*, which included a translation of Encisco's *Suma de Geographia* and which he had written at Slebech. It is claimed that he was the first Englishman to set foot in the Argentine.

His brother, William Barlow, was appointed Prior of Haverfordwest on the recommendation of Anne Boleyn as the Marquess of Pembroke, and he later became the rather infamous Bishop of St David's.

The last of the Barlows left an only daughter, who married, in 1773, John Symmons of Llanstinan, near Fishguard. Symmons razed the house of the Barlows to the ground and built the present house at Slebech. He had overstretched his purse in doing so, however, and was forced to sell his estate, in 1783, to William Knox, who had been Under-Secretary for America under Lord Shelburne. In 1792 Slebech was purchased by Nathaniel Phillips, who owned considerable sugar plantations in Jamaica. At the age of sixty he married a young lady of nineteen, and lived another twenty-three years. One of the daughters of this marriage became the Countess of Lichfield, while the eldest married the Baron de Rutzen, whose title had been granted to his ancestor by Ladislas IV of Poland.

John Frederick Foley de Rutzen, the last Baron, married Sheila, the daughter of Sir Erasmus Philipps of Picton Castle, and was killed in action in 1944 while serving with the Welsh Guards in Italy. His widow, who married Randal Plunkett, later Lord Dunsany, sold Slebech to William Speke Philipps, son of Lord Milford, whose widow is the present owner.

No trace of the Commandery remains, and its church was allowed to become a ruin by the first Baron. Within its walls lie buried Sir William Hamilton and his first wife, Catherine Barlow. A service is held annually, on the Sunday nearest to the Feast of St John, by the Order of St John of Jerusalem.

In 1838 the first Baroness de Rutzen persuaded Queen Adelaide, the widow of William IV, to head a list of subscribers towards building a new church, dedicated to St John, on the main road to Haverfordwest, but she and her husband met most of the cost. Effigies which may be of Sir William Wogan and his wife, Margaret, daughter of Sir Dafydd Gam, were removed there from the old church. The arms of the de Rutzens are displayed over the entrance to the church, and the royal arms over the chancel arch.

Canaston Bridge crosses the Eastern Cleddau where the river ceases to be tidal. It was here, it is maintained, that the bluestone boulders, which men had hauled on dry-ground sledges from the summits of the Presely Hills, were transferred onto dug-out canoes, lashed together, and punted down river to the deeper waters of Milford Haven, where they were placed on sea-going rafts that carried them across the Bristol Channel and up the Bristol Avon before they were lugged overland again, to their final destination at Stonehenge.

Deep in Canaston Wood are the remains of a moated house, marked on the Ordnance Sheet as Castell Coch and described, in 1613, when it was the seat of Philip FitzPhilip, as 'Newhouse alias Redcastle'. It had a large hall, in the corner of which a circular staircase led to an upper storey, and an adjoining kitchen with a great fireplace in its partition wall. When the need for defence had diminished, a roadway was built across the moat. In a nearby field, above Pen-glyn brook, are the scanty ruins of a church, now merely the haunt of owls and jackdaws.

A hoard of Roman coins, of the third century AD, weighing a hundredweight and buried in a skin, was found at Newton Farm in 1857, on land belonging to the Baron de Rutzen. The Baron gave the finder a cow for his treasure trove.

The remote free chapel of 'St Michael's alias Monkton', now Mounton, was a small edifice with no font which served those who worked in the forest or on the upland pastures.

The road from Canaston Bridge to Minwear runs through varied woodland past Blackpool Mill, which was built where there was previously an iron forge, in 1813, with a horizontal millwheel driving stones for barley, wheat and maize. Grain-laden schooners, carrying up to eighty tons, were able to tie up at the mill, which continued to function until 1945. It has been renovated and is now a craft centre. The picturesque bridge beside the mill was raised by the Baroness de Rutzen in 1830.

Minwear church was granted in the middle of the twelfth century to the Commandery of the Knights of St John of Jerusalem at Slebech, across the river. Not even the font of that building has survived but another has taken its place, in the present church, decorated with four human heads and cartouches upon which it may have been intended to inscribe the names of the four evangelists which the heads are considered to represent.

On the river bank, opposite the Commandery but lost in a dense thicket, are the remains of the Sisters' House, so called in a

Patent Roll of 1546. The building was about a hundred feet in length and had no fireplace or chimney, no window or stair, and is considered to have been a hostel for female pilgrims to St David's. After the dissolution of the monasteries it came into the possession of Roger and Thomas Barlow of Slebech, along with the manor of Minwear.

The bellcoted church at Martletwy is dedicated to St Marcellus although it is thought that the original dedication was to St Martin. The broken effigy of a tonsured priest of the early fifteenth century, now set in the west wall of the chancel, is faintly inscribed to the memory of one Sir Philip Rhys. The church was granted to the Slebech Commandery by Raymond FitzMartin.

In a field known as Hallwalls, just south of the church, are traces of a medieval building said locally to be those of 'the squire's house'.

Landshipping stands at the dead end of a road that led to a ferry across the Eastern Cleddau. When the last ferryman put up his oars, Landshipping became isolated and approachable only along a narrow, winding lane. Although the name is derived from 'long shippen' (cowshed), Landshipping was a centre of coal mining and coal exporting. The colliery was closed in 1788 on the orders of Colonel John Colby, the rapacious administrator of the Orielton estate during the minority of Sir Hugh Owen, but it was reopened in the following year as a result of local pressure. The first steam engine to be used in a Pembrokeshire coalfield was installed here, by Sir Hugh Owen, in 1800 at a cost of £1,900 and was employed to great advantage, for in the following year 10,912 tons of coal were exported. In 1844 disaster struck when the tide broke into the workings of the Garden Pit and forty-two miners were drowned. 'They're down there, poor beggars,' old Tom Scourfield told me, whose father remembered the time, 'shovels an' all!' The colliery was abandoned, leaving scarred land surfaces and ruined quays on the riverside.

The 'respected old mansion' at Landshipping, where Sir William Owen of Orielton spent much of his time, was neglected after his death in 1781. His son, Sir Hugh, died five years later, leaving a four-year-old son, another Sir Hugh, to succeed him to the considerable Orielton estates, which included Landshipping and suffered from the maladministration of the trustees during the boy's minority. In 1789 the sum of £210 was spent on repairs to Landshipping House and outbuildings, but a few months later Lady Owen, the boy's mother, who spent most of her time in London and Bath, ordered that the house should be closed and the furniture covered in dust sheets. It was never lived in again, and by 1810 it was roofless and fast becoming the ruin it is today.

Lawrenny is reached by lanes that snake their way through pleasantly wooded countryside, or by water. Lawrenny Quay stands at the confluence of the Cleddau and Carew rivers and was once busy as a port exporting coal, limestone, corn and oysters. Sixty vessels were built here during the first half of the last century. Today it is a haven for those who sail for pleasure. Above the road leading to the quay, flanked on the river side by ancient oaks, twisted by time and tempest, on an eminence, stood the house of the Barlow family, 'a tall cube and in its external as to form not much entitled to admiration, yet is within disposed of with much taste and convenience'. Here, in 1800, lived Hugh Barlow, Member of Parliament for Pembrokeshire, who owned a coalmine at Cresswell. The house boasted 'a park well stocked with venison, extensive and well managed hot-houses, and has the command of fish'. A castellated building was erected in place of the 'cube-house' in the nineteenth century, but it was taken down after the last war.

The palace at Cresswell, a residence of William Barlow, Bishop of St David's (1536-48), had a round turret at each of its four angles, one of which was used as a dovecote. It had a garden reaching down to the banks of the Cresswell river and a fishpond supplied with water from a well called Christ's Well. Beside the well stood Christ's Well Chapel. The Barlows abandoned Cresswell during the seventeenth century and moved to Lawrenny. Cresswell Quay exported anthracite coal from the nearby colliery.

Limestone has been quarried at West Williamstone from 1500, if not earlier, and taken by lighters along deep canals to Lawrenny for export to north Pembrokeshire and elsewhere. The Haven forts were built of stone quarried here, as were the warehouses on the Old Quay at Haverfordwest.

Carew Castle was established, at the navigable limit of the Carew river, by Gerald de Windsor, the custodian of Pembroke Castle, but there is no written reference to it until the year 1212, when King John seized 'the house of Carrio', then in the possession of William de Carew, great-grandson of Gerald. The earliest remains date from the twelfth or early thirteenth century. The chapel tower, with the adjoining hall, and the south-east tower, near the entrance, were built around 1280, while the great hall and western towers were erected before 1320 to provide a fortified residence for Sir Nicholas de Carew.

Gerald de Windsor had married the beautiful and prolific Nest, 'the Helen of Wales', daughter of Prince Rhys ap Tewdwr and progenitrix of Henry FitzHenry, by King Henry I, of the FitzStephens, by Stephen, castellan of Cardigan, and, by Gerald, of the FitzGeralds, the Carews and the de Barris, among others.

The Carew family occupied the castle until about 1480 when Sir Edmund Carew disposed of it to Sir Rhys ap Thomas, who rebuilt the outer gatehouse and generally enhanced the magnificence of the building. He held a tournament there in 1507, to celebrate the bestowal upon him of the Order of Knighthood of the Garter by King Henry VII.

The tournament was one of the most spectacular events in Welsh history. Knights and 'men of prime rank', gathered from all parts of the Principality, joined in the celebration, which lasted for five days. The first day was spent in 'choosing out five hundred of the tallest and ablest men', and the second in 'exercising them in all pointes'. On the third day the party visited the Bishop of St David's at his palace at Lamphey, where they were entertained, and they returned with the Bishop and his entourage in readiness for the tournament to be held on the morrow. There Sir Rhys, arrayed in fine gilded armour, with his heralds and trumpeters in attendance, acted as umpire and saw to it that visiting jousting knights did not lose. The last day was spent in the chase and in feasting and carousing. A chronicler of the time thought it worth recording that 'there was not a quarrel, cross word or unkind look that happened between them' throughout the celebration, 'such care Sir Rhys had taken ...'.

Sir Rhys's grandson, Sir Rhys ap Gruffydd, however, was attainted for treason and beheaded in 1531. Carew reverted to the Crown and was granted, in 1558, to Sir John Perrot of Haroldston. Sir John built the great Elizabethan block, with its mullioned windows and projecting oriels overlooking the estuary.

He brought a piped water supply to the castle, furnished it with damasks, Irish rugs and Turkish carpets, stocked its library with learned books in several languages and introduced all manner of musical instruments. When he was condemned to death for treason, but died in the Tower in 1592 before sentence could be carried out, Carew again reverted to the Crown, and in 1597 it was bestowed by Queen Elizabeth on Robert Devereux, Earl of Essex. Four years later, he was executed for treason, and the castle was leased to Sir John Carew, who had married a Courtenay heiress and had settled at Crowcombe in Somerset. In 1619 the tenancy was granted to Sir John Philipps of Picton Castle but during the Civil War it was garrisoned for the King by the Earl of Carbery and held against a siege in 1644 and again in the following year, when the south wall was destroyed. It later came into the possession of the Carews of Crowcombe.

The high cross of Carew stands on the side of the road, near the entrance to the castle. It is decorated with plaits and knotwork and a swastika pattern, in a manner similar to the Nevern cross. On the front of the monument is a double panel on one half of which is inscribed *Margiteut rex Etg. fili* – 'Maredudd the King, son of Edwin'. Maredudd was a descendant of Hywel Dda, King of the west Wales kingdom of Deheubarth, and he and his brother, Hywel ab Edwin, obtained possession of that kingdom in 1033, but two years later Maredudd was killed by the sons of Cynan; the vacant half of the panel may have been intended to commemorate his brother.

Carew Mill, generally known as the French Mill, is the only tidal mill that remains intact in Wales. It is powered by water, stored at flood tide above the causeway that forms a dam across the estuary, and released through sluices to drive two undershot mill wheels. It was leased in Elizabethan times to one John Bartlett at a yearly rental of 10 sovereigns, and it continued to grind corn up to 1937. During the nineteenth century, bones were ground in a mill adjoining the grist-mill, to make bone fertilizer, but maggots found their way from the bones to the flour, despite the installation of double steel doors. In 1804 the mill was leased for 16 guineas per annum and four fat hens at Christmastide. It was restored in 1972 and is open to the public.

The parish church at Carew Cheriton – or Carew Churchton, as it was originally – has a fine tower, with a corner steeple, that is visible from afar. It contains monuments, with effigies, of members of the Carew family, including one to Sir John Carew, who died in 1637, and his wife, Elizabeth, sons and daughters, and one to another Carew and his wife. These monuments are duplicated in the Carew chapel at Camerton in Somerset. An effigy of a little girl, with her hands enfolding a heart, is of the early fourteenth century and was formerly believed to represent 'a boy bishop'.

The chapel in the churchyard may be older than the church and was originally an ossuary but was used as a school in the seventeenth and eighteenth centuries. The tomb of William Francis, who promoted cockfights at the cockpit at Well Hay and who died in 1827, is inscribed:

There now he lies in lasting rest.
Perhaps upon his moulding breast
Some spiteful fowl builds her nest
To hatch and breed.
Alas! No more he'll them molest.

When Sir Thomas Malefant was buried at St Bartholomew-the-Less in Smithfield, London, the epitaph on his tomb described him as 'Sir Thomas Malifant or Naufant, Baron of Wenvoe, Lord of St George in Glamorgan, and Lord of Ockeneton and Pill in the county of Pembroke, 1438.' Ockeneton, or Ucton, was the old name for Upton where Walter Malefant built a castle at the end of the thirteenth century. Alice, daughter of the last of the Malefants, married Owen, the son of Gruffudd ap Nicholas of Dinefwr, and their descendant Rhys ab Owen adopted the name Bowen, after the English manner, in 1564. Upton remained in the Bowen family until the latter part of the eighteenth century, when it was purchased by John Tasker, who had made his fortune in India. He died a bachelor and left Upton to his niece and her husband, the Reverend William Evans, whose descendant sold it, in 1927, to Stanley Neale, a trawler owner and a keen naturalist. He landscaped the castle grounds and planted them with exotic shrubs and trees. Camellias, magnolias and rhododendrons run riot in springtime; outstanding among them is the towering *Magnolia Campbellii* planted to commemorate the coronation of King George VI in 1937. The grounds are now managed by the

Pembrokeshire Coast National Park Committee by arrangement with the present owners, and are open to the public on certain days.

A small chapel, standing close to the castle, has effigies among which may be those of a later Walter Malefant, who died in 1362, and his wife, Margaret Fleming. An unusual taper-holder, in the shape of a clenched fist, is set in a wall.

The village of Cosheston was originally a ribbon of farmhouses on the English manorial pattern, but it took its name from Cystennin (Constantine), maybe he of that name who was the son of Erbin, a prince of Dyfed.

14

Pembroke

Pembrokeshire, 'the premier county of Wales', was so called because the domain of Gilbert de Clare, when he was made Earl of Pembroke in 1138, became a county palatinate, in which the Earl had quasi-royal jurisdiction. Cheshire, Durham and Lancaster still retain such a title, but Shropshire, Kent, Hexhamshire and the Isle of Ely have lost the designation, and their jurisdiction is vested in the Crown. In the case of Pembroke, the palatinate ceased to exist when the county palatine was combined with other lordships, under the Act of Union of England and Wales in 1536, to form the new county of Pembrokeshire.

The old Welsh name *Pen-brog*, meaning 'land's end', has become *Penfro* in accordance with the laws of mutation in the Welsh language, whereas the English form *Pembroke* has more closely retained the original enunciation.

Pembroke's past is well represented on its coat-of-arms – the chevrons of Strongbow and a bordure of martlets of Valence, supported by the red lion of the Marshals and the white lion of the Herberts each gorged with a naval crown to denote the dockyard and charged with the portcullis and Tudor rose badges of Henry VII. The dockyard is now partly developed as an industrial estate, and a part is now the new base for the B & I ferry to Ireland. Pembroke itself rests on its reputation as a historic town to which people travel from afar to visit one of the finest castles in the kingdom within the walls of which the founder of the Tudor dynasty first saw the light of day.

The town lies along a narrow limestone ridge, at the end of which a castle, 'a slender fortress of stakes and turf', was built in 1093. Roger de Montgomery, Earl of Shrewsbury, close upon the death of the powerful Prince Rhys ap Tewdwr, swept across

Wales, through Ceredigion and on to Pembroke, along with his son, Arnulf, but they soon retired, leaving their castle in the custody of Gerald de Windsor, son of Walter FitzOther, custodian of Windsor. Gerald had to face a formidable attack by the Welsh, under Uchtryd ab Edwin and Hywel ap Gronw, in the following year. The castle was closely beset but Gerald was able to confound the besiegers by deliberately losing a letter stating that he did not require reinforcements, and by throwing over the castle fence his last flitches of bacon so as to make them believe that he had enough food to withstand a long beleaguerment. The gullible Welsh withdrew, and one might say that 'Little England beyond Wales' was born that day. When the Montgomerys fell out of royal favour in 1102, Gerald held Pembroke for the King, Henry I, but his successor on the throne, Stephen, granted it to Gilbert de Clare, whom he created Earl of Pembroke.

Gilbert's son, Richard de Clare, succeeded in 1148 and, in response to a request for help from Dermot McMurrough, the usurped King of Leinster, led an invasion of Ireland; as a reward, he received the hand of Eva, Dermot's daughter and heiress, in marriage. For the next two centuries, the earldom passed by marriage to the families of Marshal, Munchensy, de Valence and Hastings, until John Hastings died without heirs in 1389 and in 1397 Richard II presented Pembroke to his queen, Isabel.

Henry VI created his half-brother, Jasper Tudor, Earl of Pembroke, who brought his fifteen-year-old sister-in-law, Margaret Beaufort, there to be under his protection while her husband Edmund Tudor, Earl of Richmond, was fighting in the Wars of the Roses. Edmund died at Carmarthen in 1456 and his son, Henry Tudor, was born posthumously at Pembroke Castle on 28 January, a cold winter's day, in the following year.

Henry VI, on his readeption in 1470, had declared, on seeing the boy Henry Tudor, that 'this is he unto whom both we and our adversaries must yield and give over the dominion', and with the fall of the Lancastrian line following their defeat at Tewkesbury, Henry became the true heir of the House of Lancaster. It was no longer safe for him to remain in this country and so he was taken by Jasper to Tenby, where they set sail, in a ship provided by the mayor, Thomas White, and sought refuge in Brittany. On Christmas Eve 1483, Henry Tudor swore a solemn oath at the high altar of Rennes Cathedral that, after defeating the usurper

Richard, he would marry Elizabeth, heiress of the House of York, and so unite the white rose with the red. He returned to Pembrokeshire in August 1485 and attracted a great following, his just cause having been widely proclaimed by the Welsh bards. After a brief encounter at Bosworth, Richard was toppled from his horse and Henry became king, making the red dragon of Cadwaladr, along with the lion of England, a supporter of his royal arms.

When William Herbert of Raglan was appointed Earl of Pembroke in 1461, he was the first Welshman to receive an earldom. Jasper was restored in 1469, but after his death the title was vested in the Crown. Henry VII conferred it on his son Henry, who in 1533 created his wife, Anne Boleyn, the Marquess of Pembroke.

During the Civil War, Pembroke was the main stronghold of the Parliamentary forces in West Wales, but in 1648 John Poyer, Mayor of Pembroke, declared for the King, fortified and provisioned the castle and appointed himself its governor. On 24 May Oliver Cromwell appeared before Pembroke and directed a siege that lasted forty-eight days, during which damage was done to the Barbican, the Bygate and the Henry VII and Westgate Towers. Colonel Poyer, Major-General Rowland Laugharne and Colonel Rice Powell were sent to the Tower of London and sentenced to death for treason, but the Protector decreed that it would be sufficient for one to die. Three bits of paper were placed in a hat, two inscribed 'Life Given of God' and the third left blank, and a child was made to draw the lot. The blank fell on Colonel Poyer, and he was shot at Covent Garden on 25 April 1649.

Cromwell ordered the destruction of the castle, which was only partially successful, but steady pilfering occurred over the next two hundred years until J.R. Cobb, of Brecon and Manorbier, undertook some restoration work in 1880. It was again neglected until 1928, when it came into the possession of Major-General Sir Ivor Philipps of Cosheston Hall who removed ivy from the walls and undergrowth from the ward, and largely restored the castle to its present splendid condition.

The entrance to the castle is by the Barbican Gate, and to the left is the tower in which Henry VII is believed to have been born. By the Monkton Tower is the Water Port through which a water supply was brought by earthenware pipes, and beyond it the Western Hall and the Chapel. On the north-east side are the Norman and Northern Halls, standing over 'the Wogan', a natural cavern in the limestone rock from which a ditch ran down to the Pembroke River. Adjoining the Norman Hall are the Chancery, the Oriel and the Dungeon Tower. The Great Keep, one of the finest of its kind in Britain, was built by William Marshal, who held the earldom from 1189 to 1219; it stands over a hundred feet high, commanding an extensive view over the surrounding countryside. The town walls, built in the thirteenth century, were protected on the north by the tidal river and on the south by marshy ground, and were pierced by three gates, Northgate at Mill Bridge, Eastgate on the road to Lamphey, and Westgate, a fragment of which remains on Monkton Hill.

Monkton Priory was originally a cell of the abbey of Séez in Normandy, the gift of Arnulf de Montgomery, along with twenty carucates of land. Its remains, including a dovecote, are partly incorporated in Priory Farm, while the choir and sanctuary form part of the chancel of the parish church, which was restored in 1887. The church contains monuments to the Meyricks of Bush and the Owens of Orielton. Dorothy Owen, who 'caused a monument to be erected' to her husband John Owen, also wished it to be known that 'Dorothy the rayser of this monument was interred here the 27th of February 1635 aged 70 years having through God's Providence and her own goodness erected a more lasting monument of her memory in that she lived a widow above 41 years, and leaving all her 7 children, being all that she ever had.'

When John Wesley visited Pembroke in 1764 he had arranged to preach at St Mary's Church but the mayor, Josiah Evans, 'sent to forbid it'. The people, however, he found 'elegant and genteel', although he must have been unprepared to find that the vicar of St Daniel's was also named John Wesley.

John Owen, born in Pembroke in 1833, became rector of East Anstey, in Devon. He was especially interested in free thought, which he called 'skepticism', and between 1891 and 1896 he published *Evenings with the Skeptics, The Skeptics of the Italian Renaissance, The Skeptics of the French Renaissance* and *The Five Great Skeptical Dramas of History.*

'The black snake among the rabbits' was Napoleon III's

description of HMS *Warrior*, which for fifty years was berthed in the Haven, below Llanion. When launched at Blackwell in 1860, she was the largest, fastest and most powerful vessel ever built, and the first iron-clad, sheathed in $4\frac{1}{2}$-inch armour plating backed by teak timbers two foot thick, with seven- and eight-inch muzzle-loading rifled guns. Yet she did not once fire a shot in anger, nor could she claim any hour of glory save to act as escort for the royal yacht bringing the Princess Alexandra from Denmark to become Princess of Wales and, later, Queen. *Warrior* was paid off as a sea-going ship in 1884, and in 1900 she became a torpedo ship based at Portsmouth. In 1929 she was brought to serve as a floating jetty for tankers berthing at the Llanion oil-fuel depot, and there she remained until she was taken to Hartlepool to be restored to her former grandeur, and then to Portsmouth to lie alongside Nelson's *Victory* and the Tudor warship *Mary Rose*.

The Welsh Triads relate how Henwen, the sow of Dallwyr, took to the water at Penrhyn Awst (Aust) and landed at Llanion where she 'deposited a grain of barley ... whence Llanion is the best place for barley, and the barley of Llanion has passed into a proverb'.

Pembroke Dock came into existence when the Admiralty decided, in 1814, to move the naval dockyard across the haven from Milford to Paterchurch, formerly the hamlet of Patrickchurch. For a century and more, the dockyard flourished and in it were built some 260 ships, which included the first steam man-of-war, HMS *Tartar*, the first propellor-driven warship, HMS *Conflict*, and the first of several royal yachts, the *Victoria and Albert*, in 1843. HMS *Windsor Castle* was launched on 14 September 1852, and when it became known that the Duke of Wellington had died that day, its name was changed in his honour, and another *Windsor Castle*, of 116 guns, was built in its place. HMS *Duke of Wellington* was the flagship of Admiral Napier during the Crimean War and led the grand review of the Fleet by Queen Victoria in 1855. The last ship built at Pembroke Dock was the *Oleander*, launched in 1922, and four years later the dockyard was closed. In 1930 the Royal Air Force established a seaplane base there, which during the war became the home of the Sunderland flying-boats. Early in 1944 I flew from the Dead Sea and landed on the Nile in a Sunderland that was bound from

Rangoon to Pembroke Dock and, having served with the Army in the Middle East for over four years, I was sorely tempted to remain on board as a stowaway.

The 'martello' towers were built, fifty years later than the original versions that were erected along the Channel coast against Napoleon, to provide an inner defence for the dockyard in support of the Pater battery.

The pier and landing at Hobbs Point, so named after one Nicholas Hobbs, were built of stone shipped from Cornwall, in 1831, to attract the packet service from Ireland. A Royal Mail coach, drawn by four horses, left Hobbs Point for Gloucester at five o'clock each morning, to catch the train from there to London, until 1856, when the railway came to Neyland.

Where the road forks at the Speculation Inn – 'the Spec' to the locals – there is a cluster of round barrows where those who could make it no further along this road in Bronze Age times were buried by their fellow travellers in accordance with the ritual of the period. Cinerary urns were found within the mounds, and the charcoal used to reduce the bodies to ashes, and some white quartz stones such as you will find on graves in country churchyards to this day. A Beaker man was buried at Corston Beacon with a riveted bronze knife-dagger at his side. A stone circle at Pennybridge was grubbed up by an ignorant farmer and its pillars placed along a hedgerow.

The mansion house of Orielton has as many windows as there are days in the year and as many doors as the month has days. The present house was built in 1743 on the site of an earlier foundation, probably established by the Wyrriotts in the twelfth century. In the house of Stephen Wyrriott, Giraldus reports, 'unclean spirits have conversed with mankind', upbraiding people with 'everything they had done from their birth': even 'the priests themselves, though protected by the crucifix, or the holy water', were not immune.

Henry Wyrriott had his own army which he took, in 1513, to join Sir Rhys ap Thomas in support of King Henry VIII at the Battle of the Spurs in France. George Wyrriott, who was sheriff in 1577, had an only daughter, who married Sir Hugh Owen, son of Owen ap Hugh of Bodowen, in Anglesey. The Owens of Orielton played a leading role in the life of the county for three centuries to come and served as Sheriffs, Lords Lieutenant and Members of Parliament.

Sir Arthur Owen is said to have galloped the 250 miles to London to cast a decisive vote for the Whigs, in the House of Commons, against the Tory amendment to the Adjuration Bill that required Members of Parliament and holders of public office to renounce the Stuart succession, and was thus credited with having secured the throne for the Hanoverians, so that 'not a mouse stirred' when George I arrived in his barge at the steps in Greenwich in a swirling fog.

Sir John Owen, who had been Tory member for Pembrokeshire since 1812, fought an election in 1831 which *The Times* described as the most bitterly contested in the United Kingdom. He had voted against the Reform Bill and put himself out of favour with his constituents. The candidate chosen to oppose him was Robert Fulke Greville, and at the end of a fifteen-day election Sir John was declared elected by a majority of ninety-nine votes. Greville objected to the conduct of the election, and another was held, on the ninth day of which he conceded victory to Sir John, but the bitterness engendered during the elections continued and led to three challenges to duels, in two of which honour was satisfied. The innkeepers of Haverfordwest submitted bills totalling more than £15,000 for food and drink supplied to the electors, but Greville denied responsibility for his share. Mrs Sally Williams of 'The Mariners', where he had his headquarters, sued him for the sum of £1,878, but he fled the country and did not return for twenty years; he died a poor man, at Milford, in 1867. Sir John Owen fared little better. The Orielton estate had already suffered through corruption during the minority of Sir Hugh Owen, who inherited in 1786, and the consequential proceedings in Chancery. Sir John had to mortgage his estate and went abroad to avoid his creditors. In 1857 Orielton, home of the Wyrriotts and the Owens for seven centuries, was sold. A century later, in 1954, the house was purchased by R.M. Lockley, who has told its story in his book *Orielton* and whose study of rabbits there, published in his *Private Life of the Rabbit*, later inspired Richard Adams to write *Watership Down*. The house is now a Field Study Centre of the Field Studies Council.

The rurality of Rhoscrowther suffered a change with the coming of the oil installations in the early sixties. The British Petroleum Ocean Terminal was opened by Queen Elizabeth the Queen Mother in 1961, with its control centre cleverly concealed within the walls of the Victorian fort at Popton. The storage tanks were sited at Kilpaison, on Angle Bay, and the oil was pumped along sixty miles of buried pipeline to the refinery at Llandarcy, near Swansea. The Texaco oil refinery came on stream three years later, and it has since been enlarged and modernized. Each has a jetty to provide berths for vessels of a quarter of a million tons.

The parish church, dedicated to St Decuman, was one of 'the seven bishop's houses of Dyfed'. It is of Norman origin with a corbelled tower and a steeple, and above the doorway is a small panel with a figure of the risen Christ with wounded hands raised. A tablet in the chancel commemorates Edward Skinner who met an untimely end nearby, on HMS *Iphigenia*, in 1792.

The fifteenth-century rectangular towered bastle-house at Eastington may have been fortified against pirates. The house takes its name from one Iestyn, who may have been of the line of Erbin, a prince of Dyfed.

A Bronze Age barrow exposed during a storm on Kilpaison Burrows was originally raised over the body of a young woman who died around 1500 BC, but it was used on no less than six other occasions for cremation burials and much later for a Christian burial. A stone standing at the centre of the mound suggests the survival of the megalithic tradition into the Bronze Age.

Pwllcrochan churchyard was the scene of a skirmish when two Royalist companies were surprised, the day after they had landed from Bristol, by Parliament troops. They stood their ground but after a while were allowed to march away with their arms and embark for Cardiff, on condition that they would not return. Two dozen cannon balls were found, offshore, by frogmen during the building of the Pembroke power station.

The power station, when completed in 1975 at a cost of over £100 million, was one of the largest in Europe. It burns four million tons of oil each year, which is brought by pipeline from the nearby refineries, and its output is carried away by 400 kV power lines across the country to Bristol and the Midlands.

An effigy in the parish church, of Ralph Beneger, in canonical habit, records that he rebuilt the church in 1342. The Benegers were of Benegerston, now Bangeston, a house near Pembroke.

'Skirting the bay of Nangle, I came to the village of that name, so called from being, as it were, *in angulo*, in a nook,' wrote Richard Fenton in 1811. But Nangle no longer affects the initial *n* which it gathered by following the preposition *in*, in contrast to Ash and Arberth, which continue as Nash and Narberth.

Angle's one street is gay with colour-washed cottages, pink and orange and, at one time, a morning-glory blue that was obtained by putting soot in the limewash. Its colonnaded hostelry has a spiral staircase. In the churchyard is a small fishermen's chapel, with a priestly effigy, and separated from it at high tide is a moated enclosure with the shell of a pele tower standing, and the vaulted undercroft of another. It is believed to have been the residence of the Sherbornes, lords of the manor, the heiress of which family married Robert Cradock, whose descendant Sir Richard Newton Cradock was Chief Justice of the Common Pleas. He died in 1444 and lies buried in Bristol Cathedral.

Across the creek from the village, on the path leading to the Angle lifeboat station, is the Point Inn where I was shown a culm fire that had burned for over a hundred years. Culm, or anthracite dust, was mixed with pounded clay and water, handfuls of which were made into wet, oval 'balls' and placed on the fire, except for the last thing at night when it was put on with a special shovel and a hole made for the flame to come through. The fire was never allowed to go out, and if perchance it did, fire was 'borrowed' from a neighbour, for if it were kindled otherwise, bad luck would follow. The custom is commemorated in an old Welsh nursery rhyme:

Pwsi meri mew
Gollodd ei blew
Wrth fenthyca tân
O tŷ draw.

(Pussy Miaow burnt its fur while borrowing fire from another house.)

A small chapel stood above Chapel Bay, and another, dedicated to St Anthony, on the shore of West Angle Bay, was raised by the missionary saints who had travelled westward along the Ridgeway, here to take to their frail craft to cross to Ireland.

Sheep Island, 'insulated at full sea', was used by the Normans, it is said, as a retreat for themselves and their cattle from the fury of the Welsh. Overlooking Rat Island are the remains of East Blockhouse, built in 1580 against 'the hand of war' and the activities of smugglers and pirates. George Clerk, the customs man at Pembroke, owned a tavern at Angle which was openly patronized by John Callice and other notorious pirates.

A calvary to commemorate those who fell in the Great War stands over Freshwater West beach, with its long stretch of golden sand and ever-rolling but notoriously dangerous sea. A submerged forest occasionally appears at low tide, and quantities of flint flakes indicate a mesolithic settlement here. In the burrows behind the beach are the Devil's Quoit burial chamber and a number of Bronze Age barrows, while there are Iron Age promontory forts at West Pickard and Castles Head. A leaden tablet bearing an embossed dragon found at Freshwater West is the only artefact left by the Norse along the coasts of Pembrokeshire.

Low driftwood huts thatched with rushes provided storage for the brownish-purple seaweed *Porphyra* which was gathered off the rocks at low tide and spread on the floor of the huts to dry before being sent to Swansea to be made into *bara lawr*, or laverbread. Laverbread rolled in oatmeal and fried with bacon was a highly nutritious item in the diet of the Rhondda coal-miners and is nowadays counted a delicacy, although one has to acquire a taste for this 'Welsh caviare'.

The coast from Linney Head to Lydstep is of considerable interest to geologists, archaeologists, naturalists and those who have an eye for beauty, alike.

The WNW-ESE trend of the rocks was produced by the Armorican earth movement at the end of the Carboniferous period, 250 million years ago, that squeezed the south of the peninsula up against that part, to the north, which had already been settled by the Caledonian movement. The land surface was levelled by the sea, which flowed over it some seventeen million years ago, leaving a 200-foot flat-topped landscape which has been eroded to take its prevent form. The sea is gradually eating away the cliffs, producing caves and blowholes, arches like the Green Bridge of Wales, and stacks like the Eligug Stack.

The discovery of Ogof Gofan in 1969, and other caves nearby, provided evidence of early human settlement: the bones of animals and of people who had fashioned small flints into artefacts, and the potsherds of those who had found refuge during neolithic and Bronze Age times, and in one cave two Roman coins of the third century AD. All along the coast are skilfully sited promontory forts, at Linney Head, Flimston, Crocksydam, Buckspool, the multivallate camp at Greenala Point, and on to Freshwater East, Old Castle Head and Manorbier. These cliff castles were occupied by the natives well into the early centuries of the Christian era, and some were supplied with Roman pottery by passing traders. Inland, hill forts of the same period provided refuges at Bulliber and Merrion, and at Fishpond camp sited at Bosherston Lakes.

The castle of Castlemartin is disappointing. Here, at the *caput* of a barony held of the earldom of Pembroke, one would expect to find something more than a mound and the scant traces of a bailey.

The church, dedicated to St Michael, stands in a hollow beside the castle mound. Its tapered tower is on the south side of the nave, and its floor rises in steps past an arcade of limestone pillars with pointed arches. There is a walk-through squint to the chancel, which is dug into the slope. The organ, built in 1842, came from Sibton in Suffolk and is said to have been played by Mendelssohn on one or more of his many visits to Britain. I once had the laborious privilege of blowing the organ for Ludwig Koch, who was a celebrated musician and *lieder* singer long before he became known as a recorder of bird song, and lost some sweat while Ludwig played interminably from his fellow-countryman's organ sonatas.

The churchyard cross has been restored, and among the ivy-hung headstones Fenton noted the grave of the 104-year-old widow of one of the three Loveling rectors of the parish, whose son published a book of poems, while he was at Trinity College, Oxford, that were 'more honourable to his muse than his morals'.

Against the east side of the churchyard is a ruin, known as the Old Rectory, which has an arched fireplace and bays, and a capital with carved faces.

Where five roads meet in the village stood the Pound, no longer used for impounding stray animals but, with walls lowered, laid out as a garden, with seats for the weary traveller.

Castlemartin Blacks derive from 'the horned, coal-black Pembrokeshire cattle' improved by John Mirehouse of Brownslade and grown big on rich pasture, although I once heard a man say that a Devon bull had swum ashore from a shipwreck and crossed with the Welsh mountain cattle to produce the breed. The Castlemartins obtained their own herd book in 1874, but by today they are largely merged in the Welsh Blacks.

I was told by a British Army officer that Castlemartin had its own sub-species of horse-fly, which was attracted by the dark colours of army camouflage and descended in hordes on vehicles and on men training on the Castlemartin ranges.

Three tall-towered churches stand as landmarks on the ridgeway that extends to the sea at Furzenip. St Petrox has one of the few brasses in Pembrokeshire, commemorating William Lloyd, rector, who died in 1674. It also has a memorial to a lady whose headless ghost rides by in a carriage driven by a headless coachman and drawn by a headless horse! St Twynnell's has a churchyard cross. Warren has an octagonal steeple and barrel vaulting of the thirteenth century in its nave and south transept. On the road from Warren to Stack Rocks, accessible only when there is no firing on the Castlemartin ranges, is Flimston chapel, which has recently been restored. The claim that it had a connection with Sir Gawain of the Round Table is an offshoot of the legend attached to St Govan's Chapel. Erratic boulders in the churchyard mark the graves of members of the Lambton family.

The sea has sculptured the Eligug Stack so that it is a jagged limestone pillar, rising to a level with the cliff edge and crowned with tree mallows in summer. Eligug is a Welsh name, forgotten elsewhere, for the guillemot and, along with stacks nearby, it is thickly occupied by these birds during the brooding season. Razorbills and kittiwakes occupy fingerholds on the sheer sides of the stacks, and of recent years fulmars glide tirelessly round them. The elegant Green Bridge of Wales will, one day, be another stack.

Flimston Castle, a promontory fort, encloses the Devil's Punchbowl, a precipitous hole which connects with the sea by arches, and below it is the Danish Landing, a natural rock harbour where, according to tradition, the Vikings came ashore, but for certain used by sloops loading limestone.

Bosherston church has two female effigies, probably of the fourteenth century, and a cross of the same period stands in the churchyard, with the face of Christ at the intersection.

From the village of Bosherston the road runs to the cliff edge above St Govan's Chapel. The chapel is wedged among the rocks, half-way down the cliff: fifty-two steps lead down to it, but never the same number coming up again. It has a single chamber with an earthen floor and an altar with a cleft in the rock behind it, in which you may turn, if you can, and make a wish. St Govan hid himself here when marauders from Lundy Island came to ransack the church.

St Govan, founder of the abbey of Dairinis, near Wexford, is believed to have landed here and, having built himself a cell, to have spent the rest of his life here, in not-so-quiet contemplation, and to have been buried beneath the altar. A more romantic legend maintains that Sir Gawain turned hermit after the death of King Arthur and came here for seclusion. But the building is no older than the eleventh century. The empty bellcote held a silver bell which was stolen by pirates, but no sooner had they put to sea than their boat was wrecked. Sea-nymphs came and carried it back to the brink of a well below the chapel where it now lies entombed in a rock which, whenever struck, gives forth the tone of the silver bell.

The huntsman who spurred his horse across Huntsman's Leap foolishly returned to view the chasm and died of fright. Bosherston Mere, to the west, has two blowholes through which the sea blows its spume when sou'-westers rage, which George Owen considered to be one of 'the divers wonders of Pembrokeshire'.

Broad Haven, with its golden sands, was originally the estuary of three streams flowing past and between Bosherston and Stackpole Warren, but blown sand stood between them and the sea, and in the eighteenth century a dam was built to impound the water so as to form the long fingers of ornamental lakes that reach inland through well-wooded valleys and beside grey limestone crags. The lakes are afloat with water-lilies in early summer, and each finger is crossed by a narrow bridge, so low that one appears to walk on the water. Roach, perch and tench abound, a rudd was landed on one occasion, and there is good pike fishing.

Stackpole Warren has long been regarded as the site of 'a prehistoric village', and recent excavation by the Dyfed

Archaeological Trust has established the existence of a Bronze Age settlement and an extensive field system with traces of cultivation. Beneath a standing stone, known as the Devil's Quoit, were the burnt remains of a wooden hut with cremated human remains in the middle of the floor, and nearby were traces of a Romano-British circular hut, with fragments of Samian and other ware, spindle whorls and dumps of oyster and mussel shells. Earlier finds on the site include a bronze sword handle and a bronze harp-shaped brooch.

The Devil's Quoit and two neighbouring standing stones bearing the same name are said to come together at Sais's, or Saxon's, Ford on Midsummer's Eve to dance the hay and, by the morrow, their 'dance over, resume their stations'.

The thin tower of the church at Stackpole Cheriton, dedicated to St Elidyr, peeps over the trees from a deep valley and rises, unusually, from the north end of the north transept. In the rib-vaulted Lort chapel is an inscribed stone commemorating Camulorix, son of Fannucus, who flourished during the fifth century. The worn effigies of two fourteenth-century ladies lie on the floor. Another may be of Margaret Turberville who was married, in 1349, to Sir Richard de Stackpole, the last of that line, whose canopied tomb lies in the chancel. There is also the seventeenth-century monument, with painted kneeling figures, of Roger Lort and his wife, with their twelve children on a lower panel, and the recumbent effigy of John Frederick Campbell, the first Earl Cawdor, who died in 1860.

Stackpole takes its name from the Stack Rock, which rises like an ichthyosaurus from the bay at Broad Haven. Stackpole Quay was a quarry, the limestone from which was exported to north Pembrokeshire and elsewhere. A footpath leads from here to Barafundle Bay, which was formerly the private beach of the Cawdor family of Stackpole Court.

Stackpole Court was built on the site of the fortified dwelling of Sir Elidyr de Stackpole. In this house, Giraldus Cambrensis relates, a spirit appeared in the form of a red-head who called himself Simon and assumed the office of steward but who later confessed 'that he was begotten upon the wife of a rustic in that parish by a demon.'

After the death of Sir Richard de Stackpole the estate passed by marriage to the Vernons of Hodnet and then to the Lorts.

Henry Lort, who was sheriff in 1619, was nominated to the office again in 1639 by his enemies who wished to cause him financial embarrassment on account of his unneighbourly conduct, but his son pleaded with the Lord Chancellor, as 'our adversaries doth use what meanes they can to have him pricked for this yeare, and I verily beleeve they will prevayle unlesse by your Lordshipp's meanes it may be prevented', and enclosed a list of the 'names of sufficient gentlemen to be shiriff of Pembrookeshire' in his place. Lort was unpopular because he had sold quantities of grain to other parts of Britain at a time when an 'extraordinary dearth' obtained in Pembrokeshire, and had also converted arable land into pasture, which resulted in depopulation of the countryside and for which he had to appear before the Court of the Star Chamber, where he was fined £2,500. He had been offered a knighthood in 1630 but declined the honour and, in consequence, had to pay £100 to the Exchequer.

His son, Roger Lort, was a poet of considerable merit and author of *Epigrammatum Liber Primus*, a book of Latin epigrams, published in 1646. He served the King during the Civil War, but when Stackpole Court was taken by General Laugharne, the commander of the Parliamentary forces, in January 1644, Lort sided with the Roundheads, of whom his brother, Sampson Lort, was the leader in Pembrokeshire. He later found favour with the King, for he was created a baronet in 1662.

When Sir Gilbert Lort died without issue in 1698, the Stackpole estate passed to his sister, Elizabeth, and her husband, Alexander Campbell, son of Sir Hugh Campbell of Cawdor. Their son, John Campbell, was Member of Parliament for Pembrokeshire for a period of twenty years from 1727, during which time he served as a Commissioner of the Admiralty. He demolished the castellated building that had 'walls so strong that the ordnance did but little execution' during the Civil War, and built a more elegant Georgian residence, in 1735, with 'two fronts, the principal facing the pleasure grounds and the grand approach; the other looking over a fine piece of water'. It was set in a park 'of great compass and well stocked with deer, but wanting a belt of trees', in Fenton's opinion, 'to hide the barren sand-banks without it, and produce shelter where most wanted by breaking the sea-breeze'. The stables formed a large detached quadrangular building and were 'in a style of princely pretension'. The old village of Stackpole stood in the way of the development, and it was therefore moved, leaving the broken remains of a village cross to mark the medieval site.

John Campbell, his grandson, was elevated to the peerage in 1796 as Baron Cawdor of Castlemartin. He is best remembered as the commander of the forces arrayed against the French at Fishguard in the following February, but he was also a keen agriculturist who carried out experimental cross-breeding in order to improve his stock of horses and sheep. His son, John Frederick Campbell, was created Earl Cawdor of Castlemartin and Viscount Emlyn of Emlyn in 1827. The third earl, who became First Lord of the Admiralty, was Lord Lieutenant of Pembrokeshire, but after his death in 1911 the family had little contact with Stackpole or the county. In 1962 Viscount Emlyn, who succeeded in the earldom eight years later, demolished Stackpole Court, despite pleas for its preservation, and later sold the estate. The site of the mansion and the adjoining land, including Stackpole Warren, was handed to the Government in lieu of death duties and became the property of the National Trust.

Among the treasures at Stackpole Court was the Hirlas Horn, a drinking horn which, it was claimed, Henry Tudor had presented to Dafydd ab Ifan of Llwyndafydd in Ceredigion in return for the hospitality he had received at that house on his march to Bosworth. A variation maintains that the horn was sent as a christening present to a son born to Dafydd's daughter as a result of that royal visit, and this was confirmed to me by a lady attending a lecture I was giving on the Tudor period, who announced that she was a direct descendant of that fleeting union! The horn was sixteen inches in length, mounted in silver and supported by a dragon and a greyhound, which were the supporters of the arms of the House of Tudor, borne by Henry VII and displayed on his tomb at Westminster Abbey. It came into the possession of Richard Vaughan, the second Earl of Carbery, when he married Bridget, the daughter of Thomas Lloyd of Llanllyr, a descendant of Dafydd ab Ifan, and it was kept at Golden Grove, near Carmarthen, until it passed with the estate, under the will of John Vaughan, to the Campbells of Stackpole in 1804.

Lamphey Palace is believed to have been a retreat for the Welsh bishops of St David's before Norman times, but the oldest surviving masonry dates from the early thirteenth century, comprising the hall in the south range, to which was added the bishop's camera, bedroom and garderobe.

By 1326 Bishop David Martin was able to relax among orchards and gardens and beside fishponds and watermills, a windmill and a dovecote, in a comfortable building set in a park in which roamed a herd of sixty deer, but the palace reached its splendour during the bishopric of William Gower (1328-47), the builder of the bishop's palace at St David's. In 1507 Sir Rhys ap Thomas brought the great party of knights and gentlemen that he had assembled at Carew Castle for his famous tournament, to Lamphey Palace, where they were entertained by Bishop Sherborne, who had with him the Abbot of Talley and the Prior of Carmarthen.

At the dissolution of the monasteries, the manor of Lamphey was granted to Richard Devereux, whose son, Walter, was created Earl of Essex. Walter's son, Robert, Earl of Essex, the favourite of Queen Elizabeth, spent his youth at Lamphey, and after his execution the building was left to decay until it was acquired by the Owens of Orielton. In 1821 it was purchased by Charles Delamotte Mathias of Llangwarren who had inherited a fortune from his aunt, the wife of William Smalling, a German Moravian who owned extensive plantations in Jamaica. Mathias built Lamphey Court, a fine Georgian house in classical style, which remained in the family until recently, when it was converted into a country hotel.

The ruins comprise a *camera*, which served as the bishop's private apartment, a hall and a great hall with garderobes, a chapel and a gatehouse. The palace passed into the care of the Ministry of Works in 1925.

The small village green of Hodgeston has the remains of a moat adjoining, within which stood a small building until it was removed about 1870. The church has a tower with a plain corbelled parapet, and in its chancel, rebuilt in the fourteenth century, is a triple sedilia and a double piscina with decorated work, flanked on either side by stone benches. In 1851 the building was in 'a state of extreme dilapidation' with windows blocked and the roof 'in a condition of complete decay', but it has been well and tastefully restored. It has the oldest Elizabethan eucharistic vessels in Pembrokeshire, with chalice and patten both restored in 1880. A pewter plate is roughly scratched 'Hotson 1786': the place is still known locally as 'Hotson'.

Thomas Young, born at Hodgeston in 1507, returned as rector in 1542 after having graduated at Oxford as a Master of Arts and Bachelor of Common Law. He came into conflict with Robert Ferrar, Bishop of St David's, and was a leader of the faction opposed to him, leading to the bishop's imprisonment for heresy and death at the stake on the Market Square in Carmarthen. Young is believed to have gone into exile during the reign of Queen Mary, but by 1559 he had returned and was appointed Bishop of St David's. Two years later he was elected Archbishop of York; he died in 1568 and was buried in York Minster.

15

The Manor and Island of Pŷr

'The Castle of Manorbier', wrote Giraldus Cambrensis in 1188, 'is excellently well defended by turrets and bulwarks, and is situated on the summit of a hill extending on the western side towards the sea-port, having on the northern and southern sides a fine fish-pond under its walls, as conspicuous for its grand appearance as for the depth of its waters, and a beautiful orchard on the same side, inclosed on one part by a vineyard, and on the other by a wood, remarkable for the projection of its rocks and the height of its hazel trees.' The vineyard and the orchard and the fishpond have long since vanished, but the walls of the castle stand obstinately dignified, overlooking the bay.

Within a roughly rectangular inner ward, the square tower by the gatehouse and the hall block belong to the middle of the twelfth century, while the curtain wall, with its towers on the north and south-east angles, represent a strengthening of the defences around 1230. A modern residence was built inside the gate by J.R. Cobb, who leased the castle in 1880.

The castle was originally built by Odo de Barri, whose son, William de Barri, married Angharad, the daughter of Gerald de Windsor by his wife, Nest, daughter of Prince Rhys ap Tewdwr. The last of the de Barri family died in 1359, and after a period of confusion the castle was vested in the Crown and leased to a succession of tenants before it was purchased by Thomas Bowen of Trefloyne, near Tenby. In 1670 it was purchased by Sir Erasmus Philipps of Picton Castle, from whom the present owner, Lady Dunsany, descends.

During the Civil War the castle was taken by General Rowland Laugharne, the commander of the Parliament forces, in 1645, and it is probable that it was surrendered or abandoned on more than one occasion during the war.

When Angharad gave birth to her youngest son at Manorbier Castle in 1147, the child was named Gerald after his grandfather, Gerald de Windsor, but he is known to history as Giraldus Cambrensis, the ambitious cleric and celebrated historian.

While his brothers built sand castles on Manorbier beach, Gerald, it is said, would build a church, and his father would refer to him as 'the little bishop'. He received his early education at St David's, where his uncle, David FitzGerald, was bishop, before proceeding to the abbey of St Peter at Gloucester and, in 1162, to the University of Paris. He was appointed Archdeacon of Brecon, and his great ambition was to follow his uncle as Bishop of St David's. When Bishop FitzGerald died in 1176, Gerald was the Chapter's favourite candidate to succeed him, but King Henry II insisted on the appointment of Peter de Leia, Prior of Wenlock, to the see. Gerald was offered the bishoprics of Bangor and Llandaff, and of Ferns and Leighlin in Ireland, but he refused them all, as his mind was set on St David's. When Peter de Leia died in 1198, Gerald was again the Chapter's chosen man, but the King and the Archbishop of Canterbury opposed his election as they were aware that his aim was to make St David's a metropolitan see, independent of Canterbury, for which he made three visits to Rome to plead his cause before Pope Innocent III. He was summoned to Court in 1183 and engaged by the King to mediate with the Lord Rhys, to whom he was related on his mother's side. Gerald could rightly say: 'I am sprung from the princes of Wales and from the barons of the Marches, and when I see injustice in either race, I hate it.' In 1185 he was commissioned by the King to accompany Prince John to Ireland, a task which he found congenial as he was able to meet his own kith and kin among those who had crossed from Porthclais to Bannow in May 1169 to invade Ireland, and he also turned his travels to good account by collecting material for his *Conquest of Ireland* and his *Topography of Ireland*. In 1188 he accompanied Archbishop Baldwin of Canterbury on his tour through Wales to preach the Third Crusade, of which Gerald gave an entertaining and illuminating account in his *Itinerary through Wales*, which was followed by his *Description of Wales*. He died in 1223 and was buried at St David's, where he had yearned to be enthroned. Had he become bishop, however, we would have been denied an inestimable contemporary portrait of Wales in the twelfth century.

The slender tower of the parish church, dedicated to St James the Great, rises from the slope across the valley from the castle. Its nave is older than the castle, and aisles were added in the thirteenth and fourteenth centuries by cutting through the thick walls of the nave; later restoration has helped to produce a somewhat cavernous interior. The oak loft leading into the tower is of the fourteenth century. A window in the north transept shows Master Richard, a monk, and Lady Margaret, the mother of Henry Tudor. An effigy of a knight may be that of Sir John de Barri, who granted the church to the priory of Monkton in 1324.

Not far from the castle, on the headland known as the Priest's Nose and beyond Parson's Piece, stands the King's Quoit, a cromlech which originally had three supporters, but one has collapsed and now lies beneath the capstone. Barrows at Norchard Beacon and elsewhere along the Ridgeway are memorials to those who could make it no further while travelling along this route during the Bronze Age, and promontory forts at Old Castle and Skomer Camp provide evidence of the defensive expertise of Iron Age men.

Lydstep Point is National Trust property presented by the Pilgrim Trust in 1936. Sloops and schooners used to load limestone here, near the Smuggler's Cave. Lydstep House was built by Viscount St David's at the end of the last century. The Palace of Arms, in the village, is described as the hunting seat of Bishop Gower of St David's (1328-47) and may have been an armour house.

St Florence lies hidden in the valley of the Ritec, a compact village grouped around the church, which is dedicated to St Florentius, a saint well remembered in the Loire valley, and the dedication may have been conveyed by William de Valence, Earl of Pembroke, whose family hailed from Poitou. The patrons of the church were variously the earls of Pembroke and the Crown. George Owen stated, in 1594, that it was 'a free church without cure of souls' under the patronage of the Queen, but in 1624 it was presented to St John's College, Cambridge, which remained the patron until 1920, when it passed to the Church in Wales under the Disestablishment Act. A brass plate in the chancel commemorates, lengthily and in Latin, both Robert Rudd, rector and Archdeacon of St David's, who was imprisoned in a hulk in Milford Haven by Oliver Cromwell for his allegiance to the

Crown, and Robert Williams, grandson of Robert Ferrar, the martyred Bishop of St David's, from whom descended William Williams of Ivy Tower, antiquary and author of *Primitive History*.

John Leland, on his visit to the village, 'rode by a ruinouse walle sometime longing to Sir Rhese (ap Thomas), now voide of dere'. This was the wall of the deer park of the earls of Pembroke which is still traceable at Park Hall Dyke. There are several interesting old houses, one of which has a fine 'Flemish' chimney.

Ships used to sail up the Ritec as far as Gumfreston. At that time it flowed into a tidal estuary, known as Holloway Water, but an embankment was built across the estuary in 1820 in order to reclaim land from the sea. The result was the spreading of the sand dunes and the silting up of the estuary to form The Marsh.

The railway line connecting Tenby to Pembroke was built across the marsh, along the embankment, in 1863. Three years later, the viaduct was built to carry the railway from Tenby to join the main line at Whitland.

Gumfreston, *villa Gumfrid* in 1291, is now no more than a farm, a rectory and a fourteenth-century church hidden among the trees. The church has traces of a fresco on the north wall of the nave depicting the martyrdom of St Lawrence, to whom the church is dedicated. A worn flight of stone steps in the churchyard leads to three wells, two of which are chalybeate. People came at Easter to cast crooked pins into the water, to 'throw Lent away'.

Scotsborough House, of which only the merest traces remain, was occupied by the Perrot family until John ap Rhys of Rickeston in Brawdy, who was sheriff in 1582 and in 1593, married Katherine, daughter and heiress of John Perrot and, in her right, acquired the property. His son, Thomas ap Rhys, sheriff in 1610, is commemorated, with his wife and children, by a many-coloured monument in St Mary's Church, Tenby. Edward Lhuyd, the biologist and antiquary and the first keeper of the Ashmolean Museum, stayed at Scotsborough in 1697 and discovered rare and unrecorded zoophytes which he obtained 'by dredging here', when the house stood on the Ritec estuary.

Wedlock, a farm, is no Gretna Green of the south but the modern form of 'widelok', a broad enclosure. Daisybank Farm was the home, from the time of Henry VII, of the Hall family, of which came Benjamin Hall, later Lord Llanover, during whose term as Commissioner of Works the great clock of Westminster was erected and named after him, Big Ben.

At the foot of Gumfreston Hill, on an April dawn in 1838, pistols were drawn in response to a challenge by Sir John Owen of Orielton, Member of Parliament and magistrate and a former mayor of Tenby, who had been called 'a calumnator and liar' by William Richards, magistrate and former mayor of the same town, while sitting on the bench the previous day. Richards fired into the air, but Sir John took aim and grievously wounded his opponent in one of the last duels fought in Wales.

In 1607 a grand jury presented that Katharine, the wife of Thomas Bowen of Tenby, yeoman, had 'by the instigation of the Devil performed diabolical artes called witchcrafts, inchantments, charmes and sorceries at Gumfreston on 27 June of that year' and had caused injury to cattle and goods. This is the only recorded indictment for witchcraft in Pembrokeshire, and history is silent as to whether the lady was sent to the pillory or worse.

A grant of land by Noe ab Arthur, King of Dyfed from 586 to 616, refers to Pen Alun, now Penally, while Guonocatui is named as the abbot of *Aluni caput*, or Pen Alun, in 706. By all the meagre accounts that exist, Penally was an important centre of early Christianity. The *peregrini*, or wandering missionary 'saints', travelling from Brittany and Cornwall, would land here and follow the transpeninsular route across Pembrokeshire, to Whitesand or Porthclais to embark for Ireland.

St Teilo, himself a *peregrinus* of the sixth century, was born at *eccluis Guinnion*, near Penally, 'where were the tombs of his fathers and where his patrimony lay'. He is said to have led a migration of Welsh survivors of the Yellow Pestilence to Brittany in 547 and to have remained there for seven years, during which time he visited Samson, the Bishop of Dol and a former abbot of Caldey. Church dedications to him stretch across south Wales, in a pattern that is similar to the dedications to St David, his contemporary and associate. His great monastery was at Llandeilo, on the Towy, and he was also the founder of Llandaff Cathedral. Such was his esteem that, when he died, Llandaff, Llandeilo and Penally claimed his body, but his skull, at his behest, was taken to Llandeilo Llwydarth, near Maenclochog, where generations drank out of it to cure their ailments, unaware that it was, in fact, the skull of a maiden.

Penally church is, nonetheless, dedicated to St Nicholas. It has a vaulted ceiling, and in its south transept is the tomb of William de Hampton and Isabel, his wife.

The Penally Cross, which stood for centuries in the churchyard, is now in the church, in the south transept, but placed too close to the wall for it to be fully examined. The monument, six foot high, has a pierced wheel-head and is decorated overall, on the back and sides, with characteristically Celtic interlacing spirals and plaited patterns, while the front has also a vine-scroll motif in the tradition of Anglo-Saxon art. The broken shaft of another cross has beasts and acanthus and other motifs of Saxon derivation, while another has knotwork and key patterns. Yet another fragment, which formerly stood in the church but is now lost, was decorated on all faces and bore an incomplete Latin inscription which proclaimed it to be '[the cross] which Mail Domnac erected'. The crosses date from the early tenth century.

Trefloyne, 'the venerable mansion ... garrisoned for the King' during the Civil War, and the Earl of Carbery's headquarters until it was besieged by Cromwell's russet-coated men, was referred to, in the eighth century, as *villa luin Teliau*, or Trellwyn Teilo.

Hoyle's Mouth and Longbury Bank, or Little Hoyle, caves, now some fifty feet above the Ritec marshes, were at estuary level when they provided shelter for some of the earliest inhabitants of Pembrokeshire. The caves were explored in the 1860s by the Reverend Gilbert Smith of Gumfreston, who found bones of mammoth, woolly rhinoceros, lion, hyena and bear, and artefacts now displayed at the Tenby Museum. It is now thought that human occupation of Hoyle's Mouth began before the end of the last glaciation and continued into post-glacial times. Fragments of red pottery bowls and amphorae found at Longbury Bank, along with human remains, suggest that it might have been a hermit's retreat in the fifth century or later.

The winds from the sea have piled sand high to form the Burrows, behind which lies the soft, wild-thyme scented Tenby Golf Course. Blackwood Tower, on the Burrows, which Fenton thought 'resembled Cassandra's tower', while 'some imagined it to have been a Pharos', was probably a watch-tower and is said to have been used later as a snuff mill.

The Norse called it Caldey, the cold island, but for centuries before they came it was known as Ynys Pŷr, the island of Pŷr, who is said to have established his monastery there even before Columba went to Iona. When he died – after falling into a pond in a drunken stupor, according to one scurrilous legend – he was succeeded as abbot by Samson, who was consecrated bishop in 521 and later sojourned in Ireland and Cornwall before settling at Dol in Brittany. When he sailed across from Ireland, he placed his chariot in his curragh and, on landing at Whitesand, put the curragh on the chariot and hired horses to draw it along the transpeninsular route to Penally. Presumably he went through the same exercise at Padstow and Fowey *en route* to Brittany. When making one of his several journeys to Paris, the wheel of the chariot came off, we are told.

Of Brittany's seven thousand, seven hundred, seven score and seven saints, Samson is the best known, as his *Vita* was written soon after his death. He was one of the *sept saints fondateurs*, the seven founding saints, all of whom hailed from Wales. Soon after he had established the bishopric of Dol, in 530, Paul-Aurelian founded Saint Pol-de-Léon, while later bishoprics were founded by St Tudwal at Tréguier, St Corentin at Quimper, St Briog at St Brieuc and St Malo at the place that bears his name. When Duke Nominoë became the first ruler of an independent Brittany, in 844, he raised Dol to the status of an archbishopric, which it remained until 1199 when it was restored to its episcopal level. It was suppressed in 1799.

Robert FitzMartin, lord of Cemais, and his mother, Geva, gave Caldey to the monks of St Dogmael's, who built the priory church and a monastery, the previous one having been destroyed by the Norse in the ninth century. The church was desecrated at the Dissolution, and the monastery became a farm. The island was purchased, along with St Dogmael's Abbey, by John Bradshaw of Presteign, and it passed through many owners, including the Earl of Warwick, before it was sold, in 1897, to the Reverend Donne Bushell, a native of Cardiff who was, at the time, a master at Harrow School. Bushell restored the priory church and other buildings before disposing of the island, in 1906, to the Reformed Order of Anglican Benedictines. Under their abbot, Aeldred, they built a new abbey which they dedicated to St Samson, a part of whose relics was sent to them by the cathedral authorities at Dol. In 1913 Aeldred and the majority of the monks embraced the Roman Catholic faith and joined the Benedictine Order, but in 1928 they left and established an abbey at Prinknash, having sold the island to the Cistercians. The monastery was occupied by monks of the reformed rule instituted by de Rancé, abbot of La Trappe in Normandy, in the seventeenth century, who were brought from the abbey of Our Lady of Scourmont, near Chimay, in Belgium. The monks rise for matins at three o'clock in the morning and continue in work and prayer, observing the Trappist vows of silence and austerity, until compline.

The old priory church, with its leaning tower and cobbled floor, has in its nave a stone pillar bearing a cross and inscriptions in ogham and in Latin. The ogham commemorates a sixth-century notable, MAGLIA DUBRACANUS, and in the early ninth century someone inscribed the Latin words: 'And I have set on it the sign of the Cross for all who pass by, that they may pray for the soul of Cadwgan.'

The abbey church was built, of limestone quarried on the island, between 1907 and 1911. Its interior was destroyed by fire in 1940 and was restored in 1951.

The limestone caves of Caldey provided shelter for a succession of people, beginning with the mesolithic, and there are traces of occupation continuing until the fourth century AD. The number of animal bones found at Nanna's Cave suggest a bigger faunal population than the island could sustain and reminds one that Caldey was once a hill on a wooded plain that now lies beneath the sea. Daylight Rock was a flint-working site of men who came from Europe when arctic conditions ended here around 8000 BC.

John Paul Jones, the naval adventurer – he was the son of John Paul, a gardener of Kirkcudbright, and assumed the addition, Jones, when he joined the American navy in 1775 – came to Caldey and anchored, out of the view of the customs men at Tenby, in Paul Jones' Bay. No one knows why his ghost roams the cliffs on moonlit nights. That Caldey was subject to piracy in the sixteenth century is affirmed by George Owen, who stated that the island 'is verie fertile and yeldeth plentie of corne: all their ploewes goe with horses, for oxen the inhabitants dare not keepe, fearing the purveyors of the pirates'.

David Jones, the artist and author of *In Parenthesis* and *Anathemata*, worked in the monastery's scriptorium on his engravings for the Golden Cockerel Press in 1925 and 1926. During the last war the Emperor Haile Selassie of Abyssinia found refuge on the island for a time.

St Margaret's Island, joined to Caldey at low tide, has shrunk by the quarrying of its limestone. The naturalist John Ray, when he visited the island in 1668, wrote in his journal: 'This island hath in it a small chapel consecrated to St Margaret,' but the chapel and other ecclesiastical building were converted, in the nineteenth century, into cottages for the quarrymen. Ray could hardly set foot on the island for nesting sea-birds, but these have by now been largely driven away by rats, although there is a strong colony of about a hundred cormorants.

16

Tenby

Tenby still retains all the charm of a small seaside town. Its smooth golden sands, its Guerande-like medieval setting, its Georgian harbourside and its floral gardens, including one planted in memory of a much-loved monk of Caldey, Brother Thomas, together with its mild climate and its splendid holiday facilities, combine to make it the most attractive resort in west Wales.

Addwyn gaer y sydd ar glawr gweilgi ...
Dinas diachor, môr o'i chylchyn.

'There is a fine fortress standing above the sea ... unyielding stronghold, sea-encircled.' So speaks an unknown poet of the ninth century as he mourns the death of the generous lord of Tenby, Bleiddudd, son of Erbin, Prince of Dyfed, now 'gone to the oaken church', his coffin, and remembers how the tumult of the revelry, as the company caroused over cups of mead and wine, mingled with the cries of seabirds, and how 'wrath was banished over the hills'. He presents a rare and joyous portrait of life at the court of a Welsh prince during a dark period in our history.

The 'fine fortress' has given the town its name, Dinbych, literally the 'little fort', anglicized as Tenby, and to distinguish it from all others it was called Dinbych y Pysgod, the fortlet of the fishes.

Little is known of the origins of the Norman castle that was built on a site which, as Leland noted, 'the sea peninsulateth'. It is first recorded in 1153 when the sons of Gruffydd ap Rhys, Prince of west Wales, marched across the sands from Amroth and slew its garrison. His grandson, Maelgwn, besieged it in 1187 and laid waste the town, which was sacked again in 1200 by Llywelyn the Last. Edward III ordered it to be newly fortified when there were rumours of a French invasion in 1377, and eighteen years later it was attacked by French mercenaries who had landed at Milford Haven in support of Owain Glyn Dŵr's rising. In 1648 it was defended against Cromwell's men, but unsuccessfully. Its remains include a double tower, one square, one round, on the limestone ridge of Castle Hill, and traces of a gatehouse with barbican and domestic buildings, and bits of the curtain wall.

The white marble statue of Prince Albert nearby was unveiled in 1865 by the Duke of Connaught, as the Welsh people's memorial to his father.

Tenby was 'strongeli wallid and well gatid' in Leland's time. The walls were built, and the streets laid out, following Llywelyn's pillage in 1260, and strengthened by Jasper Tudor, Earl of Pembroke. They were further fortified for fear of the Armada, and yet again before the Civil War. The five-arched barbican of St George's Gate and the surviving walls were preserved by an injunction of the Court of Chancery in 1873, but the North Gate and the gates that opened to seaward were demolished.

The Tudor Merchant House, although it has had many additions since it was built in the fifteenth century, is a fine example of the domestic architecture of the period and is now safe for posterity in the hands of the National Trust.

Leland also observed that there was 'a sinus ... and a peer for shippes'. At that time Tenby was the leading port in the county, and its two hundred households made it twice as large as Pembroke. Its breakwater, built in 1328, was much in use until the Royal Victorian Pier was completed in 1897 and used by passengers to board pleasure steamers and by keen anglers, with tackle and bait, until it was closed during the last war to discourage invaders, and then demolished in 1953.

The bollards on the harbour walls were taken from cannons used during the Civil War when Tenby was garrisoned, and besieged, both by Cavaliers and by the Parliamentarians.

The Tenby Museum, part built within the castle walls, was opened in 1878 largely to house the geological and archaeological collections of the industrious vicar of Gumfreston, the Reverend Gilbert Smith. It now has a widely representative collection of exhibits and bygones reflecting life in the locality from the time of the cavemen of Caldey to the present. The picture gallery, named after the honorary curator Wilfred Harrison, has paintings by Augustus John and his sister, Gwen.

Augustus was born in a large mauve house on the edge of South Cliffs, now the Belgrave Hotel, in 1878, and he returned to Tenby to live when his mother died and his father sold their home at Haverfordwest six years later. In 1897, while he and his sister Gwen were bathing, Augustus dived into the sea from Giltar Point and split his head open on a submerged rock. 'The universe seemed to explode,' he recounted later, and the doctor who stitched his torn scalp said he owed his life to his uncommonly thick skull. When he returned to the Slade, where he was a student, he wore a black velvet smoking-cap to hide his wound and sported a pubescent red beard, and so created the image that stalked his life. 'If I appear at all cracked at any time in the future,' he wrote in a letter, 'I trust you will put it down to my knock on the head and not to any original madness.' But on the back of a Brooke Bond Tea card, in a series on famous people, Virginia Shankland states that, 'He hit his head on a rock whilst diving, and emerged from the water a genius!'

Charles Norris brought his family, with all their possessions, on board his yacht *Nautilus* from Bristol to Tenby in 1805. Norris was born at Hughenden Manor in 1779, the son of a wealthy London merchant, and is said to have been attracted to Tenby by his cousin, the poet Walter Savage Landor. After being expelled from Rugby and rusticated from Trinity College, Oxford, Landor came to Wales in 1794 and spent much of his time at Swansea and Tenby, where he fell in love with the 'golden-haired Nancy Jones' at Tenby, whom he commemorated in verse as Ianthe, and it was during this time that he met, and lost, the inimitable

> Rose Aylmer, whom these wakeful eyes
> May weep but never see,
> A night of memories and of sighs
> I consecrate to thee.

Norris lived in a house in Bridge Street, now marked with a commemorative plaque, before moving to Waterwynch, where he spent the rest of his days. Landor, having seen Napoleon in Paris, wrote that 'his figure and complexion are nearly like those of Charles Norris', whose sturdy figure must have been a familiar sight as he tramped the countryside with his artist's equipment ready always to sketch the contemporary scene. At his death, in 1858, he left behind him more than twelve hundred drawings, of which less than a tenth have ever been published. His grandson, Charles Norris Williamson, became editor of the magazine *Black and White* and, as C.N. and A.M. Williamson, he and his wife were the authors of several popular novels.

The naturalist Philip Henry Gosse published his *Tenby: A Seaside Holiday* in 1856, giving an account of his visit studying the marine fauna of the area. In the same year George Henry Lewes came 'to ransack the sea' for his *Seaside Studies*, and was critical of local services when he failed to find a tin box in which to send a specimen of the orange-tentacled sea-anemone to a friend. He eventually packaged it in a cardboard case which a Post Office clerk stamped with such vigour as to squash the contents. With him came his companion Mary Anne Evans, who was soon to achieve fame, as George Eliot, with her novel *Adam Bede*.

Sir Gardner Wilkinson, the explorer and Egyptologist, discovered 'a new British oyster' at Tenby, and during his visit in 1867 he was instrumental in saving the old gateway at South Gate when it was threatened with demolition.

The unique Tenby Daffodil was given its specific name *Narcissus obvallaris* by R.A. Salisbury in 1796; its most closely related forms are found in the Pyrenees and south-west France. Its singularity was its undoing, however. A brisk trade in the bulbs, together with the ploughing of permanent grassland, led to its extermination in and around Tenby, and it is now to be seen mainly in hedgerows in Ceredigion and occasionally in Pembrokeshire, as an escapee from old gardens.

The church of St Mary is one of the largest and finest in the whole of Wales. It is said to have been slighted by Maelgwn in 1187 and destroyed by Llywelyn in 1260, after which it was rebuilt, with the tower alongside the chancel. The octagonal spire built in the fifteenth century is only one of the similarities with features found in West Country churches, traceable to the close maritime connection. The splendid waggon-roof, with its carved bosses bearing figures, patterns and grotesques dating from about 1470, is supported by an elegant arcade of the previous century. The church has a wealth of monuments, from the cautionary cadaver resting in a wall to the gilded memorial depicting Thomas ap Rhys of Scotsborough, his wife who died in childbirth in 1610, and their seven surviving children. Thomas White and his son John, prosperous merchants who filled the office of mayor thirteen times between them, repose in effigy, end to end, on alabaster-sided tombs. Thomas it was who hid the boy Henry Tudor in his wine cellar in 1471 and shipped him to safety in Brittany, and was later rewarded with the gift of the surrounding Crown lands. The kneeling figure of William Risam received a ball from the musket of a Cromwellian trooper who mistook him for real. Robert Recorde is commemorated by a medallion bearing a portrait which may be not of him.

The mathematician and physicist, Robert Recorde, was born in Tenby, the son of Thomas Recorde and his wife, Rose Jones of Machynlleth. Having graduated at Oxford he proceeded to Cambridge where he qualified in medicine and continued his study in mathematics and became the pioneer of mathematical writers in this country. His works include *The Ground of Artes*, a popular arithmetic published in 1543, *The Pathway to Knowledge* (1551), an introduction to geometry, *The Castle of Knowledge* (1556), on elementary astronomy, and *The Whettstone of Witte* (1557), an advanced arithmetic and algebra in which he introduced the equals sign, for the invention of which he has been wrongly credited. He published a medical work, *The Urinall of Physicke*, in 1547 and is thought to have been physician to the young King Edward VI and to Queen Mary. He was appointed Comptroller of the Mint at Bristol in 1549 and became General Surveyor of Mines and Money in Ireland in 1551 but was later summoned before the Court of the King's Bench on a charge of defamation of magnates and ordered to pay £1,000 and costs. Unable to meet the fine, he was confined to the King's Bench Prison at Southwark, where he died in 1558.

At St Julian's Chapel, which formerly stood on the harbour wall, the Tenby fishermen prayed for fair winds and heavy hauls and paid tithes of fish and oysters to the rector. In 1781 the chapel was converted into a bathing house by John Jones, apothecary of Haverfordwest, which marked the beginning of Tenby's history as a holiday resort, although it had been commended for its sea-bathing some years earlier by Dr Richard Russell. A more splendid bath house was built in 1805, designed by the architect S.P. Cockerell at the expense of Sir William

Paxton. It was fitted with dressing-rooms and 'a fashionable morning lounge ... and a spacious vestibule for servants to wait in, without mixing with the company', and above its door are carved, in Greek, words from Euripides' *Iphigenia in Aulis*: 'The sea washeth away the ills of men.' Sir William also endowed Tenby with other benefits, including the provision of a water supply, and before his death in 1824 he established a new theatre, in place of an old one, at which the celebrated Edmund Kean performed.

The Tenby Observer, which first appeared in 1853, made history when its proprietor, Frank Mason, fought a High Court action which produced an Act of Parliament in 1908 establishing the right of admission of the Press to meetings of local authorities.

St Catherine's Rock was named after a chapel, dedicated to the patron saint of spinners, which once stood upon this intertidal islet. In 1859 the chapel was flattened and a fort built on its site to complement the defences of Milford Haven.

> My sound is good, my shape is neat,
> 'Twas Bayley made me so complete.

The inscription, on a bell in the belfry of Begelly church, proclaims that it was made by Bayley, the eighteenth-century bell-founder of Bridgwater. The slender church tower, used as a look-out as late as the last war, surveys 'the wide unfertile common, disdained by the land-grabbers, and populated only by a few cattle, geese and gypsies' where, Augustus John records in his autobiography, *Chiaroscuro*, he and his brothers and sisters 'ran happily wild' when staying in the house on the hill and found that 'the example of the nomads in their caravans below, our desultory but voracious reading and unfettered day-dreams – all conspired to stir up discontent and longing for a wider, freer world.' His feeling of kinship with the gypsies, which began at Haverfordwest, was here enhanced and was to remain with him for the rest of his life.

The motte-and-bailey of an unknown Norman stood near the church, but all traces of it have been removed by the hand of man during the present century.

So many new coalpits were being dug around Begelly in 1581 that the highway through the village threatened to subside and become too dangerous for carriages and carts to pass by.

The small colliery at Loveston, which had been reopened in 1932, suffered an inrush of water from an old working four years later and seven miners were drowned.

Jeffreston church stands in a circular churchyard, suggesting a pre-Christian site, and contains a pillar bearing an incised ring-cross of about the eighth century. The Kelly brothers, born at Jeffreston, formed an independent sect in the middle of the eighteenth century, which had meeting-houses at Templeton and Pembroke. James Kelly, a farrier, had been converted to Methodism by George Whitefield in 1743 and, after a preaching tour of the west of England, had established the sect, which became known as the Kellites. He later moved to London, where he died in 1778. His younger brother, John, remained in charge of the meeting-houses and was in close touch with the Pembrokeshire Moravians. After his death, the sect faded away, and most of the Kellites became Congregationalist. The brothers are remembered mostly for their hymns.

The village of Kilgetty developed as a settlement for miners working in the surrounding collieries. Kilgetty House formerly stood on a hill overlooking Stepaside and was the residence of the Canon family, rather than a house of the Canons of St David's, as sometimes stated. Here John Canon built himself a mansion complete with a deer park and adorned by swans and statues and stately oaks. Sir Thomas Canon was Member of Parliament for Pembrokeshire during the reign of James I and left £30 in his will for the poor of the parish. In 1691 Elizabeth, daughter and heiress of the last of the Canons, married Edward, son of Sir Erasmus Philipps of Picton Castle, and after his death, three years later, the estate passed to his brother, 'the Good Sir John', and brought with it additional riches from the 'black diamonds' of the anthracite deposits of the area, and the additional votes of 'the Black Hundred', as the Kilgetty freemen were known, to sway many a Parliamentary election in favour of the Philippses. Sir Richard Philipps, born at Kilgetty House in 1742, was created Lord Milford in the peerage of Ireland.

George Borrow came to Saundersfoot in 1857 and found it 'a small straggling place on the bottom and declivity of a hill'. A century earlier it was no more than a couple of houses, and in 1600 'Sannders foot' is described as a manor in the great forest of

Coedrath, where Cadell, son of Gruffydd, was set upon, while hunting, by Norman knights from Tenby in 1151.

The hollows of bell-pits that men dug in the forest, in medieval times, in search of coal are still visible in places. The Earl of Pembroke received an annual rental of 16s.4d. for 'a mine of sea-cole' at Coedrath in 1324. George Owen states, in 1600, that the colliers worked 'sundry holes, one for every digger ... each man workinge by candle light and sitting while he worketh', while boys 'beare the coales in sitt baskets upon their backes going all waies stooping by reason by the lowness of the pitt'.

The quality of the anthracite that was mined, and the proximity of the coalfield to the sea, led to its shipment to a number of European countries and even as far as Hong Kong.

The Pembrokeshire Iron and Coal Company was formed in 1846 for the purpose of 'working the Iron, Coals and other Minerals' of the Saundersfoot district. By now there were collieries, in the immediate vicinity of Saundersfoot, at Thomas Chapel, Moreton, Bonville's Court and Kilgetty, yielding between them close on a hundred thousand tons of anthracite per annum.

In 1849 the Stepaside Ironworks was established in Pleasant Valley. Ironstone was extracted from the cliffs between Saundersfoot and Amroth, both for export and to supply the ironworks. The Grove Pit was sunk in the slope of Sardis Mountain to provide anthracite for the furnaces, and limestone was brought from the Gellihalog quarries at Ludchurch for the production of pig iron, which reached its peak in 1863 when 4,684 tons was exported from Saundersfoot. Competition and industrial depression forced the furnace to close in 1877, however.

The increase in industrial activity led to the laying down of a tramroad and the building of a harbour at Saundersfoot, under the authority of an Act of Parliament secured in 1829. One branch of the tramway connected the Thomas Chapel, Moreton and Bonville's Court collieries with the harbour, while the other led from Kilgetty and Stepaside through three tunnels cut in the cliffs before it emerged along Railway Street, now 'The Strand'. The trams were drawn by horses until a locomotive, called *Bonville* at first but later *Rosalind*, was purchased in 1915. The harbour was completed by 1834 at a cost of £7,000, but two years later it suffered considerable damage during a storm that also undermined the railway near Coppet Hall. A canal between Stepaside and Wiseman's Bridge was so badly constructed that it soon ceased to be functional.

Few of the collieries survived the 1870s except for Bonville's Court, which was the largest undertaking in the Saundersfoot coalfield. It produced 35,000 tons of coal annually until 1926 but closed down four years later. Kilgetty, Broom and Bonville's Court were re-opened in 1934, but by the outbreak of war they had all ceased to function.

The fleet of smacks and schooners that kept the harbour busy has given way to gaily coloured pleasure boats, and Saundersfoot has developed into one of the most popular holiday resorts in Wales. The Lady Cave anticline on the beach is a geological monument.

St Issell's Church stands in a well-wooded hollow. It has a Norman tower but the rest of the church was restored by Kempson in 1864. It was one of 'the seven bishops' houses of Dyfed'.

Hean Castle, an anglicization of *hen castell*, the old castle, may stand on the site of an early earthwork. In the thirteenth century it was held by Nicholas de Bonvile, and later it became part of the vast possessions of the earls of Pembroke. During the eighteenth century it passed by marriage to the Wogans of Wiston, and so remained until a coheiress married Thomas Stokes, whose son sold it to his brother-in-law, Edward Wilson. His son, Major-General Sir Charles Wilson, marked the boundary between British Columbia and the United States of America, carried out a survey of Jerusalem in 1864 that led to the establishment of the Palestine Exploration Fund, and became director-general of the Ordnance Survey. Edward Wilson sold Hean Castle to Charles Ranken Vickerman, an Essex landowner who had acquired the surrounding collieries and Saundersfoot harbour and who built the present castellated mansion in 1876 from stone brought as ballast by coal-carrying vessels returning from Liverpool. In 1899 the castle was purchased by Sir William Thomas Lewis, owner of the Lewis-Merthyr colliery in the Rhondda Valley, who was created Baron Merthyr of Senghenydd in 1911. Lord Merthyr, the third baron, was Chairman of Committees and Deputy Speaker of the House of Lords.

The cliffs between Saundersfoot and Amroth reveal the intense folding and faulting of beds, coal measures among them, during the Armorican earth movements.

The Wisemans who gave their name to Wiseman's Bridge were said to have come to Pembrokeshire with Aymer de Valence, Earl of Pembroke, during the early part of the fourteenth century. The sandy beach, separated from the coast road by a pebbled ridge, was the scene of a rehearsal for the invasion of Normandy, in April 1944, watched by the Prime Minister, Winston Churchill. It was a day of inclement weather which was to be replicated during the landing on D-Day, the following June.

Between the groynes on Amroth beach, when the tide is low, the remnants of the submerged forest of Coedrath appear as black ebonized stumps, and among them have been found flint arrowheads lost by hunters eight thousand years ago, and a Roman coin embedded in a piece of timber.

Amroth appears to have been a Norse settlement, when it was known as Earwere. Near the church is the motte of the Norman castle of Earwere, first occupied by Picot de Sai, whose daughter and heiress was married to Cadwgan ap Bleddyn, Prince of Ceredigion. It was here, at a great feast held at Christmas 1108, that Owain, son of Cadwgan, heard tell of the beauty of Nest, daughter of Rhys ap Tewdwr and wife of Gerald de Windsor. As the assembled company sang her praises and spoke of her loveliness, his blood was fired and, in company with a few of his friends, he set off for Carew and stormed the castle. Nest hid her husband in a garderobe and allowed herself to be abducted by the dashing princeling. The abduction infuriated not only her husband but also the King, by whom Nest had had a son, Henry FitzHenry, *filius regis*. Owain fled to Ireland for his life but was eventually allowed by the King to return and employed by him in Normandy and in west Wales against Gruffydd, son of Rhys ap Tewdwr, who had emerged as the Welsh leader against the Normans. Owain, a skilful soldier, ruthlessly attacked his fellow-countrymen as they fled for refuge in Carmarthen Castle, and seized their cattle. As he returned leisurely with his booty, however, he was surprised by an armed force of Flemings, led by Gerald de Windsor, who was quick to avenge the assault upon Carew and upon the honour of his wife eight years earlier.

Earwere was in the possession of Cadell, son of Gruffydd ap

Rhys, in 1151. While he was out hunting in the forest of Coedrath one day, he was attacked by a party of Normans from Tenby and was wounded to such an extent that he had to relinquish his princely powers and retire to a monastery for the rest of his life. His brothers, Maredudd and Rhys, took revenge by marching across the sands to Tenby Castle and putting its garrison to the sword.

David Elliot of Earwere was bailiff to the widowed Countess of Pembroke in 1347 and was the founder of a family that was to remain in possession for the next $4\frac{1}{2}$ centuries. The castellated house, near the beach, known as Amroth Castle, was built, about 1800, by Captain James Acland. The house had a garden of 'most excellent outdoor fruit in season' as well as a 'conservatory and grapery'.

The church, dedicated to St Elidyr, was granted, together with fifty acres of sanctuary, to the Knights Hospitallers at Slebech in 1150. It was enlarged in 1856 by R.K. Penson, when the nave was considerably extended.

At Amroth vicarage, in 1623, was born 'the Independent Apostle of Pembrokeshire', Peregrine Phillips, who preached to the Roundheads besieging Pembroke Castle at the request of the Protector. He was appointed rector of Llangwm-cum-Freystrop but was deprived of his living when he refused to conform under the Act of Uniformity of 1662. Ten years later he received a licence to preach at his own house in Haverfordwest, and he ended his days on a small farm outside the town, living on £8 a year, raised by his followers when times were favourable.

To the east of the church, on sloping ground, at Trelissey, is an earthwork which was occupied in the fourth century, possibly as a military outpost from which a watchful eye could be kept on any sea-going craft.

Colby Lodge, hidden among the trees in the delightful Craigyborion valley, was designed by John Nash and is now the property of the National Trust.

17

The National Park

When Hugh Dalton, Minister of Town and Country Planning, came at Whitsuntide in 1951 to walk along the Pembrokeshire coast, we expected him to announce that here was to be the tenth national park to be established in England and Wales. Instead, he loudly denounced the practice among farmers in those days of setting gin-traps on open ground and, while still in full voice, he crossed over a stile and planted his foot firmly on such a trap. The Pembrokeshire Coast National Park was designated, nonetheless, in the following year, to include the coastal area, Daugleddau and the Presely Hills.

The park is administered by the Pembrokeshire Coast National Park Committee which is charged with a duty to preserve and enhance its natural beauty and to promote its enjoyment by the public. These conflicting aims, difficult enough to achieve in an agricultural area, were made more so by developments that could not have been envisaged at the time of designation. The conversion of the Milford Haven waterway into a major European oil port presented a serious challenge to the committee within the first ten years of its existence, but it succeeded in containing the development to middle reaches of the waterway and made every effort to integrate the massive industrial architecture into a landscape of high scenic character. Nor was it anticipated that tourism would become, within so short a time, the second industry of Pembrokeshire, with its demands to accommodate up to a million visitors that bring over £20 million annually to swell the local economy.

Most of the holidaymakers come to seek the pleasures of the coast. Whereas, at one time, they were attracted by sandy bays that offered safe bathing, they now come to partake in a wide range of recreational pursuits: sailing and pleasure cruising, sea angling and tope fishing, skin diving, wind surfing, sand yachting. Others come to enjoy the environment: coastal scenery that is as beautiful and impressive as any in Europe; a wealth of archaeological, geological and historic features; wildlife and the profusion of plants and wild flowers.

The naturalist will find nowhere in England and Wales that is richer in sea-birds. Skokholm was the first bird observatory to be established in Britain. Skomer is a national nature reserve, and Grassholm has one of the largest gannet colonies in the world.

Manx shearwaters arrive, on dark nights in February, from their winter quarters off the coast of South America to breed in familiar rabbit burrows. A daytime visitor to Skomer would not know that beneath his feet the largest concentration in the world, over 100,000 pairs, of these birds have their breeding sites. They spend the day out at sea and return after nightfall lest they become prey to the great black-backed gulls. The solitary fluffy grey chick remains silent in its burrow for ten weeks before migrating by instinct to the southern hemisphere. Another 35,000 pairs breed on Skokholm. Thousands of puffins reach the islands in April, also to occupy the rabbit burrows in which they, too, lay a single egg. Skokholm has a colony of storm-petrels, so named because of their habit seemingly to walk upon the water, as St Peter did on Gennesaret, but known to sailors as Mother Carey's Chickens.

Next to Scotland and the Farne Islands, Pembrokeshire has the largest population of Atlantic grey seals. They breed primarily on Ramsey and also on Skomer and under the mainland cliffs, and produce around 400 pups each year. Porpoises, dolphins and basking sharks are frequent visitors and, more rarely, killer and other whales. About a hundred species of fish have been identified around the coast, and the rivers yield salmon, sewin or sea-trout, and brown trout.

The fox and the badger are common, and polecat and feral mink are sometimes seen, but the otter and the red squirrel have virtually disappeared within the last decade.

The Pembrokeshire hedgebanks, long renowned for their rich flora, have suffered from road improvements and mechanical trimming, but there are still stretches of country lanes that are a joy to behold at most seasons. The lesser celandines, primroses, stitchwort, dog violets and gorse of early spring are followed in

May by red campion, germander speedwell, cow parsley and hawthorn, and in June by honeysuckle, sorrel and hogweed, and later by purple loosestrife, field scabious, foxglove and meadow sweet. The moorland is covered in heather and western gorse, while bogs and flushes have sundew, bog asphodel, butterwort and bog myrtle. The cliff tops are carpeted with thrift and sea campion, vernal squill and bird's-foot trefoil in the spring. The rare prostrate broom and hairy greenweed hang on cliff faces, and two species of rock sea lavender each have only one station in Ireland and one in Pembrokeshire. The perennial centaury is known in Britain only near Newport and in west Cornwall.

The term 'national park' is sometimes misunderstood and people believe that they have free and open access to any land within the boundaries of the park. In fact, less than a tenth of the area is in public ownership: the rest is private property, most of it farmland, to which there is no right of access except along designated footpaths and bridleways, or on to land for which there is an access agreement. Neither is it a park in the sense of Capability Brown designed parkland, or land laid out for pleasure or public recreation. It is, rather, an area of land that is considered to be of national importance on account of the high quality of its environment and which deserves to be protected for ever.

Although it is the smallest in area, at 225 square miles, the Pembrokeshire Coast National Park is more densely populated than any of the other nine parks. Unlike the others also, the greater part of the land within its boundaries is agricultural, with arable cultivation pursued to the edge of the cliffs in places. It is also unique in that it is the only national park that is predominantly coastal. No place is more than ten miles from the sea, and most places are less than three.

The warm sea currents give it an equable climate. Winters are mild, so that grass growth remains dormant only for a short period, and celandines bloom before February is out. Rainfall is low, the lowest in Wales, at thirty inches on the coast, but it increases progressively inland so that the Presely Hills get twice that much. Dale is the sunniest place in Wales and other parts of the coast share in this abundance. Trees blown into plumes indicate the persistence of the prevailing wind, and the windborne sea-spray produces a bleak landscape in exposed parts along the western coast.

The Pembrokeshire Coast National Park Committee comprises eighteen members, twelve of whom are appointed by the County and District Councils and six nominated by the Secretary of State for Wales for their specialist knowledge, and also to ensure a balance between local and national interests. It is serviced by a National Park Officer and his staff, who deal with day-to-day administration and implement the Committee's policy. It is an autonomous body and its decisions cannot be overruled by the County or District Councils.

The Committee is primarily a planning authority, responsible for development control and forward planning within the boundaries of the park. Its activities and policy objectives are published in its National Park Plan which acts as a focus for public consultation and discussion. It provides an information service and a warden service. Information centres at Haverfordwest, Pembroke, Tenby, Kilgetty, Broad Haven, St David's and Newport are visited by some 200,000 people each year. The Committee produces informative and interpretative publications on a wide variety of subjects relating to the park and has arranged an exhibition at the Kilgetty centre, on Kingsmoor Common, illustrating the coal mining and ironstone working features of that area in former times, and another at the Broad Haven Countryside Unit that specializes in marine life. A Youth Hostel providing special facilities for the disabled adjoins the Broad Haven Unit and is dedicated to the memory of John Anthony Price under whose guidance, as National Park Officer, the park was established.

A programme of more than 200 walks and talks is arranged annually for the benefit of visitors and all those who wish to gain a better understanding of the local environment. Wardens patrol the park and assist in its upkeep. They maintain contact with local residents and liaise with landowners and with the coastguards, police and other services.

The Committee has provided car parks, boating facilities, picnic sites, viewpoints, and country parks at Llys-y-frân and at Scolton. It has entered into a number of access agreements, and has made a special arrangement for the management of the splendid grounds of Upton Castle.

A year after the designation of the national park, a proposal to establish a coastal footpath was approved. The coast had been walked by the naturalist R.M. Lockley in order to investigate the feasibility of creating a path along its full length of 180 miles, from St Dogmael's to Amroth. The path was not completed, however, for another seventeen years.

The reason for the delay was the refusal of a few landowners to co-operate. The majority readily agreed and signed footpath dedications where it was necessary to establish new rights of way, but a few raised every possible objection. When agreement was reached eventually, the difficult task of making the path began, and every effort was made to follow the cliff edge as close as possible. In certain places this could not be done, however. At Castlemartin the tank ranges prevent access and the path leaves the coast at Freshwater West and follows the road through the village of Castlemartin to Warren, where it turns and rejoins the coast above the Green Bridge of Wales. It also circumvents the Pembroke Power Station and makes short detours at a few places for practical reasons. Otherwise it remains close to the sea and marches with what is, in the words of Professor J.A. Steers, 'one of the finest coastlines in Britain'.

The Pembrokeshire Coast Path was eventually declared open, at a ceremony held on 16 May 1970 above the knife-back promontory of Monkstone Point, by Wynford Vaughan-Thomas, the celebrated broadcaster and traveller, who described it as 'a shining girdle round the county' and pointed out that no path is as easy to maintain as a well-used one.

Welsh Place-names

Nothing annoys a Welshman as much as people who take pains to pronounce Drumnadrochit or Drogheda, Anguille d'Arves or Wickambreux properly, yet content themselves to enunciate Betws-y-coed as 'Betsy co-ed', Mynydd Bach as 'money back' or Gelliwastad as 'jelly-wasted'.

Welsh place-names sound so much better when they are pronounced properly, and as Welsh is a phonetic language, this should not be difficult once the sounds of consonants and vowels are observed.

In addition to the English vowels, Welsh has *w* and *y*, and each has two values, long and short. They are short when followed by *c, m, ng, p* or *t*, or by two or more consonants, and long before *b, ch, d, f, ff, g, s, th*.

The consonants *b, d, h, l, m, n, p, t* have the same sound as in English, and the following are pronounced:

c like *k*, *ch* as in *loch*, *dd* as *th* in *thine*.

f like *v*, *ff* as *f* in *fish*, *g* as in *go*,

r as in *merry*, *s* as in *essay*.

The sound *ll* may be produced by placing the tongue against the roof of the mouth and hissing like a gander.

The mutation of initial consonants may present problems, especially when searching for a word in the dictionary, and so it should be remembered that, in certain circumstances, the consonants *p, t, c, b, d, g, m, ll* soften to *b, d, g, f, dd* (*g* disappears), *f, l*, respectively.

Welsh place-names are meaningful, and the following brief glossary may assist in identifying the more common names:

aber	estuary	*gwaelod*	bottom
afon	river	*gwastad*	flat, plain
allt	wood	*gwaun*	moor
bach	small	*gwern*	alder
bedd	grave	*gwyn*	white
blaen	source	*hafod*	summer dwelling
bryn	hill	*hen*	old
bwlch	pass	*hendre*	winter dwelling
caer	fort	*hir*	long
canol	middle	*isaf*	lower
carn	cairn	*llan*	church
carreg	stone	*llethr*	slope
castell	castle	*llwyn*	tree
cefn	ridge	*llyn*	pool, lake
cil	corner, retreat	*llys*	court
cleddau	sword	*maen*	stone
clegyr	rock	*maes*	field
cnwc	hillock	*mawr*	big
coch	red	*melin*	mill
coed	wood	*morfa*	salt-marsh
coetan	quoit	*mynydd*	mountain
cors	bog	*nant*	brook
craig	rock	*ogof*	cave
croes	cross	*pant*	hollow
crug	tump	*pen*	headland
cwm	valley	*penglog*	skull
deri	oak	*pont*	bridge
dinas	fort	*rhos*	moor
dôl	meadow	*rhyd*	ford
du	black	*sych*	dry
dŵr	water	*tir*	land
dyffryn	valley	*traeth*	beach
eglwys	church	*tref*	town, homestead
foel	bare hill	*trwyn*	nose, point
ffos	ditch	*tŷ*	house
ffynnon	well	*tywyn*	sand-dune
glan	river bank	*uchaf*	upper
glas	blue, green	*waun*	moor, meadow
glyn	valley	*ynys*	island
godir	steep slope		

Index

Abercastle, 76
Abercuch, 33, 34
Abereiddi, 78, 79
Aberfelin, 77
Abermawr, 74
Ambleston, 85
Amroth, 16, 210
Angle, 181, 182
Ap Thomas, Sir Rhys, 128, 170
Asser, 22, 73
Arthur, King, 41

Barlow, Catherine, 140, 144, 166
Barlow, Roger, 165
Barlow, Bishop William, 88, 96
Barrallier, Jean-Louis, 143
Barry Island, 78, 79
beavers, the last, 29
Bedd Morris, 60
Bedd yr Afanc, 50
Begelly, 206
Bek, Bishop, 87, 98, 133
Benton, 133
Bishop's Palace, 99
Blackpool Mill, 167
Black Prince, 65
Blackwell, Revd John (Alun), 31
Bletherston, 46
bluestones, 18
Boleyn, Anne, 109
Boncath, 32
Bosherston, 185
Doulston, 163
Bradford, Earl of, 85
Brawdy, 103

Broad Haven, 162
Broad Haven (east), 186
Brunel, Isambard, 72, 87, 134
Brynberian, 49, 50
Buckland, Lord, 106
Burton, 134

Caerfarchell, 102
Caldey, 16, 17, 198-200
Callice, John, 24, 111
Camrose, 105
Camrose, Viscount, 106
Canaston, 19, 166, 167
Canon family, 207
Cantre'r Gwaelod, 16-17
Capel Colman, 32
Carew, 21, 169-72
Carn Ingli, 20
Carn Menyn, 18, 37
Carreg Wastad, 67, 68
Castellan, 34
Castlemartin, 184
Castlemorris, 76
Cawdor, Earl, 69-71, 122, 144
Ceibwr, 56
chambered tombs, 17, 51, 57, 76, 134
chess, 48, 82
Cilgerran, 27, 30
Clarbeston Road, 87
Cleddau Bridge, 134
Clegyr Boia, 17, 95
Colby Moor, 121, 160
coracle, 30
Cosheston, 19, 173
Cresswell, 169

Croesgoch, 79
Cromwell, Oliver, 23, 110, 137, 176
Crugiau Cemais, 20
Crwys, 77
Crymych, 34
Cwmgwaun, 61
Cwmyreglwys, 60

daffodil, Tenby, 204
Dale, 150, 214
David, Lewis, 125, 126
Davies, Revd Howel, 32, 76, 86, 119
De Clare, Gilbert, 109, 174
De Clare, Richard, 175
Deisi, 21
Demetae, 21
De Rutzen, Baron, 166
De Vale, Robert, 85, 150
Dewi Emrys, 73
De Windsor, Gerald, 28, 169, 175, 192
Dinas, 60
Druidston, 107
Dyfed, 21

Eastington, 181
Eglwyswrw, 47
Eligug Stack, 185
Essex, Earl of, 104, 149, 190
Evans's Gambit, 82

Felindre Farchog, 51
Fenton, Richard, 10, 41, 65-7, 133
Fishguard, 64, 72
FitzGerald, Bishop, 122
FitzMartin, Robert, 26, 56, 64, 198
Flemings, 23
Fleming's castle, 85
Flimston, 185
Foel Cwm Cerwyn, 41
Foel Drygarn, 20, 34, 37
Foel Eryr, 41
Foley, Admiral, 24, 124, 143

French invasion, 67-72
Freni Fawr, 34
Freshwater West, 16, 183

Gambold, John, 43, 115
Garn Fawr, 20
Garn Turne, 77, 84
Gatholm, 153
geological features, 11-15
George, David Lloyd, 137
Giraldus Cambrensis, 9, 10, 23, 27, 29, 56, 57, 97, 122, 192-3
Glandwr, 35
Glogue, 35
Goodwick, 72
Gordon, General, 139
Gors Fawr circle, 19, 36
Goultrop, 161
Gower, Admiral, 24, 29
Gower, Bishop, 96
Grassholm, 158
Greville, Charles, 140-4
Greville, Robert Fulke, 144
Greville, Robert Fulke Murray, 144
Griffith, George William, 23, 48, 52
Grimes, Professor W.F., 50, 51, 156
Guest, Lady Charlotte, 55
Gumfreston, 195
Gwaun Valley, 61

Hamilton, Lady Emma, 141, 143, 144
Hamilton, Sir William, 121, 140, 144, 166
Haroldston House, 119, 146
Harris, Joseph (Gomer), 84
Harry, George Owen, 23, 48
Hasguard, 149
Haverford, Pennsylvania, 127
Haverfordwest, 108-20, 126, 160, 206

INDEX

Haverfordwest Priory, 112, 146, 150
Henry's Moat, 43
Herbrandston, 148
Hobbs Point, 135, 179
Hodgeston, 190, 191
Hook, 132
Houghton, Bishop Adam, 98
Hubberston, 140, 142, 148

Jack Sound, 154
Jeffreston, 207
John, Augustus, 137, 203, 206
Johnson, Dr Samuel, 127, 136
Johnston, 136
Jones, Revd John (Tegid), 55
Jones, John Paul, 65, 199
Jordan, Mrs, 99

Keeston, 105
Kemsley, Viscount, 106
Kensington, Lord, 65, 136, 144, 153, 154, 160
Kilgetty, 207, 215
Kilpaison, 181
knappan, 49

Lampeter Velfrey, 128
Lamphey, 190
Landor, William Savage, 203
Landshipping, 168
Laud, Archbishop William, 88, 114
Laugharne, General Rowland, 23, 109, 121, 160, 176, 192
Lawrenny, 160
Letterston, 81
Lewes, Sir Watkin, 52
Little Haven, 162
Little Newcastle, 82
Llanddewi Velfrey, 125
Llandeilo Llwydarth, 37, 196
Llantyrnach, 35
Llangolman, 37

Llanion, 178
Llanllawer, 62
Llanrhian, 78, 94
Llanstadwell, 135
Llanwnda, 72
Llanychllwydog, 61
Llawhaden, 122-4
Llechryd, 30, 31
Llechydrybedd, 18, 57
Llwyngwair, 55, 56
Llys-y-frân, 45, 86
Lockley, R.M., 93, 154, 180, 216
Longhouse, 17, 76
Ludchurch, 129, 130, 208
Lydstep, 16, 194

Mabinogion, The, 22, 33, 34, 48, 55, 127-9
Maenclochog, 38, 39, 41, 46
Magnus Maximus, 34, 46
Maiden Castle, 84
Manorbier, 17, 192-4
Manordeifi, 31
Manorowen, 65, 78
Marloes, 153
Martin, Bishop David, 47, 96
Martin, Nicholas, 58
Martin, William, 56-8
Martin's Haven, 153, 154
Martletwy, 168
Mathry, 17, 75
Merlin's Bridge, 120
Moour-y-dorth, 79
Methodists, 24, 43
Mevrick, Sir Gelly, 149
Midland Island, 154
Milford, 25, 139-45
Milford Haven, 138-45
Milford, Lord, 70, 143, 164, 165, 207
Minwear, 167
Monk Haven, 150
Monkton Priory, 177
Monmouth, Duke of, 104, 105

Montgomery, Roger de, 22, 28, 174
Moravians, 24, 43, 115
Morris, Lewis, 138
Morvil, 42
Mounton, 167
Moylegrove, 56
Mynachlogddu, 36

Nab Head, 161
Narberth, 127, 128
Nash, John, 32, 96, 108
Nelson, Admiral Lord, 124, 142, 143
Nest, 'the Helen of Wales', 170, 210
Nevern, 16, 21, 49, 53
Newchapel, 32
Newgale, 16, 102
New Moat, 44
Newport, 16, 49, 57-60, 126
Neyland, 134
Nicholas, Jemima, 69
Nolton, 106, 107
Normans, 22, 138
Norsemen, 22

ogham, 21
Orielton, 179, 180
Owain Glyn Dŵr, 58, 85, 109, 150
Owen, George, 10, 23, 51, 52, 138
Owen, Henry, 89
Owen, Col. John, 38, 40
Owen of Orielton, 168, 179, 180

Parc-y-meirw, 19, 63
Pembroke, 174-9
Pembroke Yeomanry, 69-71
Pembrokeshire Coast National Park, 25, 212-6
Penally, 21, 196
Pencaer, 17, 67, 73
Penrhydd, 49
Pentre Ifan cromlech, 17, 51, 84

Perrot, Sir John, 23, 87, 112, 113, 119, 120
Phaer, Thomas, 23, 29
Philipps, Sir John, 164, 207
Phillips, Edgar (Trefin), 78
Phillips, Peregrine, 114, 211
Picton Castle, 143, 163, 164
Picton, General Sir Thomas, 24, 89-91
Pill Priory, 136, 146
Pointz castle, 103
Pontfaen, 61
Porth Clais, 41, 94
Porthgain, 78, 79
Poyer, Colonel John, 176
Prendergast, 118
Presely Hills, 17, 19, 22, 92
Puncheston, 42, 126
Pwllcrochan, 181
Pwllderi, 73
Pwllgwaelod, 60

Quakers, 23, 42, 115, 125, 142

Ramsey, 92, 94
rath, 88
Rebecca Riots, 24, 36
Recorde, Robert, 23, 205
Redstone, 125-7
Red Roses, 129
Rees, Evan (Dyfed), 43
Rellites, The, 207
Rhoscrowther, 180
Rhos y Clegyrn, 19, 75
Rhydwilym, 45
Rhys, The Lord, 27, 28, 56, 97
Roberts, Bartholomew, 24, 82
Robeston Wathen, 125
Roch, 9, 11, 103, 104, 133
Rosebush, 39-41
Rosemarket, 135
Rudbaxton, 88

St Ann's Head, 151, 153

INDEX

St Bride's, 149, 154, 160, 161
St Brynach, 44, 54, 60
St Catherine's Rock, 206
St David, 54, 94, 95
St David's, 17, 92, 95-9
St David's, Viscount, 165
St Dogmael's, 26, 27, 36
St Dogwell's, 83
St Edren's, 81
St Florence, 194
St Govan's, 186
St Ishmael's, 150
St Issell's, 209
St Justinian's, 93
St Katherine's, Milford, 146
St Margaret's Island, 200
St Mary's College, 98
St Meugan's, 48
St Nicholas, 74
St Non, 78, 94
St Patrick, 92, 100
St Petrox, 185
Saundersfood, 207-9
Scolton, 87
Scourfield family, 44
Scotsborough, 195
Scoveston, 135
seal, Atlantic grey, 93
Sealyham terrier, 83
Skokholm, 154. 156-8, 213
Skomer, 20, 154-6, 213
slates, 37, 39, 59, 78
Slebech, 88, 140, 163, 165, 167
Smalls, The, 101, 158-60
Society of Sea Serjeants, 81
Solva, 100
Spittal, 87
Stackpole, 143, 186-9
Starbuck, Samuel, 142

Stepaside, 208
Steynton, 137
Stokes, John Lort, 117
Stonehenge, 18, 37, 152

Talbenny, 161
Tate, Colonel William, 67, 70
Tavernspite, 129, 145
Templeton, 128, 130, 131
Tenby, 144, 160, 196, 197, 201-6
Trecwn, 24, 44
Treffgarne, 11, 14, 84, 85
Trefin, 76-8
Tudor, Henry, 23, 151, 152, 175
Tufton, 44

Upton, 172-3
Uzmaston, 163

Walter, Lucy, 23, 104, 151
Walton West, 162
Walwyn's Castle, 148
Warrior, HMS, 178
Wesley, John, 24, 87, 114, 177
West Williamston, 169
Whitchurch, 100
Whitechurch, 48
Whitesand Bay, 92
Williams, Anna, 136
Williams, Thomas, 69, 100, 159
Wiseman's Bridge, 210
Wiston, 121
Wizo the Fleming, 121
Wogan family, 87, 122, 134, 164
Wolfscastle, 84
Woodstock,. 32, 86, 87
Wyrriott family, 123, 179

Young, Archbishop Thomas, 191